THE BU
L(

C000212646

THE WEDDING PARTY
Judith Herzberg

DRUMMERS
Arne Sierens

BURYING THE DOG
Karst Woudstra

THE STENDHAL SYNDROME
Frans Strijards

Other volumes in the International Collection

AUSTRALIA PLAYS
ed. Katharine Parsons
Jack Davis: No Sugar
Alma de Groen: The Rivers of China
Michael Gow: Away
Louis Nowra: The Golden Age
David Williamson: Travelling North
ISBN 1 85459 056 1

CZECH PLAYS
ed. Barbara Day
Vaclav Havel: Tomorrow!
Ivan Klima: Games
Josef Topol: Cat on the Rails
Daniela Fischerova: Dog and Wolf
ISBN 1 85459 074 X

HUNGARIAN PLAYS
ed. László Upor
András Nagy. The Seducer's Diary
Andor Szilágyi: Unsent Letters
Ákos Németh: Muller's Dances
Péter Kárpáti: Everywoman
ISBN 1 85459 244 0

LATIN AMERICAN PLAYS
ed. Sebastian Doggart
Octavio Paz: Rapaccini's Daughter
Jose Triana: Night of the Assassins
Griselda Gambaro: Saying Yes
Carlos Fuentes: Orchids in the Moonlight
Mario Vargas Llosa: Mistress of Desires
ISNB 1 85459 249 1

SOUTH AFRICAN PLAYS
ed. Stephen Gray
Anthony Akerman: Somewhere on the Border
Maishe Maponya: Tile Hungry Earth
Susan Pam-Grant: Curl Up and Dye
Paul Slabolepszy: Over the Hill
Pieter-Dirk Uys: Just Like Home
ISBN 1 85459 148 7

STARS IN THE MORNING SKY
ed. Michael Glenny
Alexander Chervinsky: Heart of a Dog
Alexander Galin: Stars in the Morning Sky
Alexander Gelman: A Man with Connections
Grigory Gorin: Forget Herostratus!
Ludmila Petrushevskaya: Three Girls in Blue
ISBN 1 85459 020 0

DUTCH AND FLEMISH PLAYS

Selected by Della Couling

THE BUDDHA OF CEYLON ■ LODEWIJK DE BOER
Translated by Della Couling

THE WEDDING PARTY ■ JUDITH HERZBERG
Revised by Rhea Gaisner and Rina Vergano

DRUMMERS ■ ARNE SIERENS
Translated by Nadine Malfait

BURYING THE DOG ■ KARST WOUDSTRA
Translated by Della Couling

THE STENDHAL SYNDROME ■ FRANS STRIJARDS
Translated by Della Couling

THE INTERNATIONAL COLLECTION

NICK HERN BOOKS
London

in association with
Theater Instituut Nederland

A Nick Hern Book

Dutch and Flemish Plays first published in Great Britain
in 1997 as an original paperback by Nick Hern Books Limited,
14 Larden Road, London W3 7ST

This volume has been produced in collaboration with the Theater
Instituut Nederland in Amsterdam and the Vlaams Theater Instituut
in Brussels and with the support of the Dutch and Flemish Ministries
of Culture in the frame of the Flemish-Dutch Cultural Agreement

Typeset by Country Setting, Woodchurch, Kent TN26 3TB

Printed and bound in Great Britain by Athenaeum Press Ltd,
Gateshead, Tyne & Wear

A CIP catalogue record for this book is available from
the British Library

ISBN 1 85459 289 0

Contents

Introduction

The five plays in this collection reflect the dynamics and the strikingly singular character of contemporary Dutch and Flemish theatre. It is an anthology which will undoubtedly arouse curiosity concerning the place of these playwrights in the tradition of Dutch-language drama. There are, however, very few western countries which do so little to elaborate on their own theatrical tradition as the Netherlands and Flanders. Even the plays of the great writers such as Vondel (1587-1679), Hooft (1581-1647), Bredero (1585-1618), Heijermans (1864-1924) and Buysse (1859-1932) are never performed with any kind of regularity. Unlike in France, Germany or Great Britain, for example, there is an absence of any tradition for performing the national dramatic repertoire. Nevertheless, dramatic writing in the Netherlands and Flanders is going through a period of unprecedented growth at the moment, and home-grown theatrical material is now being performed more than at any other time in history.

The fact that companies are no longer automatically looking abroad when putting together their repertoire is a recent development. For centuries it was quite normal to present cultured townspeople visiting the playhouses with well-known international master-pieces. Native dramatic works were a curiosity. There was the occasional revival, but theatre history in the Low Countries is pitted with black holes in which not a single important Dutch-language playwright can be seen. Theatre historians and critics, too, hardly ever paid attention to Dutch-language drama. The rare exception who did, was usually concerned with questions about the causes of this 'deficiency'. Fortunately, such a negative term is now outdated. Anyone interested in recent Dutch-language drama no longer has to steel himself for a rude awakening. On the contrary, a generation of playwrights has now appeared that will not easily be dismissed from the Flemish and Dutch theatrical landscape.

The Netherlands and the northern part of Belgium, Flanders, have always had one important common denominator: the Dutch language. Culturally there has traditionally been a certain amount of interchange. Nevertheless, it is important not to lose sight of the geographic, political and cultural borders, for the development of the playwright's art in Flanders and the Netherlands was not synchronous. At the beginnings of our history, however, we are still referring to the Low Countries, by which we mean both the Netherlands and Flanders.

That history had its start way back in the 14th century: Dutch-language dramatic art is no recent phenomenon. Flanders is in possession of the oldest preserved dramatic text in Europe: the Hulthem manuscript. This manuscript must have been written around 1375, and the plays were probably performed by itinerant actors. The four plays included in the manuscript, referred to as 'abele spelen' (noble or superior plays), are *Esmoreit, Gloriant, Lanseloet van Denemarken* and *Van den Winter ende van den Somer*. They are chiefly concerned with courtly love and, entirely in keeping with the spirit of the times, they are highly moralistic.

The 'Rederijkerskamers', the chambers of rhetoric, also regarded drama as an educational medium and not as an independent artistic form. These organisations were rather like guilds, partly dedicated to practising the art of rhetoric, and they provided an important stimulus to the growth of professional theatre in the 15th and 16th centuries. Theatre, which was a flourishing feature of medieval cities and was mainly performed on the street, took an institution-alised form. At the head of every chamber of rhetoric was a 'factor', the director and artistic leader of the group who wrote the plays himself. So in the beginning the playwright was directly involved in the creation of theatre. For many playwrights, this intense col-laboration between the author and the people on the stage proved to be a precondition for success. Literary gems from the 15th and 16th centuries are the miracle play *Mariken van Nieumeghen*, which is regarded as the masterpiece of Middle Dutch dramatic art, and the morality play *Elkerlyc*. The latter was also the basis for many other plays with the same motif. The Latin play *Homulus* and the English *Everyman* are translations of this work.

The Capture of Antwerp by the Spanish in 1585 meant a parting of the ways for Flanders and the Netherlands. This political division caused the first 'Flemish wave' in the Netherlands (during the 1980s there was evidence of another Flemish wave flooding into the Dutch theatre landscape). Many artists from the southern Low Countries fled to the north, where they participated in the develop-ment of the Dutch-language culture. The strict censorship imposed by the Spanish occupying power, which found the chambers of rhetoric too progressive, bears much of the responsibility for the collapse of the theatre in the south.

The gallicisation of the southern culture created an increasingly repressive environment for Dutch-language theatre. It wasn't until the end of the 19th century that Dutch was once again recognised as an official language in addition to French, opening the way for a revival of native drama. The many years of repression by various foreign cultures and the necessity to live with the French-speaking Walloons was undoubtedly an important reason why the art of the native playwright lagged behind in the south.

During the prosperous north's Golden Age, the decline was postponed for a time by the dramatic work of authors like G.A. Bredero (e.g. *Moortje*, 1615 and *De Spaanse Brabander*, 1617), P.C. Hooft (e.g. *Warenar*, 1617) and the greatest poet from this period: Joost van den Vondel. In Amsterdam in 1637 the first Dutch playhouse opened its doors with Vondel's *Gysbreght van Aemstel*. *Gysbreght* continued to be performed every year on New Year's Day in the Amsterdam theatre, an interrupted tradition that came to an end in 1969.

Despite the exceptional quality of Vondel's plays in particular, the Netherlands began to fall behind in comparison with foreign theatre. The playwrights grew more and more distant from the actual theatrical experience. They were more interested in theory and study than in practical aspects of the theatre, while writers such as Shakespeare and Molière were proving that an important condition for good dramatic material could be collaboration with the actors. At the same time, a gap began to develop between the theatre and the surrounding community. During the second half of the 18th century theatre hardly performed any direct function in society. Imitations of French works and other translations from foreign authors served as entertainment for the upper strata of the population. From that time on, originality in the Dutch theatre became a rare commodity. New ideas, styles and plays were imported from across the border. In Flanders the year of Belgium's independence, 1830, was the start of a period in which the national repertoire was added to again: moral plays fighting Frenchify and depravity.

During the 1960s, when the focus of the theatre moved back to questions of social relevance, the work of the native playwright began to be valued once again. The only other brief revival came around 1900 and can be credited to an exceptional Dutch author with international appeal: Herman Heijermans (1864-1924). Heijermans was a socialist who, in addition to being a playwright, was also a critic, a director and the leader of a theatre company. He was furious about the terror of the box office and how it had turned into an industry. His portraits of Dutch life, such as *Op hoop van zegen* (1900), *Schakels* (1903) and *Eva Bonheur* (1917), reveal deep social commitment. Rooted in naturalism and realism, the themes and particularly the dramatic structure of his work reveal an obvious kinship with Chekhov and Hauptmann. His work was

performed in the Soviet Union, America and especially in
Germany. However, Heijermans's influence reached further than
the plays he wrote. He stimulated young writers, and more than
thirty percent of the repertoire performed by his company, De
Nederlandsche Tooneelvereeniging, consisted of Dutch-language
plays. But after his death this situation quickly altered.

Flemish writers from this period included Nestor de Tière (1856-
1920), who was known as the 'Flemish Heijermans', and Cyriel
Buysse. Herman Teirlinck (1879-1967), with expressionistic plays
such as *De vertraagde film* (1922) and *De man zonder lijf* (1925),
brought about a revival during the twenties. But these occasional
highlights were always followed by silence, and the wall between
theatre professionals and writers was raised once again. In both
Flanders and the Netherlands, men and women of letters regarded
dramatic literature with disdain, and whenever they did hazard a
glance they often mistakenly looked at the plays only as an
expression of a specific literary art. And neither producers nor
government made much of an effort to change the situation.

It sounds paradoxical, but the art of the playwright really took off
when the text lost its central and previously unassailable place
within the method of performance. The changed notions about
theatre, which developed during the mid-sixties and which were
marked in the Netherlands by the turbulent events around the
'Tomato Revolt' (see below), provided a new source of fuel for
many writers.

The Flemish and Dutch theatre after 1945 was dominated by a
number of large companies who seemed to have nodded off at the
beginning of the sixties as far as the artistic form and content of
their work was concerned. This situation, as it concerned the
Netherlands, for example, was partly a result of the fact that the
companies were trapped in a subsidy system that placed enormous
stress on the so-called 'horizontal distribution principle'. The big
cities in the west of the Netherlands – Amsterdam, Rotterdam, The
Hague – had to provide the rest of the country with theatrical
productions. After running for a brief period in the company's own
city, a production immediately went on the road to be performed in
the provinces. As soon as the company returned, the members had
to rush to get a new production on the boards. Under this intense
pressure, with from fourteen to twenty productions per season, it's
hardly surprising that little attention was paid to the development
of individual style or the stimulation of writing talent.

The only Dutch-language writer who was able to make a break-
through and to claim a permanent place in the big companies'
repertoires was the Fleming Hugo Claus. In 1955, Ton Lutz and
the Rotterdam Toneel introduced Claus's play *Een bruid in de*

morgen (A Bride in the Morning). Claus was the founding father among post-war playwrights, and his oeuvre consists of dozens of translations and adaptations as well as no less than forty original plays which are impossible to categorise in one style or genre. The power behind his dramatic poetry is a great expressive ability and an almost physical directness. One important theme in Claus's work is the conflict between desire and morality in our society.

With the big conventional theatre companies in those days the purpose of the theatre was to serve the cause of literature; performance was not recognised as an autonomous form of art. But just as in other parts of Europe during the fifties, small-scale groups emerged along the periphery which tried to give the theatre a different artistic and political slant.

In Flanders the groups performed in attics, basements and annexes, and were given the name 'chamber theatres'. A new kind of dramaturgy evolved, in which theatre was no longer regarded as a derivative of literature but as an independent medium. New ideas, themes, and views on the relationship between human beings and the world (existentialism, absurdism) demanded different means of expression. The spoken and written word were no longer regarded as the only forms of communication; psychological realism was no longer the bearer of universal happiness; and the distance between actor and audience diminished. In addition to the modern repertoire of Pinter, Adamov, Beckett, Ionesco and Albee, the work of the Flemish playwrights was performed: Hugo Claus, Tone Brulin, Piet Sterckx, Walter van den Broeck and Johan Boonen. The Flemish company Vandaag, for example, brought the Hugo Claus play *Thyestes* in an 'Artaud-acting style'. The company Het Nieuw Vlaams Theater became a laboratory in which only the Dutch-language repertoire was staged.

In the Netherlands there were two smaller companies that fulfilled this function: Studio and Toneelgroep Centrum. Kees van Iersel, director with the experimental Studio, brought the modern repertoire to the smaller theatre, but he also commissioned work from important Dutch writers: Cees Nooteboom, Harry Mulisch, Bert Schierbeek and Anton Koolhaas. Van Iersel also introduced Lodewijk de Boer, whose four-part theatre serial *The Family* (1972) was performed by Studio at the beginning of the seventies. Toneelgroep Centrum occupies a unique place in Dutch theatre history. This was the only company that concentrated consistently on Dutch drama. Its successes included *Ajax-Feijenoord* (1969) and *Kees de Jongen (Kees the Boy*, 1970) by Gerben Hellinga and *Een zeer bijzondere dag (A Very Special Day*, 1972) by Herman Lutgerink. Since 1975 the group has even had its own in-house playwright, Ton Vorstenbosch. Centrum also invited unknown writers, and rather than show them the door immediately following their first play or a less than successful piece, they actually offered them the support of a dramaturg.

But these changes were marginal, and the repertory companies grew more and more fossilised. As the sixties came to a close the protest increased. In Flanders, playwright Hugo Claus, dramaturg Carlos Tindemans and actor Alex van Royen drew up the manifest 'T68', and in the Netherlands, on October 9, 1969, after a performance of *The Tempest* by the Nederlandse Comedie, the stage exploded in a shower of tomatoes: there in the Amsterdam Stadsschouwburg (the Amsterdam City Theatre), two directing students at the Amsterdam drama school took matters into their own hands and gave expression to the steadily increasing dissatisfaction with conditions in the theatre. The frivolous actions from that period, which were a call for more social awareness and a different repertoire, have gone down in Dutch theatre history as the Tomato Revolt.

For a number of young theatre professionals, the Tomato Revolt was the starting signal to step out of the established theatre system. The Dutch government, which also recognised that the theatre had reached a dead end, reacted to the situation more quickly than the Flemish subsidisers. In the Netherlands at the beginning of the seventies many new plans were rewarded with subsidies, giving the Dutch theatre a brand new look in one fell swoop. Theatre groups such as Werkteater, Baal, Onafhankelijk Toneel and De Appel, and political companies such as Proloog and Sater were a breath of fresh air to the existing moribund system. In their search for new forms and a new audience they fled from the playhouses, with their limiting box stages. In smaller flat floor theatres or at totally different locations they tried to reconnect theatre with society. Since then, there has never been a hint of uniformity on the Dutch stage. A lively circuit of small theatres arose featuring colourful and progressive work. Some of the large repertory companies tried to renew themselves, others simply petered out, and after a time new repertory companies cropped up: the Publiekstheater, the Ro Theater and Globe.

In Flanders, the initiatives for theatre renewal, which occurred along the fringes, took much longer because of the inflexible policy structure. Artists such as Jan Fabre, Jan Decorte, Josse de Pauw and Jan Lauwers mostly worked outside the subsidy system. For a long time many theatre professionals could only survive with help from venues that offered them a roof over their heads, such as Monty (Antwerp), Kaaitheater (Brussels) and De Singel (Antwerp). Often they were forced to set up complicated international networks of co-producers. It was only a few years ago that the

Flemish authorities showed a willingness to make conciliatory gestures. They recognised the importance of a number of new companies by awarding them subsidies and making it clear that large, unadventurous companies could no longer take state support for granted.

One feature of the new theatre climate was the blurring of borders between the various disciplines. Ritsaert ten Cate made it possible to follow artistic development in other parts of the world by inviting the international avant-garde to his Mickery Theater in Amsterdam. There the public were confronted by important movements and groups such as La Mama, Tenjo Sajiki, Mabou Mines and the Pip Simmons Theatre Group. These companies involved the public in their performances and often even forced them to take a personal stand on various issues.

In Flanders the Kaaitheater of Hug de Greef developed a unique model of exchange between the foreign avant-garde and Dutch-language theatre artists (Robert Wilson, Wooster Group, Gosch, etc.)

A typical exponent from that period and an important stimulus for the art of the Dutch-language playwright was the collective Werkteater, founded in 1970. The emancipation of the actor and the banishment of the literary text from the centre of the perform-ance were two striking developments that were consistently implemented by this group. The traditional hierarchy of director and writer was no longer tolerated at the Werkteater. The actors created their own pieces, improvised on socially relevant themes and turned writing into a group process. Written material did not necessarily have to be grammatical or to dominate the action. Indeed, the process did not end with the first performance, for discussions with the audience often provided material for further changes. The Werkteater searched for target groups and performed in prisons, hospitals and old people's homes. Werkteater's actors were admired for keeping language to a minimum, yielding a lovely poetry that had not lost its natural qualities. Political theatre groups such as Proloog and Sater (in the Netherlands) and De Internationale Nieuwe Scène and Het Trojaanse Paard (in Flanders) worked in the collective mode, and wrote most of their own material. Few of the writers from this collective period are still active, something that perhaps can be blamed on their temporary position, or on their working from a basic assumption that was not always artistically challenging. But they created a climate in which other writers, who were usually directors themselves, were stimulated to take on the playwright's task.

During the eighties, a generation of theatre professionals defined themselves by creating their own theatre language. The period of

dogmatic political theatre was now over, and the focus turned
from content to form. The new directors examined their material,
especially the language, undermining conventional production
methods and audience reaction. No longer did they make the effort
to create a 'make believe' situation or to hold up a mirror of
reality. No longer did they concern themselves with immediate
recognition and identification. Rather, they worked with
associative material that had a whole range of interpretative
possibilities.

As a result, the text increasingly became part of a greater whole.
Less time was spent working on new themes and stories and more
on the form, the way in which the narrative was presented. The
plastic arts, mime, dance, music and video were very helpful in
this effort. Incidentally, this attention to form did not mean
excluding a sense of social or political awareness. But the changing
face of the world had led to less certainty and fewer dogmas and
to a more personal response in which the director has more or less
become the performance's author.

This blurring of disciplines can be seen in the work of Jan Fabre.
Fabre is a Fleming who began his career as a visual artist. He sees
text, image, acting and movement as equivalent components. Fabre
is not interested in conventional theatrical codes concerning
duration of the performance, rhythm, narration and identification.
As in *Power of Theatrical Follies* (1984), his written material
consists of disconnected sentence fragments, bits that are plucked
from daily existence and which at first seem to exhibit little
coherence. He often uses different languages, or sound only. His
material takes on meaning only in combination with images,
sound, choreography and acting. In 1989, in addition to his artistic
and major theatrical projects, he began making productions in
which the text was central, works such as *Het interview dat sterft*
(*The Interview that Dies*, 1989) and *Vervalsing zoals zij is,
onvervalst* (*Falsification as it is, Genuine*, 1992).

Through these theatrical innovations, the dramatic text has become
more and more rooted in the stage experience. The new playwright
no longer creates his text in isolation, seated at his desk, but is
closely involved in the process on the acting floor. Often the writer
plays a double role. Directors such as the Flemings Jan Decorte,
Willy Thomas and Josse de Pauw, and the Dutchmen Gerardjan
Rijnders and Frans Strijards have begun writing themselves.

The eighties were also a period when the ties between Dutch and
Flemish theatre professionals were drawn tighter once again. Just
as when around 1600 a 'Flemish wave' flooded over the Dutch
theatre landscape. This time the wave was the result of the Flemish
government's subsidy policy, whose investment in the theatre was

lower in comparison with the Netherlands. A large group of
Flemings (Ivo van Hove, Jan Fabre, Sam Bogaerts, Jan Decorte,
Guy Joosten, Luc Perceval, Jan Lauwers and Lucas Vandervorst)
were no longer interested in working with rigid companies in huge
playhouses. This surge of young theatre professionals developed
theatre groups with an entirely new image, usually free of existing
structures. The Netherlands was indispensable for their survival.
It functioned as an 'outlet' for their productions, but it also made
sure that they were given artistic recognition. The presence of
Flemish actors and directors in Dutch companies (and vice versa,
to a lesser degree) is now a fact of life.

This Flemish wave was a powerful stimulus for the Dutch theatre
climate. Differences between the Flemish and Dutch theatre are
difficult to define, and the dividing lines cannot simply be drawn
along the border. As with the language (the difference between
Flemish and Dutch being roughly comparable to the difference
between British and American English), speaking of a difference
in nuance in the theatre comes closer to the mark. These nuances
have to do with the more rational attitudes of the Dutch, who still
feel the need to explain and describe reality, as opposed to the
tendency of the Flemings to create a different reality on the stage
which allows more room for the physical, the irrational and the
poetic.

In recent years, the situation has improved slightly for Flemish
theatre professionals. It is striking that practically all innovations
have taken place outside the big repertory companies. In the
Netherlands, more innovative, controversial directors have moved
on to the major theatres. With them the new dramaturgy has found
its way to the larger stages. An important example of this movement is Gerardjan Rijnders: director, actor, film-maker, writer and,
since 1987, the artistic director of Toneelgroep Amsterdam, for
whom high-risk interpretations of international classical and
modern repertoire alternate with new dramatic material by Dutch
playwrights. Rijnders's own material is often called provocative,
hard and cynical. It reflects a sombre picture of the world in which
violence, lovelessness, hypocrisy and small-mindedness have the
upper hand. Plays such as *Pick-Up* (1986) and *Tulpenvulpen*
(1988) depict broken relationships, *De hoeksteen* (*The Cornerstone*, 1987) opens fire on the family as the cornerstone of society,
and large montage productions such as *Titus, geen Shakespeare*
(*Titus, no Shakespeare*, 1988), *Ballet* (1990) and *Count Your
Blessings* (1993) are examples of an open textual structure in
which all sorts of verbal fragments are forged together.

In 1995 the premiere of Toneelgroep Amsterdam's *Rijgdraad*
(*Tacking-thread*), written by Judith Herzberg, took place. It was

something of a sequel to *Leedvermaak* (*The Wedding Party*), whose content and form made such a great impression on the Dutch public in 1982. In *Leedvermaak*, with its more than eighty fragmentary scenes, Judith Herzberg for the first time expresses the problems and especially the guilt experienced by the second generation of Jewish war victims. Herzberg sketches her characters with few words and a wry humour; the dialogues are almost all remarks made in passing, but there's not a single sentence without a double meaning. The sound of her language betrays Herzberg's background as a poet. Her work usually takes shape through interplay with the actors. Herzberg is a genius at suggesting backgrounds and at weaving many threads together at the same time, and very slowly the puzzle-pieces come together in the audience's head. She also uses this montage technique in some of her other plays, among them *En/of* (*And/or*, 1985), *Kras* (*Scratch*, 1988) and *Some of my Best Friends* (1995). Many of her plays have been performed in Germany as well.

Frans Strijards, artistic director of Art & Pro, in his plays and performances also goes a step further with techniques involving deconstruction and alienation. The actors in his company have perfected a physical style in which they use enlargements and comedy to expose their characters' motives, thereby breaking down traditional theatrical forms. Faced with these fragments, the audience is simply incapable of creating fully-rounded characters' or logical narratives. The use of obscure language, the identity crisis of the individual and the unmasking of theatrical illusion are central to such plays as *Hensbergen* (1985), *Gesprekken met Goethe* (*Talks with Goethe*, 1988), *Het syndroom van Stendhal* (*The Stendhal Syndrome*, 1989) and *Toeval, voorval* (*Accident, Incident*, 1991).

These are only a few aspects of the work of a varied crowd of Dutch-language writers that resists simple categorisation and is growing bigger all the time. Together with the people on-stage, writers such as Rob de Graaf, Willy Thomas, Jan Decorte, Paul Pourveur, Peter Verburgt and Tom Lanoye have developed their own theatre idiom. They no longer hold up a mirror to reality, a 'task' that has probably been taken over by television, but they search for the specific means of expression to be found in their own medium. With the linking of cause and consequence, plays can be created from several different perspectives, and dream and reality are woven together.

Arne Sierens, one of Flanders' leading writers at the moment, also deserves a place in this group. Sierens, who wrote several pieces for the Blauwe maandag Compagnie, was formerly director and actor in his own company, De Sluipende Armoed. His frag-

mentary pieces are associative and poetic, and they describe
the everyday tragedy befalling the common man. His musical
language is very direct and he often writes in dialect with a great
deal of humour. A few titles are *De drumleraar* (*Drummers*, 1994),
Mouchette (1990), *Boste* (1992) and *Moeder en Kind* (*Mother and
Child*, 1995).

The Dutch playwrights Karst Woudstra and Lodewijk de Boer are
more in the tradition of classical text theatre, or rather their work
exhibits a greater degree of traditionalism. Woudstra is also a
dramaturg, director and translator of plays, and his pieces have
a realistic framework and an internal logic. The psychologically
credible, frequently contemporary characters converse in recogniz-
able, flexible dialogues. But beneath the surface is hidden a deeper
symbolic layer, a dark past, which often emerges in extreme
situations or during confrontations. Woudstra's work includes
Hofscènes (*Court Scenes*, 1980), *Een hond begraven* (*Burying the
Dog*, 1989), *Een zwarte Pool* (*A Black Pole*, 1990) and *Na de
middag* (*Ante Meridium*, 1995).

Lodewijk de Boer began his career as a violinist with Concertgebouw Orchestra, and moved on by way of a student theatre
group to the Toneelgroep Centrum. Now his *oeuvre* consists of
more than thirty plays, pieces incorporating both music and text.
De Boer directs his own work, not only in the Netherlands but also
in Sweden, which has sometimes been called 'poetic naturalism'.
Several other titles in addition to the previously mentioned four-
part *The Family* (1972) are *Darts* (1967), *Angelo en Rosanna*
(1986) *The Bouddha van Ceylon* (*The Buddha of Ceylon*, 1990),
the trilogy *Ingeblikt* (*Tinned*, 1991), the opera *Naïma* (1985) and
the youth theatre play *The Wedding House Party* (1994).

It's easy to see that the art of the Dutch-language playwright is
quite colourful at the moment, and the climate extremely fertile.
And we still haven't spoken of all the successful playwrights
for young people's theatre whose work is regularly performed
abroad, and the relative newcomers such as Koos Terpstra, Frank
Vercruyssen, Marian Boyer and Jeroen van den Berg.

The new playwrights don't occupy an unassailable position by any
means. The text has become just one of many elements used in
contemporary theatre, and it is adapted as necessary. The plays
usually emerge from a common stock of ideas and a lively
exchange between the writer and the producer. Conflicts are
always lurking in such an approach, of course, and there's a certain
amount of flexibility required of both the writer and the producer.
But it is only through this renewed, intense relationship that the art
of the Dutch playwright can be assured a lively future.

The past thirty years have brought us to a point where the Dutch-language playwright is no longer a curiosity. Unfortunately we don't regularly see the texts, perhaps because now more than ever they are associated with original productions or with a particular director. Often a play ends up on the shelf after one production, never to have its merits tested again by anyone. It's slowly becoming time for more new productions of old work. Only when old and new plays, original productions and reinterpretations enter into dialogue with each other will we be able to speak of a real tradition in the Dutch-language region as well.

Petra de Kock

DUTCH AND FLEMISH PLAYS

THE BUDDHA OF CEYLON

by Lodewijk de Boer

Translated by Della Couling

Lodewijk de Boer was born in Amsterdam in 1937, where he attended the Amsterdam Conservatory, specializing in the viola, an instrument he subsequently played professionally with great success, including a period from 1961 to 1968 in the world-famous Concertgebouw orchestra. But already by 1963 De Boer's interest in the theatre had led to his first play, *De kaalkop luistert (The Baldhead is Listening)*, inspired by the emergent absurdist movement. Since then he has written over thirty plays for the theatre, and other work for radio and television, plus libretti and screenplays. He is also a composer and director.

Since the mid-seventies, De Boer has frequently tried in his plays to achieve a form of theatre combining text and music. The constantly recurring elements in his work of an inner world at variance with an outer world, different agendas followed by different characters simultaneously on stage, echoing the complexities of opera ensemble writing, clearly demonstrate the continuing influence of music in his creative process.

The Buddha of Ceylon was premiered in 1991 in The Hague, directed by the author. Set in a Dutch colony 'somewhere in South America' in 1943, the play has one strand that is an experience familiar to the British: colonial guilt. Woven into that strand is also the Nazism of the German occupiers of the Netherlands, the waves from which have washed up on this far colonial shore a refugee Jewish violinist, Alban, his wife, Hannah, and a mysterious German-speaking agent from Prague, called Prager. They all gravitate to the residence of the Governor, Theodor, and his wife, Athalie. Theodor's ambivalent attitude towards Nazism and towards the native population he has been sent out to govern, is an often unacknowledged factor of Dutch colonial experience. Tensions spark off constant small explosions which together eventually destroy all the characters in some way or other. The play ends with a quirky and surreal coda.

'Only a musician can write a play like this, in which the events follow each other like the themes and motifs from a piece of music,' wrote the critic of the *NRC Handelsblad* after the premiere in February 1991. Although there is very little music in this play, it is true that the spirit of music hangs over it and dictates its progression.

Characters

THEODOR DE BOUSSELAERE, *colonial governor*
ATHALIE, *his wife*
ALBAN ZADOK, *a refugee*
HANNAH, *his wife*
PRAGER
SYLVIA

The play is set in the governor's residence somewhere in South
America in 1943.

ACT ONE

Scene i

Fade in.

Music: from 'In Memoriam' by Schnittke, Tempo di valzer.

Enter ALBAN ZADOK. *He is carrying a small suitcase and a violin case. He opens the violin case, looks in it, runs his finger over the strings and closes the case. Looks around. He goes to an alcove in which there is an expensive looking Buddha statuette, picks it up, inspects it from all sides and puts it in his suitcase. He closes the case and leaves the room. All this is observed from one of the entrances by* SYLVIA, *who now crosses the room and disappears . . .*

Fade out.

Scene ii

Fade in.

THEODOR *and his wife* ATHALIE *enter the room.*

THEODOR *(taking off his jacket)*. God . . . I just can't get used to this climate, or the country, or the people.

ATHALIE. Like a drink? Or have you had enough?

THEODOR. I've never had enough.

ATHALIE *(pours, there is the chink of icecubes)*. Any special requests?

THEODOR. A lot of ice . . . My sworn allegiance to the crown, the heavy responsibility towards the mother country going through such trying times . . . All this, in combination with my physical condition, makes the desire for ice even greater. *(Sits.)*

ATHALIE. Here's your whisky.

THEODOR. Why there?

ATHALIE. I've just no desire today to run behind you with your whisky. Why don't you take a shower?

THEODOR. Yes, why not . . .

ATHALIE. You've been sitting there again drinking and chattering on at the club. And we're expecting a guest.

THEODOR. That's true. It will be a pleasure for me to confront a deserter like that with the insurmountable problems of an overseas territory.

ATHALIE. Why don't you give it up? Ask for a transfer. Some consulate or other on a little insignificant island. There you could try to forget everything.

THEODOR. Oh no!

ATHALIE. An unimportant man on an unimportant island trying to forget his unimportant life. I think that would be just the thing for you.

THEODOR. I don't want to forget anything. On the contrary. We have to remember everything. Keep everything in our heads right down to the smallest detail. Life only has meaning if you forget nothing and no one forgets anything.

ATHALIE (*after a silence, thoughtfully*). How is it that in fact I met a failure while I thought the opposite. Was that the influence of your father? Back then?

THEODOR. I have never asked you what you thought when we met. I had little to say for myself at that time.

ATHALIE. And later things didn't get any better.

Silence. Sounds, a woman's voice humming.

THEODOR (*stands up, listens*). What are they up to now . . . ?

ATHALIE. Screwing up courage.

THEODOR. What for?

ATHALIE. To overthrow us.

THEODOR (*scornful*). Don't make me laugh! As though that would be in their interests! This ridiculous country, this bottomless pit . . . (*Somewhere in the distance stands* SYLVIA.) Mark my words, it wouldn't take much for us to let them have this country back again. And then I'd like to see how quickly these clowns send the whole place to buggery.

ATHALIE (*in the alcove*). Where's the Buddha?

THEODOR. Europe is in flames, bauxite has never been so high on the market and do you think that boosts production? Of course not! That pack of black idiots withdraws into that disease-ridden malarial back garden and SCREWS UP COURAGE!!! What for? To raise their miserable living standard? To be converted to a decent religion? Oh no! Stirred up by an alcoholic witchdoctor they are busy sharpening their bows and arrows to overthrow us! Sorry, but I have to laugh . . .

ATHALIE. The Buddha, have you by any chance . . .

THEODOR. There comes a time when we have to tackle it differently. Put things straight. No wishy-washy sentimental humanism but drastic eradication of hotbeds of rebellion. What did God do when man really made a mess of things? The flood! Mass drowning. Two white trusted agents and a menagerie were spared.

ATHALIE. Are you listening?

THEODOR. Yes.

ATHALIE. The Buddha's gone.

THEODOR (*in the alcove*). Damn it! It's been stolen. How often have I told you you can't trust the servants. How often?

ATHALIE. Often.

THEODOR. This country makes me sick. They laugh in your face and steal behind your back or the other way round.

ATHALIE. Nothing has ever been stolen by the servants in this house.

THEODOR. And in other houses?

Silence.

ATHALIE. I fear for Europe . . .

THEODOR. You!? Well, a fat lot Europe will care about that. And what do you mean exactly? (*Acting.*)Ah! You mean the goddess who was overpowered by Zeus in the guise of a gigantic bull on the Phoenician shore and raped.

ATHALIE. No . . . Please don't bore me with your encyclopaedic knowledge –

THEODOR. Oh no? I know what you mean long before you know it yourself.

ATHALIE. Of course you know.

THEODOR. Because I have an intellectual lead. Intellectually I am a few lengths ahead of you. That is pretty obvious.

ATHALIE (*gapes*). Now listen . . .

THEODOR. I went to grammar school and you went to domestic science college. That's the difference. But that's why I still love you. We need one another. Because just as this black country needs its white masters, so decadent Europa provoked the white bull. She was raped and Minos was the result of that alliance, founder of Crete . . . (*In a different tone.*) National Socialism is raping Europe, Minos stands for the new idea, the 'new man' in fact, and Crete is one powerful united Europe standing firm against the primitive balalaika-playing hordes from the east . . . See, that's what I mean by a strict classical education. You learn to see the connections. My father beat me without mercy with his walking stick, while I, bent over, read Ovid's Metamorphoses in Greek by the light of an old candle.

ATHALIE. In Latin, Ovid wrote in Latin –

THEODOR. That doesn't matter! I read the classics in their own dead language and Father kept on beating. At first I had my doubts about the violence of his pedagogic methods that caused me a lot of pain. It could escape no one, however, that my zeal in getting to the bottom of the classics was almost superhuman. But later, much later, I understood the old man . . . Just as in the Middle Ages a nobleman was dubbed a knight, my father dubbed me a governor.

ATHALIE (*vehemently*). Sometimes I think you're suffering a chronic brain haemorrhage.

THEODOR. Ha! How I love your anger. If you were black I'd probably have you flogged to death. But you're white and I love you.

ATHALIE. Yes . . . what else could you do.

Silence.

THEODOR. Oh yes, Verschoor sends his regards. District Commissioner Verschoor. They were here once at a party. You seem to have made an indelible impression on him. He's married to a pale-faced woman from Drenth with a psychosomatic inflammation of the uterus.

ATHALIE. Inflammation of the kidneys.

THEODOR. Do you know better again?

ATHALIE. He told me at the Prince's reception that malaria was totally destroying the foundations of his body. He said that, literally. I still remember it exactly. You were standing there in that grotesque governor's uniform of yours, surrounded by a swarm of your top officials who were hanging like flies on the Prince's lips. Verschoor stared at you all with his pale eyes. And without turning his head he said: 'Malaria is totally destroying the foundations of my body.' I found that a fitting image for our position in this country.

THEODOR (*scornful*). Malaria? Syphilis you mean. Caught from some coolie servant girl. You always get the wrong end of the stick.

ATHALIE. A memorable reception. How busy you were. Exalted visitor, the Prince. The whole evening I was thinking: what have we landed here. Friend or foe? That was of course because of that suspicious German accent. A thought I couldn't get away from. While of course I knew very well that he was commander in chief of the Dutch Armed Forces . . . But why did the Armed Forces get beaten so quickly, I kept thinking. While they have a commander in chief who speaks such fluent German too. I was really confused, that evening . . .

THEODOR. Not only that evening.

ATHALIE. You even introduced me to him. Right at the beginning of the evening.

THEODOR. At the end of the afternoon.

ATHALIE. Strange . . . Somehow or other men in uniform all look alike. Germans certainly. They have a special talent for uniforms. It's as though the uniform and the man sort of synthesise to, for example, just to name one, a German. I'm saying that not to hurt you, but because at the moment there are again so terribly many of those animated uniforms marching around. And all in places where they don't belong.

THEODOR. You're giving me a headache.

ATHALIE. May I just?

THEODOR. Well . . .

ATHALIE. I'd just like to finish saying something about that strange evening.

THEODOR *stands up, goes upstage, into the corridor, turns on the shower. Half visible, he undresses, stands under the shower. Half visible, he dries himself and puts on a pompous governor's uniform.*

ATHALIE. Do you remember that adjutant? A pasty-faced Friesian hayseed from the Prince's retinue. Twienstra was his name, I think. Yes. Twienstra. Sjobbe Twienstra. (*Laughs.*) May I introduce myself, Madam . . . Sjobbe Twienstra, the Prince's adjutant. Well, of course he might. Why not? What immediately struck me, apart from his operetta uniform, was that little sabre. Such a short, coquettish little ornamental sabre, that dangled at a sort of angle over his thigh. It was totally useless of course, but it gave me a strange excited feeling. Look, from a military standpoint it was of course a ridiculous spectacle. Against the enemy that Twienstra would have cut a pretty silly figure. Instead of that stupid little sabre he should have had a big axe hanging or a bunch of hand grenades . . . But this greenhorn existed only through the grace of the shining boots of his superiors. Martial bootblack in fixed employment with the Prince and his fellow actors. Shocking, but also very exciting. And while he was telling me about suffering Europe I keep staring fascinated at that little sword. And at a certain point I felt a fatal misunderstanding was arising. I had that with you too, when we began that ridiculous marriage. May I accompany you to the garden, he asked, suddenly husky. Husky. Why? I've never understood that. But at a certain moment they go hoarse. The sex drive in men seems to hit the vocal chords. So I followed him, just as obedient as I always am, right into the garden. Of course in fact he followed me. Where were his thoughts? In the kitchen garden in Ureterp? Where a gang of helmeted Teutons with bayonets were stabbing the haystacks?

God, how I admired his courage. In a tropical night, while the mosquitoes carried out divebomb attacks like Messerschmidts on his close-shaven neck, Sjobbe Twienstra stood there flirting with me with his desperate soldier's courage. Are you listening?

It doesn't matter anyway if you are listening. I stood there, far behind our house and talked, hissed and whispered. Like now, more or less. About the sadness and the little joys of love. About secret animal desires. Very open, very honest and very false. (*Slaps her hands to her eyes.*) And suddenly I was assailed by an intense feeling of femininity. A feeling that came up so powerfully that the tears choked me. I felt that everything was irrevocably lost. I was powerless. It was a final convulsion. I remember the ground started to sway beneath my feet. I couldn't get it on an even keel any more and was hoping and praying someone would come and set it all right way up again. A father, a child or if need be a heart attack. Not Twienstra with his calf's eyes and his little sword, but something liberating, a comfort for the lost feeling. (*She turns round and sees* ALBAN ZADOK *standing in the room.*) I'm glad you're here.

THEODOR (*in the splendour of his governor's uniform, entering the room*). We are glad you are here.

ALBAN. My apologies. The plane was delayed. The war has the world in its grasp and shuffles the cards.

THEODOR. Quite, yes . . .

ATHALIE. How was your journey?

ALBAN. Under the present circumstances not uncomfortable. As stowaways we were in a military transport plane. More or less forced to make conversation with the great-grandchildren of cattle thieves.

ATHALIE. The Americans, you mean. The future liberators.

ALBAN. Ah! You are informed.

THEODOR. Please sit down.

ALBAN. Thank you. (*Remains standing.*)

ATHALIE. Are you alone? No luggage? No family?

ALBAN. Our departure was somewhat hasty. Moreover we had too little time to lug all kinds of useless things. To save our lives seemed enough. We have a room in the Tokai Hotel. My travelling companion and I. If I'm not mistaken she is lying on her bed now.

ATHALIE. What would you like to drink?

ALBAN. Scotch, please.

ATHALIE. With ice?

ALBAN. Neat. In a tall glass, if you have one. Do you have one?

THEODOR. What?

ALBAN. Tall glass.

THEODOR. I think so.

ALBAN (*cheerful*). My travelling companion has a rather lighthearted character. That is the result of a carefree youth. Her father was the Belgian ambassador in Hong Kong, her mother a beautiful soloist in the local folk dance group. I believe they married one another out of a sort of fascination. That often happens with people from different cultures. A strange sort of attraction. Chinoiserie in fact. Madam Butterfly, we must look for it in that corner.

THEODOR. Yes, yes . . . Rossini.

ATHALIE. Puccini. Madam Butterfly is by Puccini.

THEODOR. Damn it! I always mix up those two.

ATHALIE (*busy at the drinks cabinet*). Interesting, what you've just said.

ALBAN. I am deeply interested in the topography of human life. The complexity of existence before it exists. I mean the topography of the inside.

THEODOR. I can't quite follow you.

ALBAN (*suddenly hard and hot-tempered*). Clarity! Clarity! Clarity!

In fright ATHALIE *drops and smashes a glass.*

THEODOR (*startled*). Sorry?

ALBAN. I'm sorry. (*Beside* ATHALIE, *friendly.*) What are you doing?

ATHALIE. You made me jump.

ALBAN (*collects up the pieces, looks at* ATHALIE). I made you jump and the glass is broken. (*They laugh.*) I have the feeling I've known you for years.

ATHALIE. And how does that feel?

ALBAN (*to* THEODOR). That is what I admire so much in women. A mysterious belief in things and at the same time that slight doubt . . . What do you think about it. You, as governor and as a European.

THEODOR. Yes . . . We are living here in a rather uncultured corner of the world. My officials are either sick or completely apathetic and you can't exchange a single comprehensible word with the natives. Art, philosophy, that is totally unthinkable in this country. Our brains are empty, we are suffering from spiritual malnourishment. We devour the riches we have accumulated in Europe through our education. But we are well aware we're going downhill.

ALBAN. What are we doing here then?

THEODOR. What do you mean?

ALBAN (*to* ATHALIE, *as he takes the glass from her*). To your beauty. (*Raises his glass, then turns to* THEODOR.) Cheers.

THEODOR *raises his empty glass,* ATHALIE *takes it from him, goes to the drinks cabinet.*

ATHALIE. My husband and I are the victims of our fate. On the one hand we have the mission to civilise this country. On the other hand this mission is eating away at our physical and spiritual health. That is the price we pay. My husband has taught me to accept this, so I do accept it.

THEODOR. We're not complaining and if we complain that is our weakness. Our position here is an heroic one. We have here an heroic-historic mission to fulfil.

ALBAN (*pensive*). Where have I heard that before . . .

THEODOR. You must know that I am quoting a great man here. My father. His words are permanently etched in my soul.

ALBAN (*sprightly*). I personally see the human communication mechanism as a collection of food tins. After opening – quick consumption, otherwise the contents spoil, if they weren't spoiled before opening anyway . . .

THEODOR (*admiring*). An original idea.

ALBAN. You are very diplomatic or you are pulling my leg.

THEODOR. I am being totally serious.

ATHALIE. Seriousness and integrity are the most obvious qualities of my husband.

ALBAN. He is a diplomat.

THEODOR. The governorship falls under the diplomatic discipline. That is true.

ALBAN (*to* ATHALIE). Isn't it amazing how a conversation can run? I tell a story, you interrupt me by offering me something to drink and via the diplomatic position of your husband we are back again in my story: The Ambassador and the Chinese Dancer. On the one hand chained to one another by marriage, on the other alienated from one another by conflicting cultures. And then Hong Kong. Do you know the city?

THEODOR. No, unfortunately. But we certainly plan to make a trip after the end of my tour. Don't we, Athalie?

ATHALIE. Of course, of course.

ALBAN. And you plan to call on Hong Kong?

ATHALIE. Where my husband goes, I go too.

ALBAN (*to* THEODOR). I must advise you against it. Hong Kong is torment. A thorn in the eye of civilisation, a wretched ant-hill. One and a half million underpaid paupers, breeding on sampans . . . (*Sharply.*) What do you think of breeding?

THEODOR. I thought –

ALBAN. Figuratively speaking. Not literally.

THEODOR. I thought . . . a necessary need for the preservation of the sort –

ALBAN. I myself am a foundling. My parents found me.

THEODOR. How ghastly . . .

ALBAN. You mustn't say that. If you're a foundling it's better if they find you than if they leave you lying there. (*Laughs.*) The tribe of Zadok is by the way famous and feared for its periodic infertility. A sort of allergic infertility, a hereditary sexual disease.

ATHALIE *laughs.* ALBAN *looks at her, smiles. Silence.*

ATHALIE. You have certainly gone through a lot. Our mother country is behaving like a whore. Before the enemy had crossed the border, Europe was already lying on her back.

THEODOR (*angry*). A typically female reflection on world history, even a little risqué, don't you think?

ALBAN (*to* ATHALIE). Our mother country . . . I've just come from there, so I can give my opinion on it. (*To* THEODOR). But to say that guerrilla war has broken out there, no. I can't say that. The resistance consists of a handful of communists, three Reformed Church members, one Jehovah's Witness and a gang of adventurers. The Queen and the government are sitting safe in England and I am here. No, no. The real heroes committed suicide or have been killed. Meanwhile transport to the extermination camps is quietly going on. Regular as clockwork.

THEODOR (*fierce*). I wish to seriously question your last remark. I have talked to the Prince –

ALBAN. We have probably all spoken to the Prince at some time or other, we have perhaps at some time been kissed awake, haven't we, Madam? We love fairy tales. But the reality cannot be understood. (*Taps his forehead.*) There is still a war on, here. Sometimes there are sudden colourful explosions behind my eyes. And at the same moment I come out with a word or idea, that as a whole has nothing to do with the situation.

THEODOR *has stood up, goes to the drinks cabinet and pours a drink.*

ATHALIE. Go on.

ALBAN (*watching* THEODOR). About six months ago I was stopped. On the Prinsengracht. By a thickset German shopkeeper in uniform. An unspeakably greasy and depressing apparition. I hand him my identity card, forged from beginning to end, and at the same time start whistling the main motif from 'Siegfried'. You have to put the enemy at his ease, don't you? Transfer yourself totally into their culture. I could have sung the Horst Wessel song at the top of my voice. But some way or other that seemed a bit too proletarian for me. A bit too modern too. Personally I don't like Wagner. His music always makes me think of a well-functioning sewer. The endless melody flows harmoniously branching off, through a system of cast iron pipes, like a stream of faeces flowing on to eternity.

So I stand there whistling and the German scarcely reacts. Stupid, I think. He's stupid. The war has destroyed his hearing. I stand there performing Wagner while the concert hall is as empty as a bombsite! Suddenly he looks at me, those glassy eyes as though they've been polished with a razor . . . 'Sind Sie Jude?' With a clatter, the safety curtain drops. In its fall it shatters the wooden toy car with a twelve-year-old kid in it happily waving his hands. Blood and wood splinters mingle horribly. Jubilant, the audience is on its feet. The curtain falls. Applause . . . I don't know why, but that image flickered through my head. (*Calls to* THEODOR.) Sind Sie Jude?!

THEODOR (*chokes*). No! Certainly not!

ALBAN. Congratulations. In Europe that answer would have saved your life. (*Wipes the sweat from his forehead.*) Is it always so warm in this country?

ATHALIE. And what did you answer?

ALBAN (*runs to* THEODOR, *slaps him on the shoulder*). 'Aber natürlich, Mensch! (*Suddenly laughing helplessly.*) Natürlich bin ich Jude! Sind wir nicht alle?!'

THEODOR (*uneasily laughing*). Would you like another drink?

ALBAN (*to* ATHALIE, *serious*). Hooting with laughter he gives me my papers back and before he turns away he says: 'A man who whistles Wagner can't be a Jew.' I'm sorry, Madam, but it is disgusting.

ATHALIE. No need to be sorry.

ALBAN (*to* THEODOR, *suddenly*). And governor. How do you feel?

THEODOR (*comes up close*). I feel a bit overwhelmed. It is just as though you are blaming me.

ALBAN. What for?

THEODOR. I see a clear parallel between our position here and that of our German cultural cousins. Europe was a fragmented, disjointed jigsaw puzzle. We don't think much of puzzles. Clarity, indissoluble unity. One great, healthy nation – (*Drinks.*)

ATHALIE. Go on, Theodor.

THEODOR. Every revolution has its darker sides. Blood flows, alas, blood must flow. But if we want to have a clean frying pan then we have to scrape away the dirt. Prometheus stole the divine fire for the ovens –

ALBAN (*sharply*). Which ovens do you mean?

THEODOR. What do we know? Well? Rumours, nothing but rumours. You are an artist, I'm a governor, we know nothing of real history.

Long silence.

ALBAN. Do you have any idea where Hannah is?

ATHALIE. Hannah?

ALBAN. My travelling companion. Fellow refugee.

THEODOR. But . . . how should I know that?

ALBAN. She hasn't been picked up?

ATHALIE. No. This is a free country.

ALBAN. So you guarantee that she hasn't been picked up.

ATHALIE. Certainly.

ALBAN. So I don't have to reckon on arrest, torture, rape, a shot in the neck at the side of a mass grave?

Silence.

What's the situation here regarding resistance? I mean, there must be some kind of resistance movement or other?

THEODOR. Resistance? Against what?

ALBAN. Against the tyrants. You, for example.

THEODOR. I don't tyrannise anything or anyone. I govern. In the name of our Queen and the government of the mother country, I represent authority here.

ALBAN. Which authority of which government, actually? I've just come from that mother country but I didn't see any Queen or government. And the authority is driving round the streets in armoured vehicles and frightening children.

THEODOR. Here is not there, my dear fellow.

ALBAN (*stands*). You're right. I'm beginning to repeat myself. (*Silence, sounds, a humming woman's voice.*) What's that I hear?

THEODOR. Those noises?

ALBAN. Yes.

Suddenly HANNAH is standing in the room; ALBAN turns to her.

ALBAN. Is that you?

HANNAH. The door was open.

ATHALIE. I'm glad you're here.

THEODOR. We are glad you're here.

ALBAN. Yes.

THEODOR. May I introduce myself? Theodor de Bousselaere, governor. This is my wife Athalie. Welcome. (*Remains staring at her.*)

HANNAH. What is it, Alban?

ALBAN (*shakes himself awake*). This is my sister, Hannah. My stepsister, actually.

HANNAH. What a delightful climate. Really. It reminds me of when I was young. The dry heat. The scents. And then the sounds. A forest full of different sounds. Just like at home, years ago. Do you still remember, Alban?

ALBAN. I was only there later.

HANNAH. Were you there later?

ALBAN. When you all came back. In Knokke. I only came then, don't you remember?

ATHALIE. Do you come from Knokke?

HANNAH. Not at first, but later on we did. How do you know that?

ATHALIE. I stayed there for a while. With a great-aunt of my husband's. I loved that place. The society was, how shall I put it, distinguished. The people, especially the older ones, radiated a kind of timeless chic. It was always peaceful there . . . It must be different now.

ALBAN. The Germans, eh? On land, at sea and in the air. Everywhere Germans.

HANNAH. I found it terrible to go back. Terrible. How old was I, Alban?

ALBAN. Ten. You were ten years old.

HANNAH. And yet I remember everything . . . I remember everything and everything comes back to me now I'm here. All those exotic people, the colourful clothes, that strange, sweet air . . . I walked the whole way here. From the hotel to here. I only had to ask the way and they knew it straight away. And do you know what I find so strange. (*Smiles, feverishly blinking eyes.*) I can understand them. And they me. We speak the same language. They speak my language. Not Chinese, like in Hong Kong, but simply my mother tongue. Mine and my father's. My mother never learned to speak Dutch well. I always felt a bit ashamed about that. As long as she kept her mouth shut she was beautiful, everyone looked at her. But as soon as she started talking . . .

Silence.

THEODOR. You must look like her. No doubt about it.

HANNAH. Am I talking too much?

THEODOR. Oh no! On the contrary.

ALBAN. Keep talking. It's a relief. As long as it doesn't bother anyone . . . (*To* THEODOR.) My wife is a little overwrought.

HANNAH. You've never said that before.

ALBAN. What?

HANNAH. My wife . . . How sweet of you.

THEODOR. Are you married?

ALBAN. A bit, yes. A bit for ourselves.

ATHALIE. Why don't we sit down. Please sit down.

THEODOR. Of course. I'll get us another drink.

THEODOR *goes buoyantly, glass in hand, to the cabinet;* ATHALIE *pulls* HANNAH *down beside her on the sofa;* ALBAN *stares out of the window.*

ATHALIE (*to* HANNAH). What would you like, my dear?

HANNAH. Something cool?

ATHALIE. Whatever you want.

ALBAN. Icewater. Water with a lot of ice, that's what she drinks mostly.

ATHALIE (*to* HANNAH). With lemon. That's good against thirst.

ALBAN. You must ask her yourself.

ATHALIE. I just have.

ALBAN (*turns round, laughs*). What confusion, eh? These are confusing times so there is a lot of confusion.

THEODOR. And you, Alban? It's easier if we're on first-name terms. The same for you?

ALBAN. Please allow me to carry on calling you governor. The same, yes. Always the same, that way people don't get led astray.

THEODOR. Then I'll call you artist.

ALBAN. You do that.

THEODOR. The same, you said? What was that again?

HANNAH. Or violinist.

ATHALIE. What do you mean?

HANNAH. Actually he's a violinist. He plays the violin very well. I fell in love with him because he played the violin so beautifully. He was in an orchestra.

ATHALIE. Which orchestra?

ALBAN. Since the occupation I've scarcely played any more. Now and then I still tune it. The violin. Check to see no strings are broken. And you know what's strange?

THEODOR. I love the violin. The noblest instrument, after the human voice, of course.

ATHALIE. I've never heard you say that before, Theodor!

THEODOR. You never listen.

ALBAN. And the strange thing is that that instrument of mine has remained in perfect tune for three years.

HANNAH. Because you never play it.

ALBAN. No . . . You have to see that symbolically. Animistically. The soul of things. We must look for it in that direction.

HANNAH (*to* ATHALIE). I find it terrible that he never plays any more.

ALBAN. I don't play any more, I write. Music has been murdered. The Germanic underworld and its hangers-on have done music in. That's what I write about.

THEODOR (*who was only half listening*). What a relief it is to exchange ideas with someone from your own culture. You have no idea how we miss that. (*To* HANNAH.) Three quarters of the expat colony here consist of brainless alcoholics. The rest are married to native women. They don't even recognise their fellow countrymen any more. They've been bewitched . . . Assimilation is the worst decadence there is.

ALBAN. It's striking!

THEODOR. You understand what I mean?

ATHALIE. Of course he understands. It's just you don't understand what you're saying.

THEODOR (*to* ALBAN). Whenever I start to feel good at all, if I get away a bit from the deadly dull humdrum life here, if I feel HAPPY, then she comes along . . . Never mind. I don't want to bore you with our tragedy.

Silence.

ALBAN. Do you know what our tragedy is? No? Poverty. Being totally down and out, being forced to leave your child behind with an old Chinese woman, eating warmed up noodles day and night, that's our tragedy.

ATHALIE. Do you have children?

HANNAH (*dejected*). No . . . I only have one. A girl. She's eight . . . she's eight years old.

ALBAN. If she's still alive.

HANNAH. She looks quite old for such a little girl. She's a little old woman.

ALBAN. You can't be old enough, as a child.

HANNAH. Alban found it better to leave her with my mother. Women together.

ALBAN. Yes, I thought that best . . .

ATHALIE (*cheerful*). And I think it's high time we had a bite to eat.

THEODOR (*rushes up, gives everyone a glass. To* HANNAH). The governor's residence has never had so much beauty within its walls. Art and beauty go hand in hand. I thank the gods that fate threw you up on these seething shores. (*Raising his glass.*) To the Kingdom of the Netherlands! (*Empties his glass.*)

All drink.

Fade out.

ACT TWO

Scene i

HANNAH, *at the empty niche, is looking.* ALBAN *appears, looks at her. Long silence.*

ALBAN. Doesn't it look empty?

HANNAH (*turns round*). Why do you always have to scare me like that?

ALBAN. I like seeing it. That sudden colour in your face. There's something touching about it. You look like your own daughter.

HANNAH. When do you think we can go back?

ALBAN. When the war's over.

HANNAH. That's not an answer. I want to get away or at least to another hotel.

ALBAN. Wars have a beginning and an end. In that they are in no way different from a human life. What's wrong with that hotel?

SYLVIA *comes into the room, looks around as though she is looking for something or someone.*

ALBAN. Can I do anything for you?

SYLVIA. Isn't the governor here?

ALBAN. No . . . I have seen him. But he suddenly remembered he had to go to a party. Why?

HANNAH *looks at him.*

SYLVIA. There is someone here for the governor. He can come back later.

ALBAN. That seems a good idea to me.

SYLVIA. The Buddha has still not been found . . . (*Looks at* ALBAN.) Strange . . . A strange business.

ALBAN. A peculiar and very strange business, yes. I heard about it and I was very surprised.

SYLVIA. When would you like to eat?

ALBAN. I don't mind. You, Hannah? Any preference?

HANNAH. I'm easy.

ALBAN. Do you hear? You can scarcely imagine more easy diners. We are just happy to be alive.

SYLVIA. Will you excuse me? (*She leaves the room.*)

Silence.

HANNAH. I'm beginning to believe you weren't meaning to go back at all.

ALBAN. There's a war on. I would never feel at home any more in that country. As far as I'm concerned they are still living there permanently under the German boot. I shan't shed a single tear over it.

HANNAH. And your daughter?

ALBAN. My daughter?

HANNAH. I hope you realise what you are saying.

ALBAN. Yes, and I don't waste any more effort on that.

HANNAH. I do. She's there and I'm here. That is a great distance.

ALBAN. We have to get away as quickly as possible. To the United States. Although I loathe the idea. Where can you go at the moment with decency? Do you know?

HANNAH (*miserably*). Why did you take me with you?

ALBAN. An embittered man in the company of a pleasant young woman, that has a softening effect. That's why. And because I can't be alone.

HANNAH. I'm going back to the hotel.

ALBAN. There's no point. I've checked out of our rooms. For the moment we are staying here.

HANNAH (*stunned*). But have they invited us?

ALBAN (*with exaggerated emphasis*). We are victims of the war, Hannah. We appeal to the basic rights of man. The so-called human rights people have been at loggerheads over it for centuries.

HANNAH. You must be crazy . . . (*Abruptly she leaves the room.*)

ALBAN. That is a rather simple solution. Running away. They all do that when the going gets tough.

He slowly gets up, stretches comfortably; SYLVIA *appears, behind her stands* PRAGER.

SYLVIA. Mr Prager. He is here for the governor.

PRAGER. And that is not you, I think.

ALBAN. Do I detect a slight tone of contempt in your voice?

PRAGER. For you or for the governor?

ALBAN. We'll let that pass, if you don't mind. All right?

SYLVIA. Alban Zadok.

ALBAN. Refugee from the occupied territories.

SYLVIA. Have the gentlemen been sufficiently introduced? (*Exit.*)

ALBAN. Do you know her?

PRAGER. I don't think so. Probably seen her, but you know, in the dark they all look alike. (*Laughs.*)

ALBAN. Oh yes?

PRAGER. Women, in the dark, towards evening when it gets dark, if you get me.

ALBAN. Not fully.

PRAGER. You haven't been here long yet. If I might give you some advice, keep your distance.

ALBAN. You mean I had better keep indoors. Holding my breath behind darkened windows? No. I never planned to stay here long.

PRAGER. You shouldn't stay in any place for too long. These are confusing times at present. How is your wife?

ALBAN. Hannah?

PRAGER. Is that her name?

ALBAN. That's her name, yes.

PRAGER. I met her a few days ago. In the Tokai Hotel. We had some very pleasant talks. Didn't she tell you anything about it?

ALBAN. No. We don't bore one another with unimportant things.

PRAGER. But she is your wife?

ALBAN. Yes, why shouldn't she be my wife?

PRAGER (*laughs shortly*). You would best know that yourself. What do you think, will the governor come home sober today?

ALBAN. I see you know him.

PRAGER. I know his reputation. But if you don't know there's nothing for it but to wait. Do you play chess by any chance? They must have a chessboard here.

ALBAN. They don't look like born chessplayers to me.

PRAGER. Pity . . . Perhaps you would rather play something for me. Your wife told me you play the violin. You do play the violin?

ALBAN. I don't play anything. Certainly not the violin and most certainly not for strangers. She's always mixing me up with her first husband. Or she just said something to save bother.

PRAGER. Strange . . . According to your wife you were a member of a famous symphony orchestra. Second desk, first violins. In connection with a decree from the occupiers you were forced to leave the orchestra. And seeing that the existence of your race was appreciated less and less, after the orchestra you also left your country.

ALBAN. And the child, did she say anything about that?

PRAGER. What does a child signify in the light of eternity. Art or child, that is the question.

ALBAN. You seem to have it all worked out, don't you . . .

PRAGER (*looks towards a corner of the room*). There stands the case with the violin! A Jacob Stainer, Absam, 1632, estimated value five hundred thousand guilders. Am I wrong?

ALBAN. Do you know what, Mr . . . Präger?

PRAGER. Prager.

ALBAN (*turns his back on* PRAGER). I think, and I'm sure I'm right, that the governor has finally found his way to the governor's residence.

ATHALIE *enters the room.*

PRAGER. Madam . . . I have a . . . (*Kisses her hand.*) My name is Prager. Please excuse my presence but I have some important matters to discuss with your husband. Public and private.

ATHALIE (*with raised eyebrows*). The governor . . . my husband is just coming. He's upstairs.

PRAGER. Please leave him to it. I have been having a pleasant talk with your guest, by the way.

ALBAN. Athalie . . . Have you seen Hannah anywhere?

ATHALIE. She's outside. With Sylvia.

PRAGER (*to* ATHALIE). Charming woman. I had a talk with her a few days ago, in the hotel. Put her wise on a few things, how things are run on the Latin American continent. Nothing complicated, just the first principles.

ATHALIE. Where do you come from, if I may ask? I've never seen you before and that means an awful lot in this village.

PRAGER. From Europe. I have instructions for the governor. In connection with the unusual political situation in our fatherland. But I have been here before.

ATHALIE. Have you just come from there?

PRAGER. No. Not directly. I took various detours to divert attention.

ATHALIE. Whose?

PRAGER. Whose not . . . (*Laughs.*) You never know. There's infiltration everywhere. It's getting more and more difficult to trust one's fellow men.

SYLVIA *appears.*

SYLVIA (*to* ATHALIE). The governor is asking for you.

ATHALIE *gets up reluctantly and disappears. Silence.*

ALBAN (*to* SYLVIA). Has our luggage arrived? (*After a questioning look from* SYLVIA.) That Tokai Hotel suddenly started to get on our nerves the last few days. That's what you get with hotels. Suddenly you meet people you take an immediate dislike to. You start to feel insecure. You can't close your eyes any more, the door creaks, your bedside cabinet has been turned upside down, the toilet is always engaged and you can't find the chamber pot.

To make matters worse, the building is in a deplorable state, not a single door closes properly and the fire escape was apparently abolished at the same time as slavery. This has all played absolute havoc with our nerves . . .

SYLVIA. Absolute . . .

ALBAN. We are completely dependent on the government. Our fate lies in their hands, as it were . . . But one thing is sure, we are easy people to live with. You don't notice we are there and if we are there then it's a rare pleasure. I don't believe in blowing your own trumpet, I know some shocking examples of that, but that typical lily-livered Dutch modesty, that toadying, submissive national character, no, that's not me, not me at all! (*After a long, painful silence, to* PRAGER.) I'm not usually this outspoken in front of strangers but I feel on the verge of a breakdown and my wife hasn't had a period for months. She will certainly have told you that, am I wrong?

PRAGER. Wrong.

ALBAN (*looks sharply at* PRAGER). I would rather you didn't keep bothering her . . . (*Sees* HANNAH, *in the background, in the corridor.*) Please forgive me. (*Disappears suddenly.*)

Silence.

PRAGER (*to* SYLVIA *who is staring fixedly at him*). I'm sorry but I'm doing what I can.

SYLVIA. That's just it.

PRAGER. We have to be patient.

SYLVIA (*stands beside him, strokes his hair*). Patient?

PRAGER. Don't do that.

SYLVIA. No?

PRAGER. Not here.

SYLVIA. Why not here?

> SYLVIA *goes to the record player, we hear Schubert's 14th string quartet, at unusually loud volume.*
>
> PRAGER *has stood up.* SYLVIA *comes up to him, hits him hard and unexpectedly in the stomach, pulls him upright, throws him against the wall, pulls him upright again, hits him . . . A one-sided, long and precise fight, an exhausting punitive expedition against the human body . . . Then, just as unexpectedly as it began, the fight stops.* SYLVIA *turns round and disappears.* PRAGER *drags himself upright, passes his hand over his face, there is blood on his mouth.*
>
> Then suddenly SYLVIA *is back, she has a towel, wipes the blood from his face, disappears again and comes back with the governor and his wife.*

THEODOR. That music is very loud!

> SYLVIA *turns down the volume.*

PRAGER (*hastily, hiding his embarrassment*). Governor . . .

THEODOR. What's the matter with you?

ATHALIE. You're bleeding.

PRAGER. Am I? I think I cut myself shaving this morning. The cut must have opened up again.

THEODOR. Are we going to keep on standing or shall we sit down.

ATHALIE. Our guest is sitting, so am I, that just leaves you.

THEODOR. What shall we drink. Would you like a drink?

PRAGER. Please.

THEODOR. What?

PRAGER. The same as you yourself usually drink.

THEODOR. Sylvia!

>ATHALIE *sees that* SYLVIA *has disappeared, she goes to get up.*

>Don't get up, darling. I'd like you to listen . . .

>*Pause. The music.*

THEODOR. Schubert . . . 'Death and the Maiden'. Wonderful, don't you think? And not just the great Schubert. We should realise that no nation in the world has produced such a wealth of great musical masters as the Germans . . . Without that rare gift of the great German composers who still amaze us daily with their immortal symphonies, operas, Lieder and string quartets, without that undying heritage a European musical culture would be absolutely unthinkable . . . Do you know the Ring? Der Ring des Nibelungen? No? My wife does. Because who doesn't know the Ring has never lived, you can clearly see that in my wife . . . Again, the cradle of classical European music lies in the lap of the German Reich. Not even our Jewish violinist can get away from that.

ATHALIE (*to* PRAGER). He didn't even make any attempt to get away from it.

THEODOR. Probably not. Because we haven't talked about it yet. You must know that a couple of artistes fleeing from Europe have ended up here. We have taken pity on them and are looking after them. Athalie?

ATHALIE. Yes?

THEODOR. Yesterday I took the liberty of looking into that case of theirs. And what do you think?

ATHALIE. Desecration of the dead.

PRAGER. Of course you thought the case was empty. An empty violin case? Ha! But did you look inside the instrument?

THEODOR. Why should I?

PRAGER (*goes to the case, takes out the violin, lets* THEODOR *look inside it*). Jacob Stainer.

THEODOR. German?

PRAGER. Absam, Tirol, Austria, property of a highly cultured German Maecenas. German, as Austria doesn't exist, Governor.

>THEODOR *sits down, the violin in his hands.*

ATHALIE. Something is happening here I really don't like.

Suddenly ALBAN *is standing in the room.*

ALBAN. What are you up to there?

THEODOR. Uh?

ALBAN (*dumbfounded*) What are you doing with that violin? That's a valuable instrument. You're damaging the lacquer with your sweaty hands.

THEODOR (*greatly embarrassed, stands up*). I'm sorry, I –

ALBAN (*really furious*). Sit down! Any moment and you'll drop it as well! Are you planning to destroy that instrument?

THEODOR (*goes to sit down again*). I didn't . . .

ALBAN (*screaming*). Keep standing! Don't breathe on the lacquer! What's the meaning of all this?

ATHALIE *goes to* THEODOR, *takes the violin out of his hands and gives it to* ALBAN, *who in his turn gives it to* PRAGER, *who puts the instrument back in the case. Silence.*

ALBAN. I get completely beside myself if a stranger touches that instrument . . . That violin is the only thing I was able to rescue. For me it's worth more than my own life. I hope you can have some understanding of that.

THEODOR. Of course. Full understanding. But you must know –

ALBAN. I lost control of myself . . .

ATHALIE (*to* THEODOR). I have asked our guests to check out of their hotel. We have enough room here.

PRAGER (*gets up*). Could I have a word with you, Governor?

ALBAN. That is very kind . . .

THEODOR. Athalie? Tell our guests they can stay here as long as they think necessary. They shall have everything they need. (*To* PRAGER.) Will you follow me?

They disappear. Pause.

ALBAN. How kind of you . . .

ATHALIE. It was only natural.

ALBAN. It's strange though . . .

ATHALIE. What?

ALBAN. Since I decided not to deceive my wife any more I feel ill at ease when I'm with other women.

ATHALIE. You mean you don't feel at ease with me?

ALBAN. I don't know whether it's something to do with you or this building here.

ATHALIE. How do you mean?

ALBAN (*looks up*). Italian?

ATHALIE (*looks*). A copy. A replica of an Italian neo-classical palazzo. Actually the imitation of something that wasn't genuine anyway. Built in the late eighteenth century by a megalomaniac slave-dealer.

ALBAN. Is that true?

ATHALIE. Let's hope so . . .

    Pause.

ALBAN. Sometimes you suddenly see everything, as though someone has suddenly turned the light on. Suddenly you see what's in front of you . . .

ATHALIE. And where you are standing and who is standing in front of you . . .

ALBAN. Sometimes I have the feeling I've been standing on my head half a lifetime. Especially the last few years. And you?

    Pause.

ATHALIE. Actually you ought to be someone different wherever you are. In Europe fascist, Jewish in Israel, here black, and uninhibited in bed.

ALBAN. What do you mean by that?

ATHALIE. That makes travelling a real pleasure. (*Goes to go away.*)

ALBAN. Listen. That bed, what about those rumours?!

ATHALIE. I'll show you something . . .

    ALBAN *follows her.*

    Fade out.

Scene ii

Fade in.

PRAGER *and* THEODOR *enter from the corridor at the rear.*

PRAGER. What did you think? Of course there are links with the motherland. It's just they are secret.

THEODOR. Why don't I know anything about it?

PRAGER. Secret links.

THEODOR. I understand that. But . . . I am here on duty as representative of the lawful government.

PRAGER. For the time being, yes. That's true.

THEODOR. A lawful representative of –

PRAGER. The government knows nothing, just like its representatives. We are protecting you and your government against yourself, as it were. You should be grateful to us.

THEODOR. But . . . this is impossible.

PRAGER. In these times everything is possible. If I might give you some advice, resign yourself to it.

THEODOR. That means making my function completely hollow!

PRAGER. Perhaps even making yourself hollow.

THEODOR. Who's to say I should trust you? Who's to say that those full powers of yours are not forgeries? Who?

PRAGER. I . . . Alas.

THEODOR. I can't accept it just like that. You must understand that.

PRAGER. Oh, governor. What does it all mean? All those goings-on of people in a world where confusion just keeps on growing. All those unanswered questions. All that knowing better. Do you know, the best thing is simply to do as you're told. And if you're told to do absolutely nothing, as it were to dissolve in a tub of hydrochloric acid, then let's do it!

THEODOR *remains silent.*

You still don't understand, do you?

THEODOR. No! Do you find that odd?

PRAGER. For an intelligent man like you, yes. And as intelligent people between ourselves I advise you to take life as it comes. Amuse yourself. Eat, drink and be merry. Go into the interior in a dugout canoe. Discover the wonderful world of Peter Stuyvesant. Take your wife with you for once to the whorehouse, it's less lonely . . . (*Laughs.*)

THEODOR. I find your humour difficult to take, Mr Prager.

PRAGER. I'm sorry.

THEODOR. As far as I'm concerned, this interview is over.

PRAGER. Are you always so peevish?

THEODOR. I don't feel a hundred per cent . . .

PRAGER (*gets up*). Those guests of yours . . . Do you actually know where they come from? The occupied territories, yes, that's what anyone can say. But the question is whether those territories are really as occupied as people say. Do you know?

THEODOR. No.

PRAGER. It is a Christian duty to take those people into your house, that does you honour. It is much better that you are all here together in the Embassy. You never know what can suddenly happen.

HANNAH *appears*.

HANNAH. Oh . . . am I disturbing? (*Stares at PRAGER.*)

THEODOR (*relieved*). On the contrary. Certainly not. We've just finished. That's so, isn't it?

PRAGER. For the moment we're both finished, governor. (*Stares at HANNAH.*)

THEODOR. You know one another?

PRAGER (*to HANNAH*). Back from your walk?

THEODOR. Strange . . .

HANNAH. I was in the hotel. I just went to lie down.

THEODOR. Your husband and I have agreed that for the moment you can –

PRAGER. Just lie down in the hotel room. I do that too when it all gets too much for me. Just lie on your back and stare at the ceiling, think about how life has to go on. Whether marriage nowadays still has any value. In short, have a complete rest.

HANNAH. I went to lie down and then I walked here. There is something odd going on in the town. I don't know what it is. A restlessness. As though there is a storm on the way.

PRAGER. A storm? Strange. I haven't noticed anything.

HANNAH. I had the same feeling in Holland, before the Germans invaded.

THEODOR. Dear Hannah, you are safe here. Believe me.

PRAGER. Don't forget, dear lady, that between these walls you enjoy diplomatic immunity. And what's more, you have the privilege of rejoicing in the respect of the governor, that is very obvious. Ah! Madam, the lady of the house.

Almost unnoticed, ATHALIE *has appeared.*

ATHALIE (*to* HANNAH). Forgive my pushiness, but I've had your luggage brought here. Your rooms are at the back.

HANNAH. I hope Alban has not abused your hospitality.

THEODOR. I just wanted to tell you that it would be a great pleasure –

ATHALIE. In view of the increasing tensions it's better you don't stay on in that hotel.

PRAGER. A sensible decision, that's just what I said, Governor. Your husband was always a good administrator, Madam.

ATHALIE. Still is, if I'm not mistaken.

PRAGER. The times are changing while we stand helplessly looking on, Madam. One moment we are the proud representatives of the crown, a second later there we are with an upturned dustbin on our heads at the side of the road. Nothing is so changeable as time. Human history is a succession of absurdities, sheer terror, blood and dog shit.

ATHALIE. What is actually going on here, Theodor?

PRAGER. I must go. There are still a few things to see to before the door slams shut for good . . . (*Begins to go, a strange smile on his face.*)

HANNAH (*excusing herself*). I did see him before, you know . . . In the hotel. We were on the same floor. He invited me to his room the other day.

ATHALIE. So . . . And how was it?

HANNAH. Rather confusing. He showed me something. A little box. And in that box was something I didn't understand. It looked like something.

ATHALIE. Like what?

HANNAH. He talked, a lot, wanted to know everything about us, talked about himself, his childhood in Germany, his grandfather from Prague . . . (*Suddenly breaks off.*)

ATHALIE. What's the matter?

HANNAH. He pulled the curtains, took out the box from under his bed and opened it. I looked, but couldn't really see what was in it. (*She appears to be crying.*)

ATHALIE. There, there. Just tell me . . .

HANNAH. He sat down on the bed, the box between his legs. I knelt down in front of him on the floor . . .

ATHALIE. And?

THEODOR (*suddenly fierce*). Your appetite for sensation is disgusting, Athalie!

HANNAH has gone to sit at the harpsichord, and starts to play.

ATHALIE. Appetite for sensation! What a sickening insinuation!

THEODOR. Leave her alone. You don't understand anything about women.

ATHALIE. It has to be you saying that, otherwise I wouldn't believe my ears, Theodor . . .

They listen to the music.

THEODOR (*quietly*). Tell Sylvia not to let that man in again. He is dangerous. Do you hear?

ATHALIE. Yes . . . I'm listening.

THEODOR. Athalie. They are trying to undermine authority, it looks like a conspiracy. He knows about everything. Don't forget to tell Sylvia.

ATHALIE. Before long when we're standing in front of the firing squad, Theodor, I want to hear the same as I'm hearing now. Do you understand?

THEODOR. For Christ Almighty's sake! Don't say things like that. You're tempting the gods –

ATHALIE. – to listen. And that's what they did, the gods. And we followed their example . . .

HANNAH plays, in snatches, but more and more firmly, now and then she sings. ATHALIE and THEODOR listen.

Fade out.

Scene iii

Fade in.

ALBAN, his case in his hand, goes to the niche. Then suddenly he sees SYLVIA who, totally relaxed, is sitting in a chair. She has a cigar in her mouth.

ALBAN. Tell me.

SYLVIA (*cigar in her outstretched hand*). Yes?

ALBAN (*giving her a light*). There's something I don't understand at all.

SYLVIA. Yes . . . Could you just pass me the ashtray?

ALBAN. I'm sure you think I'm too awful for it. Or too male, or too white.

SYLVIA. I don't think anything.

ALBAN. I can see everything here but no ashtray.

SYLVIA. No ashtray. Strange. I saw it a moment ago.

ALBAN. I find that amazing.

SYLVIA. But it's the truth.

ALBAN. If you just rubbed that ash into your hair, how about that.

SYLVIA (*looks at him smiling*). And if I just stubbed this cigar out in your hand. Is that good for playing the violin?

ALBAN. To my knowledge that has never been proved. But I'll talk it over with my teacher.

Pause.

SYLVIA (*gets up*). Do you want to continue this conversation or shall I go and get you something. In this heat you are all drinking gallons the whole time.

ALBAN. You all?

SYLVIA. You are the guest of the Governor. Not of us. We didn't invite you.

ALBAN. I'm not intending to complain, although I would like to, but my fostermother taught me that I have to be capable because my fosterfather was too. They are both dead and forgotten so I can be a weak and wretched man. And I am, in spite of my white skin.

SYLVIA. What do you expect? Sympathy? Understanding?

ALBAN. God, no. That's the last thing I want. Understanding? Like a cast-off shadow I wander all over the world. I drag a woman with me, she's left a child behind, I curse the land I was born in, and I hate just about everything that's been created, starting with myself. Did you really think I'd come to you for help?

SYLVIA. You've run away at the wrong time to the wrong place.

ALBAN. You don't have any choice.

SYLVIA. Very soon things are going to change here. New winners and new losers. It's wrong for you to be mixed up in it.

ALBAN. We're not here of our own free will. Good God! Free will! Hands up anyone for whom that still means anything. Anyone for whom that still means anything should put his hand up. I'll chop it off for him personally.

SYLVIA (*suddenly in a different tone*). How late must I reserve? You don't have to decide straight away. Think it over calmly with your host and the ladies. The restaurant and its black staff are as usual waiting to serve you. Hurry up, as it could well be the last time.

ALBAN. How come? 'No whites allowed'?

SYLVIA (*about to leave*). Who knows . . .

ALBAN (*opens the case*). What shall I do? (*Takes out the Buddha.*) Put the Buddha back and tell the governor you confessed in tears to the theft? So that we can confirm his prejudice? Or shall I saw it in half, one half each, so we're brother and sister. Well?

SYLVIA (*laughs*). Saw it in two . . .

ALBAN. You saw the whole thing, didn't you?

SYLVIA. We always see everything and everywhere.

ALBAN. If that's the case then you probably know how I can get away from here. You see, I'm taking your warning to heart.

SYLVIA. The only way is the way back. This country is not an asylum.

HANNAH, *flowers in her hair, and* THEODOR, *in shorts, appear.*

HANNAH. Have you seen our rooms? The view stretches as far as you can see. Sometimes even further. Theodor is a darling, did you know that?

ALBAN. Of course he is.

HANNAH (*forced enthusiasm*). We've been into the interior. I sat in a dugout canoe, I've seen a native village, so primitive and yet so unique in its simplicity, so odd, no comparison with Hong Kong.

ALBAN. And certainly not with Knokke.

HANNAH. And with none of those countless other places they dragged me to earlier . . . Theodor is a darling.

ALBAN. So you've already said.

SYLVIA. Is there anything else you need? Anything of importance? No? Then I'll go.

THEODOR (*sharply*). What I've noticed recently, my good Sylvia, is that you're always in a hurry. You were little liable to that earlier. Hurry? I had the impression we had missed out on that concept when we freed you from your darkness . . . Well?

SYLVIA. Do you want me to react seriously to that, Governor?

ALBAN. We'd better go for a little walk. Get a little wind through our hair.

HANNAH. There isn't any wind.

THEODOR (*to* SYLVIA). No, just wait a bit. It appears you have suddenly emancipated yourself lately. It's getting more and more difficult to find you too. What's up? Are you in love or something?

SYLVIA. Let's just assume that, governor.

THEODOR. One more minute. In love with the revolution perhaps? With anarchy and lawlessness? I should watch out. Before you realize it you're on the wrong side of the road. And then it's difficult to cross over.

SYLVIA. Should I go? Or will this go on long.

THEODOR. I see you smoke cigars. Are you intending to become a man?

SYLVIA. If you don't need me any more –

THEODOR. For the moment you're not needed. I shall expect you tomorrow in my office. Then I'll tell you exactly where you can go. Good afternoon.

SYLVIA *smiles and disappears.*

ALBAN. What do you plan to do with her? Deportation?

HANNAH. Don't act so obsessive, Alban.

ALBAN. Back to Africa? Chained in the hold of a ship?

THEODOR. I assume this is another sample of your usual cynicism.

HANNAH (*slight despair, to* THEODOR). It's hardly bearable any more, believe me . . . For as long as I remember, my parents dragged me from one place to the other. Always fleeing from something, intent on changing the world, chased away by local circumstances. So that finally I could end up in his arms. I don't know what was there first; he, the war or everything at the same time. But the world only started to look really awful when we got married and the Germans invaded the country. After that he was thrown out of his orchestra, then there wasn't

a note of music to be heard in our house any more. Never more.
Nor in all those other houses we ducked into time after time,
behind the darkened windows. Never more. We hardly ever
spoke any more. Just bitterness. A dreary life with terror as
daily bread . . .

At night I held him close to me, and tried to comfort him. It was
like holding a lump of cast iron. I thought he would come to
love my little daughter, and he probably tried too, but it never
really worked, it had no substance, false posturing, imitation, a
worthless love . . . (*Suddenly embarrassed, she looks around,
smiles entrancingly.*) Goodness . . . What a session in the
confessional, eh? I have a mind to undress, you know. I
suddenly feel like letting you all see my body, strange, eh?
I suddenly feel a strong need to lie down on the floor naked
in front of your eyes and masturbate. What can that mean?

ALBAN. Tropical frenzy, I think. Just put your head under the tap.

HANNAH (*looks at him as though seeing him for the first time,
the same smile*). Do you know in what backstreets my thoughts
are lurking? Where I'll commit my body. All the things that
happen to me behind your back?

ALBAN (*between clenched teeth*). Hannah . . .

HANNAH. What do you actually know about the woman you're
married to? And, what do you want to know? Well?

THEODOR. Me?

ALBAN (*unusually sharp*). Yes! You!

Fade out.

Scene iv

SYLVIA, *running through the corridors, can be still be seen, then
disappears again as though something or someone is pursuing
her. Then she suddenly stands still.*

SYLVIA. 'Un luku na un konton' jerewa
        Obia sa tan brewa fu tego . . . '

*She is busy with something, some task or other, and loudly
sings while doing it. She runs to the radiogram, and baroque
music is heard: Vivaldi's concerto grosso in D-minor. She
leaves the room.*

Scene v

The music . . .

Then suddenly it seems as though all the doors of a frantic 18th-century salon have been thrown open. From all sides and in varying stages of high spirits, ecstasy and paranoia, they enter the room: ALBAN, HANNAH, THEODOR, ATHALIE and, a little later, PRAGER.

THEODOR (*flamboyantly*). Wasn't that an absolutely beautiful meal. Everything imported, so first-class. I'm not complaining, personally, but it's imported food that keeps us going. Even more, it keeps our thoughts bright and our bodies white and hairless. Do you understand the nuance?

ALBAN. With or without nuance, I have never ever eaten so well. Imported, did you say?

THEODOR. What did you think! But not from the mother country, this time. That good old mother country has other things on its mind.

ALBAN. Yes . . . At home with Mother in the mother country a sort of famine winter has broken out. And here –

PRAGER (*enters*). Thirty-eight degrees in the shade. An excessive meal. We are privileged, on all fronts.

THEODOR (*good-humoured*). Do you know, I had completely the wrong idea about you, my good fellow. You are much more likeable than you look.

PRAGER. Thank you for the compliment, governor.

ATHALIE (*with scarcely concealed irony*). A terrible climate but an enchanting evening. And how wonderful that we could lightheartedly make use of that beautiful American freezer. I propose that we observe a minute's silence for our frozen and hungry fellow countrymen.

ALBAN. Isn't that a bit on the long side? I feel a bit overheated. We could fall asleep and I would find that in rather bad form.

HANNAH (*giggles*). Did you see that lieutenant? I've never seen such a brute of a lieutenant. Have you?

PRAGER. That sergeant? A handsome man, in his own way. Personally I fancy Chinese more. (*To* ALBAN.) Your wife has an honest but primitive libido . . . (*Raises his glass, to* THEODOR.) Gesundheit, Governor!

THEODOR. Zum wohl . . .

ALBAN. Now we're on the subject, Governor, a military escort like that, now was that necessity or a show of respect?

THEODOR (*with a deprecating gesture*). A safety measure, I think, in connection with internal tensions prompted by the situation in the mother country, nothing special . . .

ALBAN. Nothing special? Then why did I have the feeling I was being rounded up?

THEODOR (*sourly*). You're the best one to answer that.

ALBAN. But I'd rather from now on they aim their weapons at the enemy and not at me.

PRAGER. What enemy?

ALBAN. You always ask the obvious. What's behind that?

THEODOR. Look, my dear violinist, this country is of course not the most ideal place to enjoy life, but here at least people do still care about our safety. And that is worth a lot in these times.

PRAGER. All right. But who guarantees it will stay that way? (*To* THEODOR.) You?

ALBAN. Safety is a relative concept. Just like luck ?

HANNAH. Luck? You only have that if you're lucky. And luckily not everyone has that . . . (*Forced laugh, coquettish.*) I'm an egoist, Alban says.

THEODOR. Beauty is a form of luck. Youth. They have beauty, obviously.

ALBAN. Youth disgusts me. There is nothing more repulsive than youth.

THEODOR. Youth has luck and the future, that's how I see it.

PRAGER. Youth? Then the future would be good luck? Fortunate you didn't know my grandfather.

THEODOR. Why is that?

PRAGER. He was a violin-maker in Germany and psychic medium in Prague. His predictions were so unbelievably gloomy and bloodthirsty that no one listened to him. But his instruments were very popular.

THEODOR. (*very good-humoured*). Is there anything I can still offer anyone?

Everyone starts talking at once, moving in different directions through the corridors.

PRAGER (*not moving*). My grandparents seem to have lived on

the Altstädter Ring . . . I was apparently there once but I can't
remember much about it. Nothing, actually. Yet my grandfather
and I seem to have gone for long walks to the Laurenziberg.
We weren't the only ones. It was a favourite spot for Praguers.
I remember that in those moments I was very happy. There,
holding my grandfather's hand . . .

But perhaps I imagine it. Perhaps from my parents' accounts,
they said things went so well for them in that time, in Prague . . .
Perhaps I've got mixed up with that. Perhaps I hadn't even been
born then, when they were there. Probably I didn't even know
my grandfather. There's no way of finding that out now. That
whole family, the Praguers, no one knows what happened to
them. Wiped out, I think. In a storm with powerful squalls,
that's how I end it. You need an explanation, they keep asking
you for an explanation. So I thought up the bit about that squall.
Nobody believes you, but they don't talk to you about it any
more. 'He's not quite right in the head', you see them thinking.
I'd better drop it. Anything better than dead and forgotten.

*The company has appeared again, freshly filled glasses in their
hands.*

ALBAN. You keep hoping, don't you. Against oppression. Hoping
your teeth don't rot in your mouth. For beautiful dumb girls to
warm up the old carcase. A healthy bank account and for the
time when your time is up, to sink back, a well-fed old man,
into oblivion.

ATHALIE (*suddenly depressed*). If only we were safely dead.

ALBAN. I didn't mean anything that drastic.

THEODOR. Almighty gods, what a cheerful wife I've got!

ATHALIE (*confused*). I . . . I don't know exactly, but I think it's
better to die early.

THEODOR. How early, that is the question. This evening?

PRAGER. Death comes when it wants.

ATHALIE. When I'm dead I'd like to be sent back to the mother
country in a lead freezer and be buried in the famine winter in
the occupied territory. Hard-frozen hungry ground. That sounds
lovely to me.

There is a silence.

THEODOR (*in a strange tone*). It's war. I feel it . . . War is
knowing the enemy sits primarily deep in yourself. War is
a school for murderers but for love of the fatherland too,
loyalty and sacrifice. I have a good feeling about the times

I'm living in. However strange it might sound, I'm not unsatisfied with myself. If I had a son I would advise him to follow my example . . .

ATHALIE. But you have a son, don't you?

THEODOR. Because the war is not just there but is coming here too. And if we believe in necessity, we should wage it . . .

ATHALIE (*pent-up, contemptuous*). You and your son certainly, for myself I see it . . .

HANNAH *starts to sob quietly.*

ALBAN. What is it . . . Hannah?

HANNAH. I suddenly had to think of my child.

ATHALIE. God, what an evening –

PRAGER. Wonderful . . . After a good meal there is always somebody who starts up about children, the war and death. Understandable.

ATHALIE. 'Death heals all wounds', I heard somebody say that in the out-patients department of a hospital. In all seriousness. I thought I was going mad . . .

THEODOR. My dear Prager, I couldn't give a damn about all that. My motto is, 'Aut vincere aut mori' –

ATHALIE. Conquer or die, his motto.

PRAGER. My dear Governor! Conquering doesn't exist. A new generation of youthful dead is getting ready again. The earth is opening its womb in expectation of new, fresh young dead. My congratulations to your son . . .

THEODOR. I don't have any son!

ATHALIE (*to* PRAGER). My husband will always be the son of his father and never the father of his son.

ALBAN (*a book in his hand*). Did you know that in the time of slavery a frequent method of committing suicide was swallowing your own tongue, which caused suffocation?

THEODOR. No. Eh . . . why was that?

ALBAN. Total desperation and the belief that their spirit would then return to Africa caused a wave of suicides among black slaves. But there too, my dear Governor, the whites thought up something. They hacked off the head of the dead slave and said to the living: 'Now see how this spirit will find the way back to Africa without a head . . . ' Inventive, don't you think?

THEODOR. I really do not understand why this evening you have to come out with those stories. What's the point of it?

ATHALIE (*to* THEODOR). Every dead person throws his shadow over the future. Just look at us.

ALBAN. The last few days I've been going into the history of this country a bit. This book is from your own bookshelves.

PRAGER. Oh, how few problems there were when we were still young, youthful and innocent. Springtime in Prague, that carefree folk music.

ATHALIE. If through old age and decay you're no longer young and innocent, does that mean automatically that you've become old and guilty?

THEODOR. Why are you all looking at me, for God's sake?! I don't know anything about it. What do you want me to say?

PRAGER. Something non-committal, something completely meaningless, perhaps?

ALBAN (*still with the book*). Athalie, do you know what they did with a married white woman if she was caught having sex with a black man? She was flogged, branded and banned for ever from the colony.

ATHALIE. And the black man?

ALBAN. He was immediately hanged or burned or something like that without any form of trial.

HANNAH (*who was not listening*). Did you see that glistening black body, those big paws clasping the butt of his rifle, those hard eyes staring at me? God, what splendid men you have here.

THEODOR. Dear Hannah, it's better not to say that sort of thing in public. It causes misunderstandings.

HANNAH. So is it still forbidden?

THEODOR. What?

HANNAH. Letting a Negro fuck you.

PRAGER. So, at least she says what she wants.

ATHALIE *gets the giggles;* PRAGER *looks at* HANNAH.

THEODOR (*as though he hasn't heard*). The reputation of the black race is extremely low. The men are in general coarse and ill-bred. Especially towards women. They are rough lovers, they have no conversation of any standard –

ALBAN. Just listen to this . . . (*Reads*.) In that slave society it was self-evident that the white woman was subordinate to the white man . . . Still is, you might say.

THEODOR. I'm saying nothing.

ALBAN (*slowly getting worked up*). A sexual relation between a white woman and a black man is a violation of the right of the white man to the body of the white woman. Moreover, it is an enfeeblement of racist ideology which states that the black race is inferior to the white! True or untrue?

THEODOR. Well then! It's somewhat different now, alas. For God's sake, put that book away.

ALBAN. A white woman who lets herself get pumped full of black seed is a disgrace to her race. She will bear a cross between something inferior and something superior and that is the destruction of humanity! (*Suddenly very calm*.) I mean, the white race . . .

THEODOR (*wearily*). I probably can't convince you, but this subject really perhaps ought to be –

ALBAN. As a Negro an Aryan certificate is not much use to you, nor to a Jew either. You'd do better, like the governor here, with your fatherland-loving, Germanic sympathies –

HANNAH (*somewhat too hard*). What a godforsaken fucking world!

PRAGER. The voice of the white race . . .

PRAGER *goes to* HANNAH, *grabs her, pulls her head towards him, kisses her on the mouth, they stand motionless a moment, then she slowly frees herself from him, goes to the rear into the corridor.* THEODOR *wants to follow her, hesitates, looks in extreme confusion at* ALBAN *who turns away.* ATHALIE *goes to* ALBAN, *takes him by the arm and drags him with her.*

THEODOR (*sharply, to* PRAGER). I urgently request you to leave this house at once.

PRAGER. I understand your problems.

THEODOR. All the better.

PRAGER. But I do hope it is still possible, I mean, I hope the embassy is not . . .

THEODOR. What?

PRAGER. I'm doing my best, governor.

We see PRAGER *going through the corridors.* THEODOR *stands aimlessly in the room, looks at* ALBAN *and* ATHALIE. HANNAH, *upstage, in one of the corridors, is leaning against the wall, her head back.*

ALBAN. All my life I've dreamt I would be murdered by a woman. What do you think of that?

ATHALIE. Depends on which woman.

THEODOR *goes slowly into one of the corridors.*

ALBAN. It's probably no more than a rather overwrought birth trauma, but it is repeated so often and so exactly the same I'm beginning to believe it will happen that way and no other.

Suddenly PRAGER *is there, he stands in front of* HANNAH, *opens her blouse, continues undressing her . . .*

I'm lying in bed, that is, I'm lying on her and I'm getting ready to penetrate her. No idea why. I don't even know that woman. But suddenly the roles are reversed, she is lying on me and starts squeezing my throat hard. Very slowly, with a slow, relentless strength . . .

THEODOR *sees how* PRAGER *is pressing* HANNAH *against the wall. He stands and watches, motionless.*

ALBAN. Everything is going black before my eyes and I'm starting a fall that goes on and on. An endless fall into infinite depths. I only notice I'm dead when I find myself back in a fresh-smelling wooden box. The box is on a raised platform in front of the altar of a big Catholic cathedral. At the same time I hear the immortal music of Mozart's Requiem. Not far from the box my widow is sobbing. My little daughter is sitting nearby looking rather pale, but carefully listening as she has her father's musicality . . .

PRAGER *leaves* HANNAH, *goes up to* THEODOR *and suddenly and unexpectedly knocks him to the ground.*

ATHALIE. What does that woman look like?

ALBAN. What woman?

ATHALIE. Your murderess. Does she look like me?

HANNAH *and* PRAGER *enter the room.*

PRAGER. Here is your wife. I don't know what the governor has been up to with her. I don't know how far she provoked him or if he . . . you never know that with women. In any case I couldn't do anything but take sides . . . The governor is lying in the corridor.

We see, upstage in the corridor, THEODOR *laboriously picking himself up. He stands.* HANNAH *sits at the harpsichord, tries to play, to sing and in this way accompanies the rest of the scene.*

Play on, my dear. Play on. Music is a wonderful consolation, balm for a mortal wound . . . (*Listens attentively.*)

THEODOR *has come closer;* ATHALIE *and* ALBAN *stare at him.*

The music . . . then suddenly SYLVIA *is in the room, she looks completely different, sexy, evening dress, splendid make-up, a stunning sight, she gives* PRAGER *a nod, he pulls* HANNAH's *hands away from the keys and holds on to them.*

A new sort of silence, the forceably cut-off music . . . HANNAH *looks at* ALBAN; PRAGER *goes up to* SYLVIA, *he offers her a fine, thin cigar, gives her a light, looks for and finds an ashtray, puts it in the empty niche.*

SYLVIA (*to* PRAGER) Just say we don't need them any more. Just say times are changing more quickly than we thought possible. (*In front of the others she slaps him hard in the face, again, again, again, until he falls . . .*)

Blackout.

ACT THREE

Scene i

Fade in.

The room looks 'closed', disorderly, as though there is suddenly a lack of space. There are a few unmade beds in it, items of clothing thrown over chairs, disorder, also in the corridors.

HANNAH is sitting at the harpsichord, playing, tired, now and then she lets one arm fall limply to her side.

At certain times someone comes, from the distance, through the corridors, stands in the room, listens perhaps, looks and disappears again.

It seems as though a climatological change has taken place, the characters shiver, as though an icy draught were going through the building.

Now and again, when a door opens in one of the corridors, the hum of voices is heard as though there are a lot of people in the building.

Then ALBAN appears, he lays his hands on HANNAH's shoulders, strokes her.

The music . . .

ALBAN. Do you know your playing is getting worse and worse? The more you play, lately, the more I can hear you deteriorate. Perceptibly . . . Maybe you're playing too much. It's not your technique, it's in your head. You'd do better to play a bit less and concentrate more on what you are playing. If I were you I'd keep just to Bach. Eighteenth century. Now that was a nice time.

He kneels in front of her, lays his head in her lap, she continues to play; then she lays her hands on his head, opens her legs, he pulls her to the ground, half under the harpsichord, lies on top of her . . . and in spite of the fact that the keys are not being touched any longer, the harpsichord continues to play.

PRAGER *enters.*

PRAGER (*after a cautionary cough*). Thanks to a mix of rumours, facts and common sense we must conclude that international communism has been defeated. Under the name Great United

Europe, the Third Reich has become fact. The Soviet Union, like the old glued-together vase that it was, has been smashed into countless pieces. In Trans Siberia, a seven-year-old child of the tsars with bandy legs has ascended the throne. The young state of Israel has been ground underfoot by the United Arab Republic. Everywhere the old pogroms are raising their heads again. And here . . . while this embassy has been completely cut off from the outside world by the Revolution, here people are lying under the harpsichord procreating.

ALBAN. Get lost, Prager!

PRAGER. Where to?

ALBAN. Go and water the plants.

PRAGER. The plants are dead. They are lying with broken heads spread through the streets of the city. Just like people . . . Tell me! Can it be that music is coming out of that harpsichord?

HANNAH (*has crawled out from under* ALBAN). That's what harpsichords are for, my old Prager. They are musical instruments.

PRAGER. Of course, yes . . . Look I'm sorry, but . . .

HANNAH *touches a key, silence.* ATHALIE *enters.*

ATHALIE. He's back again.

PRAGER. Didn't I tell you so?

ATHALIE. I can't understand it. It's as though his soul has left his body. Not that you can see anything on him, they didn't even touch him, but . . . it's just as though they had turned his head inside out, like a glove . . .

ALBAN. And? What's going to happen now?

ATHALIE. I get the impression all his powers have been withdrawn. They want a sort of public confession of guilt from him. (*To* PRAGER.) You certainly know more about it.

ALBAN. Yes, Prager. What's going to happen. The governor with smashed kneecaps in the market square, a placard round his neck: 'I am a rat, an enemy of the people, a traitor of the revolution', on the East European model?

PRAGER. Eastern Europe doesn't exist any more.

ALBAN. Not there perhaps, but there is not here.

ATHALIE. He's still confused. Actually he just keeps going on about his father. (*Short laugh.*) But . . . of course you don't know him.

PRAGER. I met him . . .

ATHALIE. Eh?

PRAGER. A year ago in Amsterdam. He was still living in that big mansion on the Amstel, you can probably still remember that. From behind closed windows he was guarding his art treasures, and maintaining very useful relations with the occupying force.

ATHALIE. What do you mean by that?

PRAGER. For the enemy he was an important source of information. We found it necessary to liquidate him.

ATHALIE. Christ, so he's been dead for a year.

> THEODOR *appears, he looks unkempt and a little sad, he is wearing a crumpled light-coloured gabardine raincoat.*

THEODOR (*childish, cheerful*). A child has just been born. Nice, isn't it? Life goes on all the time, that's a hopeful thought. I just ran into Sylvia. At least I think it was her. She was standing in for the midwife, she said. You should have seen her hands! Yesterday they were still black, now they are red with blood. Athalie, that skinny wife of Verschoor's, you remember her?

ATHALIE (*absent-mindedly*). Yes . . .

THEODOR. Good God, how those people had to wait in pain and sorrow for that baby. And now suddenly, while that woman is just approaching the menopause, bull's eye. Actually I don't think she was really made for having children. Much too narrow in the hips. She would have had problems giving birth to a mouse. (ATHALIE *disappears,* THEODOR *looks after her.*) The world is foundering, gentlemen! Very slowly.

ALBAN. Don't be so gloomy, Governor.

HANNAH. What do they want from you?

THEODOR. No idea. (*Declaims.*)
'Chase me away now, away with me!
Get out of the country, now, immediately!
Friends, chase me away, the damned,
Greatly accursed, by the gods
Most hated of all mankind!'

I did murder my father, yes! I screamed at those black dolts, and slept with my mother, but I didn't KNOW anything, I only did my duty! Duty to the fatherland, that beloved country for which I uselessly solved the riddle of the Sphinx. Beat me, I screamed at them, I can take it, I'm used to it. My father –

(*Stops, in quite a different tone.*) Athalie always had a strong dislike of my father. And that is understandable. He was to the end a fierce opponent of our marriage. Just imagine . . . the only son of a noble house has set his heart on the daughter of a flourmill owner from Oostzaan! That drove my father almost to the brink of madness. But when I took her home once, he was at once bewitched by her blinding beauty. That made you look, didn't it? (*Sadly, overcome by the memory.*) Unfortunately, the tropics have hardened her features. Before, she looked different. She was young and my father was a widower. A rough, sensual man, for the first years, forced by necessity, we lived with him . . .

ALBAN. So, if I understand it right, classical declamation and revealing family stories, that is what the revolution is after.

THEODOR (*bitter*). By God, when this is over I'll call him to account. Just to account, no forgiveness.

PRAGER. The governor has lost his thread a bit.

ALBAN. What's the situation regarding the diplomatic immunity of this embassy. Are we safe here or can we be taken away any moment. Do I have to get my star of David out of my suitcase or would it be better to black up. I mean, what are race relations like at the moment, governor?

THEODOR (*wary*). Don't ask me what I don't know. If there's something to be asked, then ask something I have an answer to. If you wouldn't mind. (*Crawls on to one of the beds, pulls the covers over himself.*)

PRAGER. There's not much left of the old glory.

ALBAN. Bit difficult if you want to call your dead father to account. An embarrassing scene in the cemetery.

HANNAH *goes to the harpsichord and plays.*

ALBAN (*to* PRAGER). Do you hear? Bach . . . One of the greatest phenomena in history.

HANNAH (*stops*). Sometimes I play something and a sad memory is associated with it. But I don't know what any more.

ALBAN. Do you know 'The Song of the Earth'? Do you think a piece like that can be performed again in Europe? Mahler was a Jew, he wrote some of that terrible degenerate music . . .

PRAGER. Mahler? Didn't he turn Catholic at the end of his life?

ALBAN. Not that I know.

PRAGER. I remember the 'Kindertotenlieder'. My uncle took me to my first concert. I can still see it; that enormous orchestra, that gigantic blonde singer. An unforgettable experience for such a small boy. No, in Europe Mahler is still being played all right.

HANNAH (*to* PRAGER). I remember it now. It was right after my miscarriage. Alban had had an audition and been taken on.

ALBAN. Miscarriage?

HANNAH. He had just got that brilliant violin on permanent loan. He was so happy, so elated. A fantastic instrument from an anonymous benefactor and a place in a world-famous orchestra.

ALBAN. Miscarriage? What kind of nonsense is this?

HANNAH. I knew I was pregnant and couldn't believe my luck. But at the same time I felt it could go wrong.

ALBAN. Why didn't you . . .

HANNAH. Must I tell someone who is so happy that there is a corpse in my body? That his semen sowed death and decay? Would you have wanted that?

ALBAN (*turns away*). No. Not then.

Silence.

HANNAH. I want to leave you.

ALBAN. I know.

HANNAH. For a long time now. It's over, it doesn't mean anything any more.

ALBAN. Yes . . .

HANNAH. I'll go back to my mother. I want to see my little girl. By now she's old enough to know her father is not her father. And that he never made any attempt to be so either. Prager is seeing to it that I can leave here. I'm going with him.

ALBAN (*looks up, coldly*). With him? You don't mean that.

HANNAH. Yes.

ALBAN. Is there something between you two?

HANNAH. Something like that, yes. In any case where relationship is concerned, differently from with you.

ALBAN. Better?

HANNAH. Better than what?

ALBAN. Is he going to be the new father of your daughter?

HANNAH. I'm going. (*She leaves.*)

ALBAN. Go, then! And don't let me see you ever again! At any
rate not . . . (*Silence.*) Well, Prager, that's peculiar . . . I've
always thought you were a frustrated queer. But I often forget
myself. I sometimes think my own wife is actually the postman.
Specialising in disaster reports. We'd only just got married
when she let me see where children came from. That was a
really traumatic experience, I assure you. Just like when I first
saw your head.

PRAGER. It's a bitter pill, I understand that.

ALBAN. Thank you for your sympathy. It's not easy to go through
life as an exile and then to lose your wife to a half-baked
masochist.

PRAGER. It's only going to get worse. I've got some more ghastly
news.

ALBAN. Do you realise that the name of my wife spelt back to
front is the same as from front to back? A palindrome. How do
you take her, by the way? From behind?

PRAGER. I don't take your wife at all. She is not my type.

ALBAN. So . . . she said something like that.

PRAGER. It's a question of common interest. I help her to get
away from here. I myself have to go back to Europe. In
exchange she provides oral satisfaction. That is the only thing I
can stand. I am rather delicately built.

ALBAN. Disgusting.

PRAGER. More like unpractical. You always have to explain so
much before they get going.

   Silence.

ALBAN. When are you leaving?

PRAGER. I'm sorry. I'm not just taking your wife but your violin
as well.

ALBAN. Eh?

PRAGER. That anonymous Maecenas of long ago is my uncle, the
brother of my fostermother . . . (*Takes a sealed envelope from
his pocket, gives it to* ALBAN.) You don't know the contents
but I know what it's about.

ALBAN (*tears the envelope open, reads*). 'By removing yourself
without demonstrable reason from the practice of music, and
contrary to the agreement leaving the country without
notification, you have definitely violated the contract between
us . . . We request you to hand over the violin built by Jacobus

Stainer and given to you on permanent loan, to our family member, Mr Prager, so that it can be returned undamaged to our possession.'

PRAGER. Our plane leaves tomorrow.

ALBAN (*his head in his hands*). I don't understand . . .

Enter ATHALIE.

ATHALIE. That child is not doing very well. A doctor is needed. Prager, please. You are the only one here who still has any influence over them.

PRAGER. Even if there was a doctor, they wouldn't let him come.

ATHALIE. That child is going to die!

PRAGER. Do you think they'll worry about that, Madam. So many children die. Revolution and dead children, they belong together.

ATHALIE. You're a swine, Prager.

PRAGER. I am powerless, Madam.

ATHALIE. You're even worse than that black scum.

PRAGER. Your frankness is a boon, Madam governor. Or is it governess? You might look on it as a stroke of luck if they allow you right away to be the governess of their children.

THEODOR *gets up.*

ATHALIE. Your threats don't worry me.

THEODOR. Don't say that, Athalie, never say that if you haven't gone through it.

ATHALIE. There is a newborn baby here about to die. But I see no one is interested in that.

THEODOR. Sometimes death is a boon.

ATHALIE. You don't decide that!

THEODOR. After what I've gone through I have a right to speak . . .

ATHALIE (*scornful*). For a while still, yes, but it's almost over. Then you'll be old and redundant. All of us, come to think of it. Redundantly we'll all sit together, staring at a little baby corpse. Without any understanding. Without courage. God, how unbelievably powerless we are.

THEODOR. That woman was not healthy, Athalie.

ATHALIE (*sadly*). No, what do you expect . . . If you're healthy you're not stuck here.

THEODOR. She's much too old to have a child. And then that man. He's a wreck ravaged by years in the tropics, as long as I've known him he's had one foot in the grave. It's a blessing the child is not mongoloid, because they survive. And mongolism is a punishment of the gods. Nothing worse can happen to anyone than the birth of such a scourge of the gods, I assure you. My wife, my dear Athalie can tell you about that . . .

ATHALIE (*standing in front of* THEODOR, *ice-cold*). If I had a gun I would shoot you dead on the spot.

SYLVIA *enters, she is wearing a military camouflage jacket over her evening dress, an ammunition belt with pistol. She hands the pistol to* ATHALIE. ATHALIE *gives the pistol back, follows* SYLVIA *out of the room.*

THEODOR (*flabbergasted*). That is something. To be executed more or less summarily by your own wife. (*To* ALBAN *and* PRAGER.) That unbelievable coldbloodedness, that merciless hardness. I think my father and Athalie found kindred souls in one another there.

ALBAN. A very special bond, I presume. Rather like between my wife and Prager?

THEODOR. There are things in life you see happening in front of your eyes without it getting through to you. You don't want it to get through.

ALBAN. Only later you understand why. And then it's too late. Isn't that an interesting idea, Prager?

THEODOR. I'm Oedipus. Except I knew what he couldn't know.

ALBAN. What do you mean?

PRAGER *starts to walk away.*

THEODOR. My father's aversion to Athalie was pretty serious. But when hate slowly but surely decreases, even turns into affection, then one should surely be glad, don't you think?

But the situation changes when you find them together in bed. The bed of your dead mother. An agonising scene: your wife in the arms of your father. According to Sophocles I should have killed my father at that moment and then with my mother . . . but she had been dead for some time . . . Perhaps I should have gone blind on the spot or had my sex chopped off, anything would have been better than standing there at the foot of the bed staring. Until he threw me out of the room . . .

Silence.

ALBAN. Athalie . . . Nice name. But she is still your wife?

THEODOR. Yes.

ALBAN. She told me it wasn't with you but your father that she lost her virginity.

THEODOR. Eh . . . yes.

ALBAN. You seem to have left more or less everything to your father.

THEODOR. Yes . . . At that time I did, my education was rather . . . unusual. No sex before marriage and afterwards I never really got started on it . . . But, because my fiancée was pregnant, we had to get married, do you see? The child was born and it seemed as though nature had played on us both a frantically jolly joke. My father distanced himself immediately from his offspring. Out of hand he had us transferred to this country.

ALBAN. She showed me the photo.

THEODOR. Oh, did she . . . It is a comfort that the gods can strike so relentlessly, don't you find?

SYLVIA *has entered, she waits.*

Not so impatient, Sylvia. I'm coming. (*To* ALBAN, *rather sadly.*) We have to go back again . . . The tribunal of the provisional revolutionary government. Always the same questions and always the same answers.

THEODOR *follows* SYLVIA *into the corridor. They pass* HANNAH *who enters the room.* HANNAH *has a suitcase, is wearing a jacket which she is clutching close to her body; she lays the suitcase on one of the beds.*

ALBAN. It seems to be getting colder and colder, have you noticed? And fuller.

HANNAH. Yes . . . an icy draught as though everything was open.

ALBAN. Whereas the opposite is true. How long ago is it since we were still sitting carefree in the garden? It would have been better if I had stayed in my underground address.

HANNAH. What are they still up to with Theodor?

ALBAN. Do you notice it's getting darker? In the middle of the day and we're sitting here in a tropical country. Or maybe I've been mistaken all this time. Maybe we're not where we think we are at all.

HANNAH. If I feel the way I feel, it's evening now.

ALBAN. I see you've left our rooms.

HANNAH. Yes . . . And any moment I'm leaving you.

ALBAN. I didn't bring you with me to lose you again.

HANNAH. You didn't bring me with you at all. You went and I followed. Now I'm going and you're staying.

ALBAN. Forced by a war situation, yes. A political hostage.

HANNAH. I'm frightened Theodor will be tortured.

ALBAN. They're blacks, not Germans.

HANNAH. Just stop going on about that war. That enemy image of yours has altered ten times since then.

ALBAN. Forgive and forget, you mean?

HANNAH. That war and the woman who belongs to it. Forget them.

PRAGER *enters, in one hand a suitcase and in the other a violin case. He has blood on his mouth.*

ALBAN. What's happened to you? Has that black charwoman given you another hiding?

PRAGER (*to* HANNAH). Just give me a hand . . .

HANNAH *wipes the blood from his face.* PRAGER *lays suitcase and violin case on the bed.*

ALBAN. Kissed on the mouth by the revolution, perhaps?

HANNAH. Your jokes are unbearably unfunny, did you know that?

ALBAN. If you say so.

PRAGER. There's total havoc in the city. If they suspect you're a sympathiser of the old regime, watch out. It would be better to get away, anyway.

ALBAN. That's just what I am doing.

PRAGER. To my amazement I hear more and more that Europe has become viable again. The rubble has been cleared away, a fresh spirit is blowing, a new energy. Berlin is the capital of the European Reich . . . These are persistent rumours.

ALBAN. As soon as I take to my heels anywhere, peace breaks out. I'm convinced, I have a fatal influence on world events.

PRAGER (*to* HANNAH). We're leaving tomorrow morning.

HANNAH. Do you feel the cold? It's as though they've piled ice blocks up against the house outside. A wall of ice blocks to freeze us solid.

PRAGER. The climate is changing. Nature is losing its grip.

HANNAH. No . . . it's in this house. Three children have died
here. And when the children are all gone it'll start with the
parents and so on, older and older, until it reaches that old
Indian woman, like water that rises up to your lips . . . I want to
get out of here as quickly as possible.

PRAGER *lays* HANNAH *on the bed, half over the cases,
kneels beside her, strokes her legs. Silence.*

ALBAN. Tell me . . . it looks a bit like the final wish of the
condemned prisoner and you have to see it like that, but, I'd
like to try just one more time to let the violin sing, see if it's
still working.

HANNAH. Oh wonderful, Alban.

PRAGER. Not too long. I always get seriously upset by violin
playing. Not too long.

ALBAN *pulls the violin case out from under* HANNAH, *goes
into the corridor – at the same moment, from another direction,*
THEODOR *enters. He has a paper in his hand, reads; from a
distance the tuning of the violin is heard . . .* THEODOR *raises
his head, a melancholy smile passes over his face.*

SYLVIA *appears, she looks at the two by the bed, without
interest, then she takes out a cigar and puts it in her mouth. She
speaks to* THEODOR, *alternately hard and humble, in Sranang
Tongo and Dutch.*

Vaguely, in the distance, we see and hear ALBAN *playing the
violin, snatches of études, scales and improvisations.*

SYLVIA. Yu wan' wan sigara? [Would you like a cigar too?]

THEODOR. You know I don't smoke. (*Gives her a light.*)

SYLVIA. Suma na yu? Yu srefi noso wan tra sani? [What are you
representing? Yourself or something else.]

THEODOR (*stares at the paper in his hands*). I represent the
Kingdom of the Netherlands.

SYLVIA. How would you like your whisky, Governor?

THEODOR (*contemptuously*). I'm telling you for the last time,
waiter! A double whisky with ice! A lot of ice. In a tall glass!

SYLVIA *gets the whisky.*

SYLVIA. A kondre fu a kownu fu den P'tata. In'suma nen? [The
land of the king of the sweet potatoes . . . In whose name?]

THEODOR. In the name of our beloved Queen Wilhelmina, Queen of the Netherlands.

SYLVIA (*gives him the whisky*). Dat'no tru sa y'e taki. A kownu pot'a makti in'den anu fu en uma pikin. [That's not right. The King has handed over power to his daughter.] Here you are, Governor.

THEODOR. I haven't been informed of that . . . Thank you.

SYLVIA. Yu no abs no wan makti moro. A kownu fu yu dede o men'langa k'ba. [You have no powers left now. That king has been dead for a long time.]

THEODOR. The King is dead? You don't know what you're saying.

SYLVIA. Can I be of service to you in any other way, governor?

THEODOR. I feel terribly cold. Is there a blanket or something?

SYLVIA. Yu agri nanga a strafu sa un'gi yu? [Are you in agreement with the punishment we have imposed on you?]

THEODOR. No, certainly not. I did my duty.

SYLVIA (*goes out, comes back with an Indian blanket*). Here you are . . . (*Almost tenderly, she puts the blanket round his shoulders.*) A grontapu kenki. Ala dat'yu no si. [The world has changed. You haven't seen it.]

THEODOR. I represent an old time. The new one doesn't interest me.

SYLVIA. Yu s'don dya giwan owru, weti, abani kondre. [You represent an old, white, criminal world.]

THEODOR. Criminal? I was never aware of that.

SYLVIA. Y'o opo'yu borsu? [Are you protesting against the judgment?]

THEODOR. No . . . There is nothing left that binds me to this world. I'm slowly starting to go blind. I can't keep up with your time, as I have often been accused. But . . . why do I have to keep up with a time which is not mine. One thing I regret . . . that now I myself am being murdered, I can't murder my father any more. That's my only regret.

SYLVIA. When you've finished your whisky, will you follow me?

THEODOR (*finishes his whisky, helpless*). Mi b'o wan'fu [I should like . . .]

SYLVIA, *back to the audience, lets the camouflage jacket fall from her shoulders to the ground, pulls down the shoulder*

straps of her evening dress, the dress falls to her feet . . .
THEODOR *stares at her body and starts slowly and silently to*
cry. This image should be continued as long as possible. Then
she readjusts her clothing again and precedes THEODOR *into*
the corridor.

Music: 'Sarabande de la Muerte Oscura' by George Crumb,
played by the Kronos Quartet, merges together with the sound
of the violin.

THEODOR. Aequo animo e vita, cum ea non placeat, tamquam e
theatro, exeamus . . .

PRAGER *opens his suitcase, takes out* HANNAH's *clothes*
and starts dressing her. At the rear, in the corridor,
THEODOR *kneels on the ground.* SYLVIA *blindfolds him,*
takes out her pistol and shoots him in the head. More or less at
the same time, one 'sees' how ALBAN *slams a chopper down*
on a block on which his left hand is lying . . . In the half-dark,
ATHALIE *is seen, moving rapidly through the corridors, a*
dead baby in her arms.

Fade out.

Scene ii

Fade in.

The room is almost empty, only the harpsichord and three rocking
chairs remain.

Music: Tallis/Kronos Quartet.

From the distance, the continuous noise of rain.

SYLVIA, *dressed as she was at the beginning of the play, puts the*
Ceylon Buddha back in its place, dusts it. It is exactly the same
statue, but three times bigger. ALBAN, *his left hand bandaged,*
watches SYLVIA's *actions.* ATHALIE *appears, after a short*
glance at the Buddha.

ATHALIE. Enormous luck that he's back again. That Buddha. I
bought him long ago from a dealer in Ceylon. We have dragged
him with us through the whole Latin American continent. My
husband was an ambassador. In one of those forgotten Dutch
colonies. A terrible time . . . That Buddha went everywhere
with us. Like a child. A very quiet, motionless golden baby . . .
How is your hand doing?

ALBAN. The pain is less but the fingers will never grow back on.

ATHALIE. You could play the other way round? I mean, the violin on the right side.

ALBAN. Then I would have to start from the very beginning again. That whole martyrdom again? No . . . you don't have to start living that kind of life again. Once is enough. I know now what it's like.

ATHALIE. Pity. You played so beautifully.

ALBAN. You scarcely heard me and understand absolutely nothing about music.

ATHALIE. More than you think.

ALBAN. You're mixing me up with my ex-wife.

ATHALIE. No I'm not. Your wife played the piano, if I remember correctly. Harpsichord. We had a sweet little harpsichord. Something like this one.

ALBAN (*taking off his jacket*). Is it always so oppressive on this island? Everything is clammy.

ATHALIE. May is the hottest month in the year. The rainy season. There's no wind. Would you like something to drink?

ALBAN. A scotch, please.

ATHALIE. With ice?

ALBAN. Straight. In a tall glass if you have one . . . Do you have one?

ATHALIE. What?

ALBAN. Tall glasses.

SYLVIA *enters the room.*

ATHALIE (*to* SYLVIA). Wait, just let me see . . . (*Looking in the drinks cabinet.*)

SYLVIA *sits down in a rocking chair, takes out a cigar.*

ALBAN. Anyway, I don't have a violin any more. A violinist without a violin is like a violinist without a violin, forgive the simple comparison, but it is apt. (*Leans forward, gives* SYLVIA *a light.*)

ATHALIE. It is apt through its simplicity. Here's your whisky. (*Comes up to him with a tray, serves* SYLVIA, ALBAN *and herself and sits down in a rocking chair.*)

ALBAN (*sits down in a rocking chair*). How wonderful that we're all sitting together here and can be on first-name terms again. That strengthens solidarity. Through such a simple linguistic formality all the differences between man, woman and our Sylvia here, drop completely away.

They listen to the music.

ATHALIE. So here we are, in the middle of the dropped away differences. A unit, as it were, if only it weren't all a sham.

ALBAN (*looks at his injured hand*). I still don't know if it was a premeditated act or a fit of madness . . . You need courage to hack off the fingers of your own hand. And I'm not courageous.

ATHALIE. Are you sure it was you? It could just as well have been someone else.

ALBAN. Who would do something like that?

ATHALIE. People. I can point them out to you. The possible criminals. Cutting off someone else's hand, you don't need any courage to do that.

ALBAN. After years of abstinence I was just starting to play again. The untold drudgery of a lost life was suddenly crystallised in that one bright violin sound.

ATHALIE. I remember . . . or has it still to happen? Sometimes past and future run together like the paint in a watercolour.

ALBAN. But I had the violin on permanent loan, just like my wife and her child was the child of someone else. There I was in a strange country, run down by my people, playing the violin, because another people, who had run down mine, were after my life. Ultimately I was completely superfluous there like a clown sawing away on an old violin. So I took the axe and –

ATHALIE. I remember now! Victor Jara! The guitarist! They chopped his fingers off because he made the people rebel.

ALBAN (*looks at his right hand, moves the fingers*). At least these are still attached . . . Now I can finally devote myself to writing. The right hand writes, the left hand rests, mutilated for ever, on the desk. From the distance music sounds. Rain is falling on the leaves . . .

The light suggests the enchanting colours of a slowly setting sun.

ATHALIE. Nightmares . . . Suddenly the ghosts jump at your neck. They wrap themselves like a more and more tightly pulled rope round your neck. You only need to fasten one end to the ceiling.

ALBAN. And then everything comes down. Like a blazing fire.

ATHALIE. What?

ALBAN. The roof.

ATHALIE. Ah . . . (*Short laugh.*) If it hadn't been for Sylvia, we
wouldn't be here. No, you don't have to answer.

ALBAN. Even if she did answer, we wouldn't be any the wiser.

ATHALIE. She's the only one who saw the town burning. We are
the survivors but she is the witness. Don't forget that.

ALBAN. How could I forget it?

ATHALIE (*looks over her shoulder*). Strange, that Buddha.
everything burned except him. Do you believe in the
supernatural?

Silence.

ALBAN. Do you hear? The music has stopped.

ATHALIE. But the rain is still falling.

ALBAN. Until that stops too.

ATHALIE. Sylvia? Put some music on. Let's hear what you like.
Everyone has a right to his own culture. So, don't be ashamed.

ALBAN. It's as though I hear a governor.

ATHALIE. Poor Theodor . . .

*SYLVIA remains sitting, motionless, at the same time we hear
'The Blue Danube' by Johann Strauss, at comfortable volume.
The three characters look into the audience, rock silently,
smiling in their rocking chairs, to the rhythm of the waltz. This
image and the music held for some time.*

Blackout.

THE WEDDING PARTY

by Judith Herzberg

Originally written in English by Judith Herzberg

Revised by Rhea Gaisner and Rina Vergano

Judith Herzberg was born in Amsterdam in 1934, the daughter of the well-known Dutch author Abel Herzberg. As a Jewish child, she was forced into hiding during the Nazi occupation of the Netherlands in the Second World War, staying with many different families. As she once stated in an interview: 'My youth was defined by the war. I was kept alive thanks to many people who risked their lives.'

Herzberg has already built up an impressive body of work, including poetry, essays, plays, film and television scripts and translations and adaptations of non-Dutch works. Her plays have been translated into different languages and staged in Germany, where they have enjoyed considerable success.

Herzberg divides her time between Israel and the Netherlands.

In 1995 *Rijgdraad (Tacking-thread)*, a kind of follow-up to *The Wedding Party,* was premiered in Amsterdam. In this play most of the characters from *The Wedding Party* reappear, but the time is twenty years later, and their preoccupations reflect current concerns on the basic questions originally raised in *The Wedding Party.*

Within the framework of an unhappy wedding, *The Wedding Party* introduces a very varied group of people. What they have in common is that in one way or another they are all involved in the fate of the Jews, which has affected all of them – usually to a traumatic degree. Lea, the bride, is marrying for the third time, this time to Nico, who was previously married to Dory. Both previous spouses are also present at the wedding.

Gradually the wedding party becomes the occasion for the revealing of relationships between the various characters and their histories. Because of the past, they do not grow closer to one another, but become more distant. The end of the party is marked by separations.

The play consists of some eighty scenes; these are short, detached dialogues that sometimes take place at the same time. There is no linear narrative as such, but it is precisely in this absence, this vacuum, that the characters are revealed. Each character tells his/her own story, which converges – or clashes – with the story of other characters.

The inserts into the text, of lists and instructions, play a special role. They express the suppressed thoughts and memories which the characters choose to leave unspoken. (In the original production, these were performed by all the characters in chorus.)

The Wedding Party was premiered in 1982 in Amsterdam by the Baal Theatre Company. 'With this play,' wrote the Amsterdam daily *Het Parool*, 'Judith Herzberg has put herself on a level with the German avant-garde writer Botho Strauss. In its construction and in the sensitive sounding out of contemporary despair, *The Wedding Party* is in no way inferior to plays like *Great and Small*. Here again, the withered relationships between typical representatives of a disintegrating society are poignantly analysed in flashes of scenes that pass like a rapidly edited film.'

The order of the scenes in this play is as it was in the first Dutch version, *Leedvermaak*, performed in the Frascati theatre in Amsterdam on 27 March 1982 by Baal theatre group. It was originally conceived as a loose-leaf volume, where the order of scenes could be altered at will.

The action takes place in the 1970s.

Characters

LEA, *the bride, second violinist*
NICO, *the groom, doctor*
SIMON, *Lea's father, successful businessman*
ADA, *Lea's mother, hat designer*
ZWART, *Nico's father, businessman with high hopes*
DUIFJE, *Nico's stepmother*
ALEXANDER, *Lea's first husband, artist*
DORY, *Nico's first wife, first violinist*
HANS, *Nico's friend, teacher*
RIET, *Lea's war mother, factory manageress*
DANIEL, *Simon and Ada's guest, a wanderer*
PIEN, *secretary at music academy*
JANNA, *young working student,*
HENDRIKJE, *working student*

Series of small rooms or balconies off a larger room which is not visible. A wedding reception is in progress in the large room. People wander into the small rooms to be alone for a moment or to have a private conversation.

The house belongs to SIMON *and* ADA, LEA*'s parents.*

ADA *and* ALEXANDER.

ALEXANDER *is standing in silence.* ADA *joins him.*

ADA. What are you doing?

ALEXANDER. I'm singing.

ADA. Really? Instead of what? Oh, I'm sorry.

*

NICO *and* HANS, *later* SIMON.

NICO. Have you got them?

HANS *(carrying flowers)*. Of course.

NICO *(unwraps them)*. No!

HANS. No?

NICO. Impossible. Exactly the same as the ones I gave Dory!

HANS. I don't believe it!

NICO. Damn it. You'll have to go and change them.

HANS. They're camellias. I bought something completely different for Dory.

NICO. What then?

HANS. They can't be.

NICO. They are. Exactly the same. *(Takes photo from his wallet.)* Look.

HANS. That sort of thing doesn't bother Dory. Actually I think it's rather apt; the same flowers for the same occasion. After all you don't have anything different to offer her. You are the same man with the same – the same – everything! I don't see how it's going to be the flowers that make the difference. Why don't you buy your own damn flowers.

NICO. Next time I certainly will.

Exit HANS, *enter* SIMON.

NICO. What do you think, Simon, should you give your second wife the same flowers you gave your first – out of a kind of honesty, or completely different ones, to show that everything is going to be different.

SIMON. Now there you have a problem that is quite beyond my experience, I'm glad to say.

*

DUIFJE *and* DORY, *later* HANS.

DUIFJE (*to* DORY). Daddy's just coming, the dog's still in the car. You know, he licks my toes! I sometimes say, 'Why don't you ever lick my toes?' But then Zwart says, 'What about women starting to lick men's toes!' But you know, men have such sweaty feet!

Enter HANS.

HANS. Dory, can I ask you something?

DUIFJE. Oh! I'm off!

HANS. Dory, you remember the flowers Nico gave you when you two got married?

DORY. Yes, camellias.

HANS. Would you mind terribly if –

DORY. Look, I know Nico. We could hardly expect him to suddenly have imagination, could we.

*

ZWART *and* LEA, *later* NICO, *then* ALEXANDER.

ZWART (*to* LEA). I was going to bring you a beautiful bunch of flowers, but there weren't any flowers. I mean, there were *flowers*, of course –

LEA. Who are those two men?

Offers ZWART *a plate of cheese cubes, and leaves.*

When ZWART *is alone, he throws a cheese cube into the air and tries catching it in his mouth. He fails. Tries again. Stops, embarrassed, when* HANS *and* NICO *join him.*

ZWART. Hello! I must say, you did that beautifully!

HANS. What?

ZWART. That entrance, that was the perfect entrance.

HANS. That goes with my profession, sixty per cent is acting, thirty per cent improvising and ten per cent conveying knowledge. Isn't it, Nico? Nico should know! Cheers!

NICO. That's just what I was going to say.

Enter ALEXANDER. *This causes a silence.*

NICO (*to* ZWART). This is Lea's first husband, Alexander.

ZWART (*to* ALEXANDER). Oh – so it wasn't to your liking.

ALEXANDER. And who are you?

ZWART. I'm Nico's father. At least that's what they say. There are no witnesses any more. Ha ha ha. A persistent rumour. From reliable sources. That's right, isn't it, Nico?

NICO. And what have you done with Duifje? (*To* ALEXANDER.) His wife, my second mother.

ZWART. It isn't easy on Duifje either, she was just getting used to Dory. Complicated business.

*

RIET *and* LEA.

LEA. Mama Riet!

RIET (*kisses* LEA). Darling! As far as I'm concerned you can't get married often enough! I so love the parties you give! So festive! Really! You don't find parties like that anywhere else! Just look at all these delicious things! There's bound to be left-overs. Do you think they'll manage to eat it all?

LEA. If it all gets eaten, my mother thinks there isn't enough. So there has to be too much.

RIET. I still can't throw food away. Funny, isn't it, the way things linger. I do all my shopping once a week now. I buy exactly what I need for each day. That way I never have any left-overs. I actually feel guilty when I have to throw things away. What a super abundance! Well, there's something to be said for it.

LEA. Don't you think Nico is a dear? You'll see what a dear he is. And did you know he's a very good doctor? You just have to say ow and he's already found the problem. Isn't that a marvellous idea? Sometimes he finds it before you've said a word. I feel like a princess! I've never been so happy in my whole life. It's as if the world has opened up for me. No, as if the world

has burst open! Can you imagine? I'll bring you back something gorgeous from our honeymoon. What would you like?

RIET. Don't exaggerate, child, I don't need anything, you know
that.

LEA. You might as well say, because you're going to get
something!

RIET. I'll think about it. I'll think it over, all right?

*

LEA, NICO, HANS *and* ALEXANDER *and some other guests;
later* DORY.

LEA (*enters*). I wanted to rope you in, I wanted to ask you . . .
(*Suddenly seeing* ALEXANDER.) – hey – Alexander!

They embrace. NICO *offers her the camellias. Enter* DORY,
who laughs when she sees the flowers.

*

RIET *and* HANS.

RIET. Marvellous party.

HANS. Yes, it is.

RIET. Have we met? I'm Lea's war mother. We took her into
hiding during the war.

HANS. I've heard the stories about you.

RIET. You can call me Riet. Everyone just calls me Riet.

HANS. Hans. I'm a friend of Nico's. We went to school together.

RIET. You're a doctor too then?

HANS. No I'm a teacher. I know Nico from before.

RIET. So this isn't the first wedding for you either. Of Nico's,
I mean.

HANS. No this is Nico's second one for me too. I'm not married
myself.

RIET. Oh I didn't mean to pry. Goodness, no. But it's certainly
always nice for a single person to meet another single person.
They are more approachable, I find.

HANS. I've never classified myself as 'single'.

RIET. Oh but you are! Unless you're cohabiting of course! It's just
a word, after all. What stories have you heard about me?

HANS. Since Nico's been with Lea. Lea talks more about you than about her own mother.

RIET. Really? I didn't know that. Is that really true? I had no idea, not the faintest. Really I didn't. (*As* HANS *is moving away.*) We'll see each other, won't we. I'll find you later – Hans.

*

ZWART, DORY, DUIFJE *and* RIET.

ZWART. When we got back we were so tanned! It was still winter here – embarrassing.

DORY. Why?

ZWART. Embarrassing to be that tanned while everyone else –

DORY. Why?

ZWART. It's as though you're – oh come on, you know what I mean.

DORY. Yes, but why did you go then?

RIET. Out of the wind, and in the sun, that's a tall order!

*

ALEXANDER *and* LEA.

ALEXANDER (*with a newspaper clipping*). ' . . . over the past ten years the scope of his technique and visual imagery has become increasingly profound; despite the comic-strip element inherent in his style of painting, the bloodshot eyes and piles of bones are imbued with a pessimism verging on the truly tragic.'

LEA. Let me see. What a ridiculous shirt. It doesn't do a thing for you.

*

RIET *and* ADA.

RIET. Alexander didn't even recognise me. He walked straight past me.

ADA. Really? A moment ago he was standing here singing.

RIET. I just don't understand it. They used to come and visit me often enough. Have I changed that much?

ADA. You?

RIET. Why else would you walk straight past someone like that.

ADA. There are things one can put up with and there are things one cannot put up with.

*

HANS *and* JANNA.

HANS. Shall we have a little dance?

JANNA. No sir. I'm here to serve the guests and I promised not to have anything to do with anyone or anything. Or I wouldn't have been allowed to come.

HANS. Strange conditions.

JANNA. Yes, because my mother said, I don't know these people, they may be perfectly decent people, some of them are, but if you have to stay there till the early hours, you have to promise not to have anything to do with any of them because you never know, after they've had a few drinks – Now I know you haven't drunk anything yet but a promise is a promise.

HANS. So your mother made inquiries first.

JANNA. Yes sir.

HANS. And?

JANNA. Completely satisfactory sir.

HANS. And the money?

JANNA. Also satisfactory sir.

HANS. Yes, some of them are all right.

*

DUIFJE *and* DORY.

DUIFJE. What a beautiful day, have you noticed, Dory, what a beautiful day it is? They've been lucky there don't you think? Exceptional, an exceptionally beautiful day.

DORY. Yes, nice weather.

DUIFJE. What do you mean, you don't think the weather is nice?

DORY. Lovely weather. Fantastic weather.

DUIFJE. Well that's all I meant.

DORY. Yes you're right, the weather is really very nice.

DUIFJE. It's not that I want to be in the right, what nonsense! In the right! In the right! I was just talking about the weather.

DORY. No offence meant.

DUIFJE. What?

DORY. Maybe it'll stay this way.

DUIFJE. What?

DORY. The weather.

DUIFJE. I was just saying something – something neutral. You're making I-don't-know-what out of it!

DORY. 'As usual'.

DUIFJE. You didn't hear me say that!

*

ADA, SIMON, HANS, DUIFJE, NICO, LEA, DORY *and* RIET.

SIMON. Have you heard about Ada's latest exploit?

ADA. No, Simon, they don't need to hear about it.

SIMON (*to* ZWART *and* DUIFJE). As you know, my wife is sometimes a little absent-minded. She'll walk into a house just because the door is standing open. She thinks it's for her, that's she's expected. (*Laughter.*) Or she'll suddenly buy a child's dress, and it's only when she gets home with it that she remembers Lea isn't a child any more. Or –

ADA (*laughing*). Now, Simon, that'll do.

SIMON. Yesterday she had to buy some ginger. She can't do that round the corner, no, she has to go into town for it.

ADA (*laughing, to* ZWART *and* DUIFJE). Before the war, we used to live in the centre. I like going to the same shops, then I know where to find things.

SIMON. Like a packet of ginger.

ADA. And I enjoy going there.

SIMON (*not sarcastic*). Because of the parking problem she takes the tram. But how does she get back? Not by tram. Guess how she gets back.

ADA (*laughing*). Simon, please.

SIMON. I'll give you three guesses.

(*Everyone talking at once.*) 'On horseback! By taxi! On foot! By plane! In a wheelbarrow!'

SIMON. In a police car.

ADA. It was just out of kindness. They were kind and helpful. It was a misunderstanding.

SIMON. What happened? Ada was sitting in the tram, clutching her ticket, duly paid for, of course –

ADA. Suddenly two of those men got on. In uniform. With boots. They were speaking German.

NICO. German?

ADA. Maybe I'm just imagining that. Maybe they weren't speaking German. But I thought it was German. So I got off. At least that's what I wanted to do, but I had to wait till the next stop. But I thought – at least, that's what I think now – I think I thought I wasn't allowed to be on the tram at all. We weren't allowed. But we did anyway. But at that time there weren't those awful trap doors that you can't open, that only open when you get to a stop. Horrible doors, especially when you're caught in a traffic jam, you can't get out, even if you're in a hurry, even if you're really close, they don't let you get out. And you can hardly breathe. So I tried to force them open. I stuck my umbrella between them and I thought, I'll wrench them open, I can always get another brolly. But those men with the boots thought that was suspicious. Do I look like a fare-dodger? So they grab me. I scream. I shouldn't have, but I got so scared when they grabbed me – God, I was confused – but what do you expect – two men suddenly grab your arms, the door won't open, I can't get out – I don't remember anything more. But when I looked in the larder it turned out I still had eight packets of ginger. I'm an old hoarder. Silly, eh?

RIET. And did they apologise?

ADA. Who, why?

RIET. The ticket inspectors.

ADA. Goodness no why should they? They were just doing their job. (*Laughing.*) Befehl ist Befehl! And they were nice, very sweet boys. At any rate the policemen were nice. The inspectors must have handed me over to the police.

SIMON. They almost got an invitation for today.

ADA. I did invite them! They were such nice boys. And they brought me all the way home!

SIMON. You see!

They all applaud.

*

LEA *and* ALEXANDER.

LEA. Last night, I had made myself a hot toddy, I went to lie down for a bit, suddenly I smelled a smell – the same smell that used to come from my blouse – after we – your smell. A mixture of your smell and mine.

ALEXANDER. Regret?

LEA. Regret? Never occurred to me – but now you ask – (*Ironically.*) overwhelming regret. Nothing but regret, isn't it obvious?

ALEXANDER. You don't look any different. If anything, more beautiful.

LEA. Even more beautiful? I used to think, when it comes to the future, people are a bit like chameleons: if you see a rosy future, that's the colour you take on. Have you tried this marvellous salmon?

ALEXANDER. You don't have to be scared of me. If you want to go, just go.

LEA (*switching to a normal tone*). I wish you hadn't come.

ALEXANDER. You invited me yourself.

LEA. But that was three weeks ago. Alexander –

ALEXANDER. ?

LEA. Do you think I'll ever get there?

ALEXANDER. You must never give up hope. Five minutes before you die you can still meet someone, someone who's just right for you. Really, I really believe that. (*Kisses her, and hurries off to where the drinks are.*)

*

RIET *and* LEA, *later* SIMON *and* HANS.

RIET. Is something the matter with your mother?

LEA. Yes, why?

RIET. I told her Alexander didn't recognise me, that he had walked straight past me, and that I didn't understand why. Because you two used to visit me often enough.

LEA. And what did she say?

RIET. She said: 'There are things one can put up with, and there are things one cannot put up with'.

LEA. You're acting as though Alexander is the most important person here today. (SIMON *and* HANS *join them.*)

SIMON (*to* HANS). Human beings have to learn to feel. But what they learn is not the feelings themselves, because they're born with them. They learn which situations are linked to which feelings. For instance, they don't have to learn what fear is. Darkness; big things that come towards you slowly; noise, being alone; strange people; snakes, spiders, wild animals; especially in combination: being alone in the dark with a noise. There are also fears that have to be taught. The fear of illness, for instance.

LEA. And what about small things that hit you at great speed?

SIMON. Fear of the dark, on the other hand, has to be un-learned.

RIET. Talking of the dark, I saw a film a while ago. A French film, a beautiful film. Really wonderful. And the story made me think of you. Don't laugh, I know nothing about history but I can't help liking films about that time. Because whichever way you look at it, it was a very special time, wasn't it? Well, this man is being chased. There's been a mistake, and they think he's a Jew. He isn't, but he can't prove it. A whole different story, with changes of identity and what have you. At long last they catch him all the same, and he disappears. In the end he's sent to a camp anyway, along with all those French Jews. And he wasn't even a Jew, he was completely innocent!

SIMON. Riet has a heart of gold!

*

ADA *and* LEA, *later* HANS, *then* SIMON.

ADA (*to* LEA). Lea is it true David has come?

LEA. David? (*Runs away.*)

ADA (*alone*). If it *is* true David has come, then I'd very much like to see him. A son-in-law is like a son, except that a son-in-law can suddenly disappear, which a son can't. Where could he be? Upstairs?

HANS *peeps round the door.*

ADA. Oh Mr Hans. Perhaps you know where David is.

HANS. David? Never heard of him, sorry.

ADA (*alone again*). Maybe he's having a bath. If you know someone has come, but you don't see them, it can be a problem. I can't help thinking he's here, David, one of my dearest sons-in-law. Oh, how I'd love to see him, even if only for a moment. Who knows who else might have come? If I can't see them, then maybe there are even more dear ones upstairs. If I think David is there, why shouldn't Selma be there, and why not Ernst, and Karl, and Max and Erna and Rosa and even Paul. And Lina and Maurits and Asser and Freddie and Jozef or did I already mention him. It makes me feel dizzy. All upstairs, all of them have come, only I don't see them.

SIMON (*enters*). Ada are you coming?

*

DANIEL, ZWART and HANS.

DANIEL (*drowsily*). Has anyone seen Theo? I'm sorry, have you started already?

ZWART. Just about, just about.

DANIEL. Theo? Did I say Theo? I didn't mean Theo, I meant . . . well . . . it was something very like Theo.

HANS. Shall we start?

*

Play within play.

A sketch the guests perform for the bridal couple.

On the street. Auf der strasse. Dans la rue.

How do I get to?

Which way is?

The hotel?

The church? The museum? The tulip fields?

Which way is the centre of town?

I've lost my way.

The toilet, please.

A taxi rank?

The tram/bus/ to . . . ?

How many stops?

How far is it?

How long will it take to . . . ?

How do you say . . . ?

What is the meaning of . . . ?

Would you please write it down for me?

I don't understand this; would you read this?

Where? When?

How much? How?

To the right?/To the left?

Nearby? Far away?

Today? Tomorrow?

Big? Small?

High? Low?

A chemist's/Hospital?

Can you tell me what time it is?

A tobacconist's.

A news-stand.

How much is it?

How much do I have to pay?

In the car. Beim Autofahren.

Which way is . . . ?

I have a flat tyre.

Check the brakes.

I'm insured. Are you?

The driver's licence.

Please tow me to . . .

How much is it?

What do I have to pay?

In the train. No comboio. Pa tag. En train.

I want . . . tickets to . . .

First class. Second. Return.

An express. A sleeper.

To reserve a seat. Reserved seats.

The waiting room.

To the . . . o'clock train to . . .

Careful, fragile.

Is there a dining car?

May I smoke?

This seat is taken. Please close the window.

Can I put my suitcase up there?

Can I open the window?

I've got on the wrong train.

Is there a hotel near here?

How much is it?

How much do I have to pay?

The hotel (1).

Which hotel is the best?

Do you have a vacancy?

Is there another hotel you could recommend?

I don't want a room at the front.

The noise keeps me awake.

Do you have a room with a sea view?

Do you have a cheaper room?

Please make me a hot water bottle.

There are no towels in the bathroom.

The sheets on this bed are damp.

Please open/close the window/the awning/the shutters.

It is too cold/hot in the room.

The radiator doesn't work.

The radiator is too hot.

How much is it?

How much do I have to pay?

The hotel (2).

The light is very poor.

This lamp is broken.

Please wake me at seven.

Please don't wake me tomorrow.

Who is that?

What time is it?

Just a minute!

Come in!

Are there any letters for me?

Has anyone called for me?

Has anyone phoned for me?

I'm expecting a gentleman/lady.

Please send him/her up at once.

The chambermaid never comes when I ring for her.

I've lost my . . . in my room.

*

Simon's speech.

SIMON. Dear daughter, dear son-in-law.

It won't be necessary to tell you that the performance we've just seen has somewhat pre-empted the performance I myself wanted to give, and which would consist of my giving you a cheque for your honeymoon. Now I know quite well you don't need the money as such, but in a way we wished to present you with this trip for our own pleasure, so when you are on foreign soil, dear Lea, dear Alexander –

LEA. Nico!

SIMON. Do forgive me. Dear Lea, dear Nico, when it comes down to brass tacks it's rather selfish of us to offer you this trip as a gift, by the way, it was Ada who insisted, since we ourselves never had the opportunity, I don't have to go into that, it was Ada who insisted that you, dear Nico and dear Alexander, please forgive me, that you should accept this trip as our contribution to this new and hopeful match, and I am sure that, as soon as you are on your way, you will no longer be bothered by the thought that it was us who gave it to you, but that you

will enjoy your young lives for what they really are: a gift of
nature.

*

Dory's song.

Where are we going, you ask me.

Where do you want to go, I ask.

And we sleep and we sleep for hours and hours

waking and sleeping, sleeping and waking

and arriving nowhere at all.

Hand in hand we sleep at last

as if we're out walking, as if we're out walking.

The path is so short

and the field is so small

and the wood is quickly passed through.

Where are we going, you ask me.

Where do you want to go, I ask you.

*

Lea's song.

In my blue blue dress in the blue blue sea

if I drown I'll drag you down with me.

The melons here are so ripe and round

juicy flesh in a dark green pod

and peaches soft with furry down

we spit the pips at one another.

Bullseye! Roll through the sand.

Without my blue dress in the blue blue sea

under water I yield to you

I yield like seaweed floating free

on the blue blue beach, in the blue blue sea

if I sink I'll drag you down with me.

*

NICO, ALEXANDER, LEA, DORY, PIEN.

NICO. If everyone would only say what he really means.

ALEXANDER. Then we would be able to enjoy the silence at last.

PIEN. Do you mind my being here?

NICO. That wasn't aimed at you.

PIEN. No, but I suddenly thought – I just came – no one invited me.

DORY. Don't worry about it.

LEA. Who'd like a piece of cake?

DORY. Cake, are you crazy. That comes later. That's part of the ritual.

*

NICO *and* LEA.

NICO. I must go and see the Rinsemas. Every year around this time I want to go, but nothing ever comes of it. After all, I have a lot to thank them for, if not everything. I have everything to thank them for and yet I never go and see them. They probably think I'm ungrateful. Will you come? Dory always used to come with me.

LEA. Riet is here. Why aren't they?

NICO. They wouldn't go to anybody's second marriage.

LEA. Then maybe they wouldn't want to see anybody's second wife.

NICO. Oh, come off it. They are a bit old-fashioned, but they accept facts. And they can't get away for long – they still do the milking by hand.

*

DUIFJE *and* LEA.

DUIFJE. Child, you look ravishing. I know I said so before, but I just have to say it again. Ra-vi-shing! What were you thinking of, when you chose this?

*

ZWART, DANIEL *and* DUIFJE.

ZWART. Who are you? Do I know you?

DANIEL (*drowsily*). No, you don't know me. Actually, I live in this house.

DUIFJE. Here? With Lea's parents?

DANIEL. For the time being.

ZWART. Strange, I didn't know about that. Where are you from?

DANIEL. Where I'm from?

ZWART. Yes. Is that a strange question?

DANIEL. No, I don't think it's a strange question. I constantly ask it myself, but the answer got lost. Is lost. Got loose. How shall I put it. I came down to stop this wedding. I'm looking for the bride. Can you tell me where I might find the bride, please, oh please.

*

LEA, ZWART, DUIFJE, NICO.

LEA. Nico has promised to stop smoking and to work less.

ZWART. Really? How are you going to do that? Fewer patients each day – referring them more quickly?

NICO. No new ones, that's all. Just as long as it eases up a bit. I never have time for anything. I want to do a bit of living.

ZWART. The illusions you two have about living! What exactly do you have in mind?

NICO. Well, eh –

*

DANIEL *and* RIET.

RIET. Marvellous party.

DANIEL (*almost asleep*) Yes, marvellous.

RIET. Have we met?

DANIEL. I know who you are. A heroine. I am in awe.

RIET. Call me Riet. Everyone just calls me Riet.

DANIEL. Daniel. I used to live here.

RIET. You're related?

DANIEL. Only to my parents.

RIET. So you're not married.

DANIEL. About to be engaged.

RIET. Really? How splendid!

DANIEL. Probably.

RIET. I didn't mean to pry. But the fact is, it's always nice for a single person to meet another single person. They're more approachable, I find.

DANIEL. I never thought of myself as 'single'.

RIET. Oh, but you are! Unless of course you're cohabiting, but you don't look the type. It's just a word, after all. To whom are you engaged?

DANIEL. I don't know yet.

RIET. Your Dutch is really excellent.

DANIEL. My parents were Dutch. They owned this house before the war.

RIET. Really, where do they live now?

DANIEL. I don't know any more. (*Waking up.*) Sorry, I couldn't tell you. Do you know where the bride is? Are they going to live in this house? I don't think my parents would like that. Not at all. Where is the bride?

RIET. I think she's in the bathroom, with her first husband, David, her second husband I mean, because Alexander is over there (*Points.*) This may sound strange, but he's in the bath, you see, so she had to, I mean, if she wanted to see him at all –

*

ZWART, RIET, SIMON, ADA *and* DUIFJE.

Beginning of a longer scene in which the older people are sitting together, to be continued on the next page.

ZWART (*relating dream*). Although the hunting season was over I went down to the estate. I had two women with me, a mother and daughter, don't ask me why. On the table were two grapefruit halves, covered with dust. The butler said: 'The worst that could have happened to him is that they should be retrieved.'

DUIFJE. My husband is furious, beside himself.

*

ALEXANDER *and* DORY.

ALEXANDER (*sketching* DORY). But she looks much older than you, because of the life she's led.

DORY. While I'm the one who's always travelling.

ALEXANDER. Different. In a disciplined way, or at least I assume so. You don't permit yourself to go out on the town for nights on end. That's what gives you the shakes.

DORY. Is that necessary?

ALEXANDER. In her profession it is. It was sheer curiosity with me, the first time. I'm not shocking you, am I?

DORY. No.

ALEXANDER. I'd heard so much about her, she had quite a reputation, and if someone like that lets you know she'd like to go out with you –

DORY. That's tempting naturally.

ALEXANDER. Irresistible.

DORY. That's what I mean.

ALEXANDER. For me at least.

DORY. And are you still together?

ALEXANDER. Well together, together. That's not the kind of person she is. Me neither, come to that. But we are mad about each other. 'My prize bull' she calls me. Why I don't know, but I like it, of course.

DORY. What else does she do?

ALEXANDER. What else does she do, good question. She's active in the anti seal-clubbing movement. Are you asleep?

DORY. What? Oh, Alexander! Why couldn't you have stayed with Lea!

ALEXANDER. So you could have stayed with Nico?

DORY. No, I just thought – you could have saved yourself all this trouble. But what business is it of mine. Shall we dance?

*

ZWART, SIMON, ADA, DUIFJE.

Continuation of scene with older people from the previous page.

ZWART. . . . devoted wife, two sons, the youngest, Nico, had just been born, she didn't take him with her 'too young for such a long journey,' we said to one another. I, as a non-Jew, was left behind with Nico, but I sent him to people in the country, also because of the food, as far as you could call that which we were eating 'food'. I was too preoccupied, I don't want to go into that, but, you know, what with the resistance, etcetera, etcetera. There were still a few letters smuggled in and out of the camp. The eldest grew and grew, she wrote, he grew very tall but was constantly tired. She had him declared sick, just to get more food for him, but in the hospital barracks he caught something which he then died of. Simon he was called, just like you. Then my wife. After the war I married again, as you see, a mother for Nico –

ADA *glances from* ZWART *to* NICO.

SIMON. Clever clogs.

DUIFJE (*who has been peering into the big room all the while*). Who would buy a cake you can't get through the door!

*

SIMON *and* ZWART.

SIMON. If man ever does succeed in summarising all the details, one question is bound to remain: How will that which is understood understand itself – in other words: how does one turn molecules into consciousness? Did you know, for instance, that feeling and reason actually reside in different parts of the brain? Yes, that's the way it is, sadly enough.

*

HANS *and* PIEN.

PIEN. Does your father brag like that? I don't believe he was ever in the resistance.

HANS. My father was in the resistance all right, but unfortunately he can't brag about it any more. At least that proves he really was in the resistance.

PIEN. That must make you very proud.

HANS. I would rather have a father who bragged now and then, even if it wasn't true, I think. But if I had a father like that – perhaps Nico is less irritated because he sees from me what it's like not to have a father at all.

PIEN. But now you're so old, it doesn't matter any more. So many people your age don't have a father.

HANS. But I don't have any brothers or sisters either. I have neither kith nor kin, nor wife, nor what-have-you. I wouldn't know how to. I've been in love, but then I didn't know how to proceed. Like a book with the second half missing. Do you think that's strange?

PIEN. Yes, weird. If I were you I'd see a shrink. I know a very nice one. Do you want his address?

HANS. No, thanks. No need at the moment.

PIEN. But you just said –

HANS. No, everything is fine. As long as I don't get – as long as I'm not in love everything's fine.

PIEN. Are you gay?

HANS. Who knows?

PIEN. Or are you impotent or something?

HANS. Yes. I'm impotent or something. Shall we leave it at that?

PIEN. Fine by me.

*

ZWART, DUIFJE, NICO *and* LEA.

ZWART. Isn't it wonderful to know your future is safe? Of course with Alexander you didn't exactly live hand to mouth but then he was always dependent on commissions, while Nico –

LEA. I'm working as well.

ZWART. Ah yes, the jolly fiddler. I've always thought, this may sound terribly naive but I've always thought anyone involved with music cannot get miserable. That always struck me with Dory. So level-headed. Is that you too?

LEA. Have you seen that fantastic cake yet?

DUIFJE. If only the things you didn't eat made you lose weight, whereas it's the things you do eat that make you put it on.

ZWART. Now about the gift. The problem is of course everything that used to belong to Nico's mother I've already given to Dory. And now I don't know what Dory's kept and what she's given back to Nico.

NICO. I don't want anything back from Dory. You gave Dory nothing but rubbish anyway.

DUIFJE *clutches the valuable necklace she is wearing.*

NICO. Exactly.

ZWART. It's not the value in gold, it's the emotional value.

NICO. Exactly.

ZWART. Just say what you want. Apart from what Duifje is
   wearing, you can have anything you want.

NICO. Shouldn't there be a pendant on this chain?

ZWART. How would you know?

NICO. Not belonging to my mother, but to Duifje. Don't you
   remember, Duifje, what a scene I made?

DUIFJE. There were so many scenes, I don't know which one you
   mean. (*To* LEA.) What a teenager. What a teenager he was.

   I never stopped to think about it, of course I knew it had
   belonged to Nico's mother, who had inherited it from her
   mother, but that it was a star of David, I hadn't noticed that,
   I just saw it as a piece of jewellery. And then suddenly, in
   puberty, he went all Jewish, the only Jew in the family, he was.
   'And you're not wearing it, and you're going to take it off.'
   So I did, for the sake of peace.

LEA. And where is it now, that little star?

DUIFJE. In some little box or other. Do you want it? You can have
   it if you want, but it's no good without a chain. I'll look for it if
   you like.

   ZWART *and* DUIFJE *are exiting but their text off-stage cuts
   through that of* LEA *and* NICO.

NICO. Don't think you'll ever get it.

LEA. I hadn't thought of your mother as someone with jewellery.
   Funny, isn't it? It must be because of that photo.

ZWART (*to* DUIFJE). Let's go and live in France, somewhere
   where it's peaceful and quiet where you never have to walk
   through long corridors.

DUIFE. Oh, and that just occurs to you, from one moment to the
   next, poof!

NICO (*to* LEAH). If only she had taken everything. My father
   buried it in the garden, for when the war was over, under a lilac
   tree. But by the end of the war the lilac had had it as well, and
   nobody knew where it had been. So then they dug up the whole
   garden to find that little tin. And later when I saw Duifje
   wearing those things, I used to think: if only she had taken them

with her, after all they bartered gold for bread, didn't they?
Maybe she'd still be alive. Nonsense of course.

ZWART (*to* DUIFJE). One has to come up with something!

*

Advice to original parents.

Your child is safe.

Do not visit.

Do not telephone.

Do not write.

Erase all traces of it.

Get rid of clothing.

Get rid of toys/dolls.

Get rid of the cot.

Try to obliterate any reference to the child from your personal
papers.

Do not keep photographs. They may endanger the life of your
child and that of its new parents.

If you have already left your house, seek some reliable person to
destroy evidence for you. Do not talk about your child to
anyone.

Ask friends and family not to mention your child.

Money is to be sent in the pre-arranged way or handed over to the
contact person.

Have a good journey!

*

ADA *and* ALEXANDER, *later* LEA.

ADA. But I have to make the choice, not him. He says he's already
made his choice. From the moment we got back here he never
talked about it again. Now we're going to build, he said. With
me it's different. I have to choose between two kinds of regret.
Here, have another one. (*Handing him something to eat.*)
They're good. You certainly haven't put on any weight. I've
got to do this, you see, even if I'm sure to lose him.

ALEXANDER *embraces her carefully, as if she were a child.*

ADA. Oh, my child, my boy. To think we had to have another wedding to see you again! Will you look up your old mother-in-law when I'm back?

ALEXANDER. Just say the word and I'll come running!

LEA *(has hurt her hand)*. Das krasseste Unlustgefühl ist der Schmerz.

ADA *and* ALEXANDER *(together)*. What's the matter?

LEA. I caught my hand between the door and the cake.

*

SIMON *and* DANIEL.

SIMON. Look, I don't have any objections to you feeding the ducks, on the contrary, I approve of it, I think it's excellent, but next time you do it – I'm not saying this because I'm annoyed or anything – would you please make sure there's some bread left over to eat – three, five slices? That's enough, that's more than enough!

*

RIET *and* LEA.

RIET *(bandaging* LEA*'s injured hand)*. There you are, my dear child, and now I would advise you to put it in a sling.

LEA. Oh, no, that's going too far.

RIET. For ordinary people maybe, but you can't take any risks. Come now, Liesje.

LEA. I like it when you call me Liesje.

RIET. Lea, I mean.

*

SIMON *and* NICO.

SIMON. There are two kinds of uncertainty. The first is the genuine, age-old, eternal uncertainty that applies to the real dangers of life. Without that uncertainty we wouldn't be able to live. We'd go straight under a car when we tried to cross the road. You agree with me thus far, I take it. Then there is this another kind of uncertainty, and that is the uncertainty Ada is suffering from, which is conditioned by the socio-historical context we are living in at this moment. If you attribute one – no, let me finish – if you attribute too great a meaning to one of those two kinds of uncertainty, you either grow apathetic, or you begin, if you'll allow me, to put too great a trust in medical science, which claims to be able to rid people of certain fears which have come about through their own personal history. So, now you may say something.

NICO. Sorry I can't stand long stories. But the fact is that some therapies can cure some people of some fears; I will defend my profession that far.

SIMON. 'The fact is, the fact is.' Nothing is a fact. I want her to talk to me and not to all those so-called therapists who haven't been through anything themselves, don't you understand? 'The fact is'! I don't want her to submit herself to some horrendous treatment in an asylum.

NICO. It isn't an asylum.

SIMON. An institution then. Have you talked her into this?

*

HANS *and* PIEN.

HANS. Of course, it could be coincidence, but I don't think it's right. Why should that crooked property dealer have to have a nose like that? I mean, anyone can be untrustworthy, and certainly with money, so why not someone with a nose. But on the stage, or in a story, it can never be coincidental. We can't permit that kind of thing, there are enough prejudices as it is, we don't need to add to them. That's dangerous, it can be used against us. I'm not saying we should all be presented as members of the nobility, but what sense does it make, I ask you, to confirm all those perverse ideas and on top of that to suggest – no, we can't afford that! Not now, and certainly not in the past! And probably not in the future either.

PIEN. How should I know? Don't ask me.

HANS. Then just say yes or no.

PIEN. Don't be ridiculous. Leave me in peace.

HANS. You must.

PIEN. D'you think I have nothing better to worry about. Lay off me, you prick.

*

ALEXANDER *and* SIMON.

ALEXANDER. I'm trying to call but I can't get through.

SIMON. Wait, the answering machine is on.

ALEXANDER. Thank you.

SIMON *leaves* ALEXANDER *alone.*

ALEXANDER. Hello, darling, how are you? You could have come, it really isn't as bad as all that. Not as bad as you thought. It's all quite normal, quite relaxed. What? No, quite normal. Yes, lots of old faces – some, yes. Don't you feel like dropping in for a while, to pick me up? I'd really like that – as you wish. No, definitely not. No, not late, I won't be late. Bye, bye.

For the rest of the play ALEXANDER *keeps phoning, doesn't get an answer, phones again.*

*

LEA *and* ADA.

LEA. But why choose the day after the wedding?

ADA. I put it off till after the wedding. I meant to do it much sooner, but I didn't want to be away when you got married. I'd like to explain it to you, but you're the very one I can't explain it to. Maybe I could if I pretended you were someone else. Shall I pretend you're someone else? I could explain it to someone else. Do you know what I dreamt last night – or was it the night before? (*Trying to recall.*) Three gentlemen were living in a sleepy house. Three white gentlemen made of eggshell. They had no eyes, they had no noses. They came outside, they walked down the street. And I was walking ahead of them. There was a child playing with a small spade, I walked past, and after me came those gentlemen men, those three eggshell gentlemen. The child suddenly let out a terrible shriek and I didn't dare to turn round.

*

NICO *and* HANS.

NICO. But who are those two men then?

HANS. They're something to do with your father-in-law, aren't they?

*

HENDRIKJE *and* ADA.

HENDRIKJE. I was in Auschwitz last year.

ADA. Were you? (*Silence.*) Don't mention it to Simon, please.

HENDRIKJE. Terrible. Unbelievable.

ADA. Yes.

HENDRIKJE. No, I don't talk about it to anyone. It's too horrible.

ADA. Yes.

HENDRIKJE *gestures despair.*

ADA. Yes.

HENDRIKJE. Only to you, because you know.

ADA. Yes.

HENDRIKJE. Is it painful to talk about it?

ADA. No, not at all.

HENDRIKJE. There was a group of American students, when I was there. They were on a holocaust tour of Europe. They were absolutely shattered, had read everything about it, of course, but still, America is always that much further off. Here one is so close, it's different. 'Children of survivors', they said. Looking for their parents' pasts. Survivor-guilt, do you have that as well? Yes, it's rather a strange question, but it's something I can very well imagine, feeling guilty to have survived, something like that. It's unthinkable. I quite understand if you don't want to answer. But on the other hand, one so often hears –

ADA. What does it look like, Auschwitz?

HENDRIKJE. But you were there yourself!

ADA. I mean, in summer.

HENDRIKJE. Oh – I was there in the autumn. Dark clouds, ominous sky, it looked like a heavy storm, but it didn't rain. Not heavily, anyway.

ADA. That's good to know.

HENDRIKJE. Does it really not bother you to be reminded of it?

ADA. No, heavens no, not at all.

HENDRIKJE. Because you always hear how painful it is that that time has been forgotten, and the fact that the younger generation lives as if it hadn't happened makes it even worse, that feeling of isolation. That's why I went there. I wasn't actually planning on going, but I was close by, and suddenly it was like a magnet, I couldn't not go. (*The memory almost makes her break down.*)

ADA (*laughing*). Yes, it was like that for us too at the time! Can I get you something to drink?

HENDRIKJE. And nobody wants to talk about it!

ADA *exits laughing.*

*

ALEXANDER and DANIEL

ALEXANDER. And have you found the bride?

DANIEL. I'm so tired. I've seen so many faces. Are you related?

ALEXANDER. To the bride? I used to be, in a sense.

DANIEL. Her first husband, I take it. Some people don't even get one chance. I'm going to sleep. If you're finished, that is. (*Suddenly quite formal.*) Are you finished?

ALEXANDER. I wasn't going to say anything.

DANIEL. Just what I thought. Sleep well.

*

LEA, SIMON *and* ADA.

LEA. Is it true you've threatened to leave if she really decides to go there?

SIMON. Yes it's true. I think it's totally unnecessary.

LEA. But are you really planning to leave. Really?

SIMON. I'll have to. I can't – after all these years – I can't live with someone who needs another person for her problems. A professional! As if I wasn't – she keeps up a monologue for hours on end, every night I hold her in my arms!

LEA. I can't imagine. You two separated. I just can't imagine it. And I must say it's rather rotten of you. Or have you got someone else, is that why you're deserting her?

SIMON. My dear child, you don't understand a thing. First of all, I'm not deserting her, she's deserting me. Secondly, there's no such thing as 'someone else'. That's precisely why I take it so seriously. At my age – or in any case I – I can't even imagine 'someone else'. We're not the type for 'someone else'. We are, at least I thought we were until now, one entity. It's her who's breaking that up, not me. I'm going to go and live somewhere else.

LEA. I can't imagine it. You mustn't blame me for not being able to imagine it. I'll stay with her, of course.

SIMON. Oh? I thought you were getting married today for the third time! Really, Lea, this is not the first time your mother has brought this up. But if she intends on leaving tomorrow, I'm leaving tonight. I won't be left here alone.

LEA (*to* ADA). Why don't you say something?

Both SIMON *and* LEA *wait for an answer.*

SIMON. If you'll excuse me, I'll go and pack.

LEA. No! Please don't.

SIMON. It all depends on your mother. If she leaves tomorrow I'm
leaving tonight. Maybe you'll understand me one day, when
you see how inadequate psychology is, and if you ever
discover, in this marriage, or in one of your next, what it
means: to have a bond.

*

DANIEL *and* DUIFJE.

DANIEL. Forgive me for not opening my eyes, but the light here
is so glaring and my eyes have been bothering me for some
time. I can hardly get them open, do you understand?

*

RIET *and* LEA.

RIET. You know that Daddy Bear went to Canada in '46. Would
he have done that if we'd been allowed to keep you? Who can
say? In any case it was a great piece of luck your parents came
back. Who'd have expected it? We certainly didn't, when all
those awful things came out. Daddy Bear went every day to
read the Red Cross lists. Every evening we grew more certain,
because their names weren't there. Not as missing persons, not
as survivors. You can't imagine how keyed up we were. Then
one day they were standing on the doorstep. Well, you could
hardly call it 'standing'. You can't imagine how glad we were
for you. But of course they weren't able to take care of you
straight away. We were allowed to keep you a few more weeks.
Meanwhile Daddy Bear got his travel documents arranged. I
had no idea at the time. But afterwards, I could understand. All
those years he had slept with a gun under his pillow, on account
of you.

LEA. It's tragic. No, I mean it: tragic. What do you want me to
say? I've said it was tragic. But I already knew. Every time I
get married you tell me the same story.

*

DUIFJE *and* SIMON.

DUIFJE. I'm cold.

SIMON. How strange. It isn't cold in here at all.

DUIFJE. But I'm cold.

SIMON. Oh dear, what can we do about it. I'll see if I can find you a blanket. Or a coat?

DUIFJE. No, don't bother, it's all right.

SIMON. But if you're cold . . .

DUIFJE. Don't bother. Really.

SIMON. No one's supposed to sit here shivering. Look at you. Come on, give me that, or you'll be spilling the rest too. (*She licks her spilt wine off the table.*) No need for that, silly, I can pour you some more. Come on, stand up. That way you'll get even colder, of course.

*

HANS *and* PIEN.

HANS. You think that's funny? It's a fact. It's something to do with not having a foreskin.

PIEN. Fairy-tales. I've been to New York. You can't tell me anything. Your kind is no different to any other. There's just one difference.

HANS. Which is?

PIEN. Jewish guys go on about themselves non-stop.

HANS. Generalisations, and you know where they can lead.

PIEN. You set me up for that, you bastard. I walked straight into it. Well done. I'll bet you do that to everyone.

HANS. It's not as bad as all that. Come here.

PIEN. No, never. Certainly not now.

*

DORY *and* NICO.

DORY. You should go and see the Rinsemas. Every year around this time you want to go and you never get round to it. After all, you have a lot to thank them for, if not everything. You have everything to thank them for, yet you never go and see them. They must think you're ungrateful.

NICO. I'm a bit scared.

DORY. Scared? Of course.

NICO. The first time I went to see them, the first time I went of my own free will and on my own, I got such terrible diarrhoea that I spent more time on the toilet than in the room with them.

And those few times with you – but you're right, of course. I should go.

*

HANS *and* PIEN.

HANS. But don't you have any scars anywhere, no marks, nothing?

PIEN. Of course I do.

HANS. What then? Where?

PIEN. That's none of your business.

HANS. But I find it interesting.

PIEN. Why?

HANS. Because then I can kiss it better.

PIEN. You're mad. Leave me alone.

HANS. You don't get an offer like that every day.

PIEN. I get offers like that ten times a day.

HANS. Oh really? Someone who asks you if you're in pain anywhere?

PIEN. That's not what you're asking. You're asking if I still have my appendix. And if I say no, then you'll ask: where did it used to be then?

HANS. You're getting to know me!

PIEN. No, I'm getting to know your game. I know your game. I don't know you, and I have no desire to, because even before I've got to know you I've had more than enough of you.

*

Duet: HANS *and* PIEN.

(She) God he kissed me on the nose.

(He) God she kissed me on the nose.

(Both) Is this getting serious?

(She) Whatever can this mean?

(He) I wonder if she's really keen?

(She) Perhaps I'll stay a little longer.

(He) I shouldn't stay a second longer.

*

DANIEL *and* LEA.

DANIEL. Madam! You have to cancel all plans of getting married to a man of the opposite kind. Nothing good can come of it. I'm baring my soul to you, not out of habit, but in order to save you. I myself was once engaged to a non-Jewish woman. Have you thought of your offspring? You must not do this Madam, you will bring unhappy people into the world, people who no longer know which group they belong to. Do you know what that means, Madam, to belong, you probably do, that's why you neglect your offspring before they are even born. You have no idea what it means to a person, not to belong. Is this what our forefathers suffered for, is this why they bore the yoke down through the centuries – so you could cast tradition away like an old slipper.

LEA. Shoe.

DANIEL. ?

LEA. Yes, that's it. A shoe that no longer fits, is what tradition is. Yes, I have rich parents, but what does that get me? A much-too-large party, as usual. I don't know who you are, sir, and to be quite frank, I'm not really –

DANIEL. I can walk on my hands just as easily as on my feet. It's all the same to me whether I eat or throw up and I can pronounce each sentence backwards or forwards with equal ease. The last sentence, for instance, is: ESAE LAUQE HTIW SDRAWROF RO SDRAWKCAB ECNETNES HCAE ECNUONORP NAC I. And do you know what 'UOY EVOL I' means?

LEA. Is that Hebrew or something?

DANIEL. No, it's 'I love you' spelled back to front. And do you know why it is spelled back to front? Because I live from back to front. I've seen everything that is to come, and at the moment that the worst appeared, I turned around in time, and am now I'm back at the beginning. Did you know my parents lived in this house before the war? Only here can I succumb to love, it's like being possessed. I've tried to fall in love in all the lives I've had, but it is only in this house that I feel the turmoil – it's as if I'd lived here myself, it's as if my memories are stored here in this attic. I only have to evoke them, and if I strive to remember them, whom do I see but you, Lea, like a memory, like a promise from the past – which still has to be fulfilled. This time I'm not just going to let go of you. My name is Daniel.

*

NICO *and* DORY.

NICO. I wish you hadn't come.

DORY. You invited me yourself.

NICO. That was three weeks ago.

DORY. And you phoned me.

NICO. That was two weeks ago.

DORY. And we saw each other in the small auditorium.

NICO. Yes, that was last week. But now I wish you hadn't come.

DORY. I'll go if you want.

NICO. Will you come and sit by my deathbed too?

DORY. If you want me to.

NICO. Don't you ever say: go to hell!

DORY. Why should I?

NICO. Because sometimes it's the only thing to say.

DORY. . . .

NICO. I wish some disaster would befall you, just for once!

DORY. It has, as you well know.

NICO. I don't believe a word of it, there's no sign of it at all.

DORY. . . .

*

ZWART *and* RIET.

ZWART. Duifje has always said: if Nico and Dory ever divorce, it will be the perfect divorce, mark my words –

*

LEA *and* DORY, *later* NICO.

LEA. Will you think it over?

DORY. No.

LEA. Do you realise what that means?

DORY. Of course I realise what that means. It's not because of you, I just don't give lessons any more. Just the few students I already have. I've got no time. Really I haven't.

LEA. But you have more time than you used to.

DORY. Because Nico's gone?

LEA. Not just because of Nico – you must have had more to do before – a bigger house, Nico's practice – I don't know how I'm going to manage it all. And the garden – (*Looks at her hands.*)

DORY. I don't mind helping you vacuum, but I'm not giving you any more violin lessons.

LEA. You don't have to be afraid. I'll never come up to your standard anyway. I just wanted to learn some new techniques, but you won't even give me the chance.

DORY. Christ, I'm not the only one.

LEA. To me you are.

DORY. And where would that happen? Have you thought about that? I'm not setting foot in my own house again. Not for the time being, anyway.

LEA. At your digs. I'll come to you.

DORY. I'll have to think about it.

LEA *embraces her affectionately.* NICO *joins them.*

DORY. The answer is no.

LEA. But I'm at a standstill, that's obvious, isn't it! All I want is to develop myself and I'm at a complete standstill!

*

DUIFJE *and* LEA.

DUIFJE. My child, you look ravishing. I know I said it before, but I just can't help myself. Ra-vi-shing! What were you thinking of when you chose this?

LEA. Well, it had to be festive, and Nico had to like it, and it had to be comfortable, and I had to be able to wear it for work. Not for concerts, of course, but matinées and that sort of thing. It so often – (*Simulates playing the violin.*) – it always pulls across here.

DUIFJE. And you were brought up with clothes.

LEA. That too, yes.

DUIFJE. But that's why – I wanted to know – what do you think of when you dress yourself, how do you present yourself, how do you see yourself, how do you choose yourself, your type –

*

What to take on the journey.

Warm clothing, waterproof

Heavy shoes, waterproof

Jewellery

Two blankets or one sleeping bag

For children:

Warm clothing, waterproof

Heavy shoes, waterproof

Jewellery

Two blankets or one sleeping bag

Furthermore, per person:

1 mug

1 plate

1 fork

1 spoon

1 small pan

N.B. It is forbidden to take superfluous items such as: books, toys, photographs, etc.

*

A variation on a very vulgar popular song is sung.

*

DANIEL *and* DORY.

DANIEL. It's your husband who is getting married, this must be a strange day for you.

DORY. Oh yes, no, yes, no.

DANIEL. But everyone stays friends?

DORY. Yes, usually.

DANIEL. But those two grey men, who are they?

DORY. So you've noticed them too! Are they different from the others here? I thought it only seemed so to me.

DANIEL. You're not paranoid, I'm the paranoid one, and I can tell you they are bad people. Respectable people.

DORY. Yes, perhaps you're right.

DANIEL (*with even more distaste*). Respectable people.

DORY. Then why do I find them so off-putting?

DANIEL. Tailor-made suits. Dog-lovers. Unscrupulous.

DORY. How do you know?

DANIEL. Headhunters. Experimenters. Button pushers. Organizers. Administrators.

DORY. How do you know? They might be quite decent. They might even take people into hiding if need be –

DANIEL. Are you Jewish?

DORY. Does it matter?

*

RIET *and* HANS.

RIET. Do you know what I don't understand, I'd like you to explain something to me.

HANS. As long as it's not about Jews again.

RIET. What do you mean? I'm not around that often.

HANS. Go on then.

RIET. Well . . .

HANS. Yes?

RIET. I go to the theatre quite often. More than I would if I lived in town. If something's on, then I go and see it.

HANS. Yes.

RIET. And now I wonder – a whole play where all the characters are Jews, that would be impossible, wouldn't it? I mean because if all the characters were Jews, then not one of them could have bad qualities, and then you'd never have a play. I mean – there couldn't be one pathological liar, for instance, because that would make it an anti-Semitic play. Wouldn't it? I mean if Shakespeare is anti-Semitic because of Shylock, what about someone who wrote a whole play with only Jews in it, what would he be? Just imagine O'Neill, with all those creepy families, just imagine if they were Jews. Or is there something I'm not getting?

HANS. Why are you so preoccupied with Jews all the time?

RIET. Well, my whole life has been . . . determined by them. Hasn't it?

*

RIET, ADA *and* LEA.

RIET. Are you in retreat? Would you like me to join you?

ADA. Retreat? What do you mean? They're in retreat. As a matter of fact, I'm turning to the others. There's more understanding out there than there is inside.

RIET. How can you say such a thing as a mother.

ADA. If it weren't for your goodness we wouldn't be alive any more. But if it weren't for the murderousness of others we wouldn't have needed your goodness, nor your courage, to stay alive. 'Yes, there is cruelty in the world but –' I'm standing here in the cruel air trying to catch my breath, if you want to stay, it's all right by me.

RIET. I used to think we could be friends. For both of us it was Liesje . . . Lea. But you've been so strange these last few years, as if gratitude had turned into –

LEA. My mothers! What are you brooding about! The cake! The cake is being attacked!

*

Duet: ADA *and* RIET.

Song based on a child's swinging or skipping rhyme, or a variation on:

There was a little girl, who had a little curl
Right in the middle of her forehead
When she was good she was very very good
And when she was bad she was horrid.

*

SIMON *and* DORY.

Silence and shyness.

SIMON. May I call you Dory?

   Silence.

   Lea has – the family constellations – it's all become rather complicated.

   Silence.

   I admire you greatly – I have for years from a distance, as a violinist. Can I get you something – a drink or something?

DORY. No, thank you.

SIMON. Something to eat?

DORY. No, really –

SIMON. Something to – (*Silence.*) yes, your tone is quite exceptional.

DORY. I never know –

SIMON. Really, no drink?

DORY. I've often wondered –

SIMON. Yes?

DORY. Whether maybe you happen to have known my father. He was in textiles too. You were in textiles before the war too, weren't you? Breslauer.

SIMON. Breslauer. (*Silence.*) No. No, I don't think so. Breslauer. Breslauer. The name does ring a bell, of course, but no, no, I'm sorry. I'm really very sorry. Can you tell me any more, which branch, where was he?

DORY. No, I don't know. I thought, perhaps. It would have been pure coincidence.

SIMON. No, God, I'm terribly sorry. No, no, really not. What did he look like? Big, small –

DORY. I don't know. Big – I still think.

SIMON. And Mrs Breslauer? Who do you get your talent from?

DORY. Talent, talent.

SIMON. Yes, you must have got it from someone, it doesn't just drop out of the sky.

DORY. I don't know. Silly, isn't it?

*

ZWART *and* HANS.

ZWART. When I was born, everyone was still alive. They didn't start dying till later. It's not true that as soon as a person is born he starts to die, first he has to get rid of everyone. He comes into the world, is at once surrounded, the world is chock-full around him, he gets to know them all, sometimes even grows fond of them and then they start dropping one by one –

HANS. My father died before I was even born, so in a way I was lucky.

*

LEA *and* SIMON.

LEA. You should have taken me with you to the camp.

SIMON. And that on a day like today!

LEA. A fitting day.

SIMON. No one likes to talk about it.

LEA. I do.

SIMON. You were so small.

LEA. That's why. You should have taken me.

SIMON. We should have done this, we should have done that! Of course! Please, Lea –

LEA. Did you ever wonder how I was? Not just in general, but how I lay in bed at night, for instance? Did you ever talk about that together?

SIMON. It would have been much harder with a little child. None of us would have survived.

LEA. Who wants to survive!

SIMON. This is pointless. Unwise.

LEA. If I had a child I'd take it with me, I'd keep it with me, I'd take it everywhere I went. I'd soothe it just by holding it against me. I can't imagine it: let's give the child to someone else.

SIMON (*as if 40 years ago, to* ADA). Maybe we'll have a better chance of surviving if we do.

LEA. What for, in God's name. There's not that much for her to look forward to.

SIMON. At the time we thought there was.

LEA. I'd keep it in my arms. Especially when things got bad. What does it matter how old you get? Dying's no disaster; being left is a disaster.

SIMON. Who says, I said to Ada, who says you'll be there to keep her in your arms.

LEA. And what did she say?

SIMON. That I was a dreadful pessimist. That it wouldn't be that bad. A long journey, freezing cold, warm clothes and we'll make it. One winter, and then home again. We had terrible arguments but neither of us knew what we were talking about.

LEA. You know, I sometimes envy Dory, who wound up in an orphanage after the war. End of fuss. (*Takes his hand.*)

SIMON. No, no, you don't have to apologise. I understand what you're saying, I do, that's all much less complicated. But there's nothing to be done about it now. We're still alive.

*

ALEXANDER *and* PIEN.

ALEXANDER. And what strikes me is how it works on other women too. As if there is a secret world everyone is curious about, in which, as it were, I'm at home. As soon as they hear that Xantippe is my girlfriend, all doors are open.

PIEN. Doors?

ALEXANDER *kisses her.*

PIEN. And does it exist, that secret world?

ALEXANDER. Do you want to know?

PIEN. Yes, I'm really very curious.

ALEXANDER. Ring me then.

PIEN. And what if Xantippe answers?

ALEXANDER. All the better!

PIEN. I wouldn't dare.

ALEXANDER. If you're really curious there's nothing you don't dare. Tomorrow night?

*

RIET.

RIET. So many didn't come back. Why should *they*, out of all the people who perished, stay alive? Liesje was already starting to look like me. 'She's your daughter', they used to say. Liesje was lucky. To me this is an hysterical sort of hospitality here. Not my cup of tea. They don't know how to live and so they cover it up with salmon. If you don't know how to live, why do it? Because no one can cover anything up with salmon. Not in my opinion. Should I have stayed a member of the church? But when he said, 'After all this, how can one continue to believe?' I stopped believing, no matter what he said after that. What if Ada died? She could. Shock therapy does go wrong at times. And she's at that age. And what if I die? I could marry Liesje's father. Not for the bed, just to be a couple. Grandparents together. Would he think of me? My breasts are as good as new. But how would he know. My nipples always used to ache when Liesje started crying, and she was already four when she

came. Seven when she left. Seven is much too young for a child
to be taken away from her mother. That's a fact. Much too
young.

*

Ten recommendations for prospective parents

If the child you are about to receive cannot yet talk, you can ignore
points: 1, 2, 3, 6, 9.

If the child you are about to receive is already talking, the
following points must be carefully observed.

1. The child's own name must be changed. Its own original name,
as well as the names of original parents, grandparents, etc, must
be forgotten.

   The new name should in no way resemble the original name.

   When choosing a new name, it should be ensured that this name
   is not based on, or similar to, the name of a person known to the
   child.

2. A new address should be invented. It should be ascertained a)
that this address exists in reality, b) whether the occupants of
this address have/have not had any connection with the child, or
with the original parents of the child. In the event of the latter,
the address may not under any circumstances be used.

3. Life history. The child will have to be drilled in a new life-
history which will replace the old life-history. The child must
learn its new life-history by heart and forget the old one as far
as possible. It is advisable to 'test' the child on its new life-
history by waking the child several times a night and asking it
questions such as: 'What is your father's name?'

4. Clothing. The child's clothing should not be conspicuous, nor
should it differ from that worn by other children in the new
environment.

5. Religion. It is advisable to have the child instructed in a new
religion, regardless of whether the original parents were/are
religious.

6. Language. The child should be made to replace its original
accent with the regional dialect of the adoptive environment as
quickly as possible.

7. Appearance. There is nothing that can be done about the shape
of the nose or the colour of the eyes. In some cases it may be
advisable to bleach the child's hair. This should be done as the
child arrives and before anyone has seen it. Repeat weekly.

8. Nutrition. The contact person will regularly provide you with ration books. The food the coupons entitle you to should be given to the child and not to other members of the family, pets, etc. The coupons marked tobacco/sweets may be used according to discretion.

9. School. It is advisable to ascertain the allegiance of a school before registering the child there. It is strongly advised not to let the child go to school unless the safety of this enterprise can be guaranteed. If necessary, we can provide textbooks with which to keep the child occupied in the home.

10. Hiding place. In case of danger there should be a hiding place, known to the child, where it can hide for several hours/days/weeks. If possible, this hiding place should be large enough to permit the child to sit upright.

N.B. Before it came to you, the child probably underwent shocking experiences which will be hard to get over. The child may therefore seem difficult at first. The child should *not* be allowed to speak about its experiences, as this would only burden you and your family. It would be best for the child to forget its experiences *as quickly as possible*.

After reading, please destroy this letter.

Thanking you on behalf of the original parents.

*

ADA.

ADA. I can creep under Riet's skin and feel what she feels. She wants me out of the way. Don't you want me out of the way? It would be a relief if you said yes, so I would at least know she were honest. I would have been better long ago if it hadn't been for you. I couldn't very well leave the house, and if I came back safe and sound, the child was gone. I had to keep my child with me or Riet would have loved to take my place. Even with Simon, just to be near Lea. Can you deny it? She hasn't slept with a man for over thirty years, so what does she know of life? Or did she have a man, how am I to know? Are you dried up? I don't want to think of her body, do you want to use my perfume? I dropped the bottle in the washbasin and the bottle didn't break but the washbasin broke. Then I cleared up the splinters of glass, how can there be splinters of glass when the bottle didn't break? And I cut myself deeply but it didn't bleed and that was rather worrying. Maybe I'm too old to bleed. Have you seen these beautiful flowers, I think they're awful. Would you like to have my awful flowers, yes, by that I mean it's been going on for long enough.

*

LEA *and* DORY, *later* ALEXANDER.

LEA. Leaving already?

DORY (*slightly drunk*). Yes.

LEA. Can't you stay a bit longer?

DORY. No, I think I'll go.

LEA. Are you going home?

DORY. Why?

LEA. No reason. I just wondered.

DORY. Don't worry.

LEA. No. I was just wondering. Shouldn't have asked, of course.

DORY. What were you wondering?

LEA. Just what it's like.

DORY. What what's like?

LEA. What it's like to go home now. Switch on the light and so on.

DORY. Sympathy.

LEA. Perhaps. Curiosity too. I've never lived alone, you know.

DORY. Yes, I know.

LEA. Do you think it's strange then that I should wonder what it is like for you to go home? God, I don't want to be mean or – pushy –

DORY. I go home. I switch the lights on –

LEA. And then?

DORY. Dear Lea. A few months ago you asked me how to live with Nico. Of course, I couldn't give you any advice. Now you're asking me how to live without Nico. What do you want of me?

ALEXANDER *joins them.*

LEA. I'll see you out.

DORY. I'll be right back.

*

ADA *and* DUIFJE.

ADA. One just steps over it, like one would step over a dug up piece of road. Just the other day, instead of the pavement, there was suddenly a tent, one of those tents with a little light. They were busy inside repairing the sewage pipes. They had put down a plank, so we could get out of the house by walking over that plank. They had intended to start on the opposite side of the road but they couldn't, so instead of starting on the other side, they started on our side. If they had started on the other side, that again would have been instead of somewhere else. Or don't you think so. I'm asking you instead of someone else. I'm asking this, instead of something else, we are sitting here, instead of others sitting here, and instead of somewhere else.

Don't you ever wonder instead of whom you're sitting here? And instead of where? Or do you just sit?

If one were to do the thing for which this is the replacement, and with the person whose place I am now taking, would one know, in that case, would one sit more solidly, not just hover, as if one could be blown away at any moment? What is the matter with you all of a sudden? What did you expect?

DUIFJE. You're vicious. You're a bitch, do you know that? You only pretend to be mad so you can hurt people!

*

NICO *and* DORY.

Standing with their foreheads against one another.

DORY. I still can't do it, Nico.

NICO. So you're leaving are you?

DORY. I'm still not generous. Still not spontaneous, not sensitive, still not impulsive or fickle. I'm still so dull, Nico, so sensible.

NICO *strokes the back of her head.*

DORY. Lea thought my coat was nice.

NICO. It is nice.

DORY. She asked where I got it. And I didn't immediately take it off and give it to her. I was just about to and then I thought, why burden her again. All that thinking – I should have just given it to her and now it's too late. In the end I'll be so sensible I'll choke.

NICO. I wouldn't have liked that, Lea in your coat. And anyway you think it's beautiful.

DORY. It's not beautiful and it's not ugly, it's just a coat. Is it beautiful?

NICO. When we bought it you thought it was beautiful. When can I see you again? What about tomorrow evening? I need to talk to you. Tomorrow evening, early, I don't want to make it late.

DORY. I can't tomorrow evening.

NICO. Why not, what are you doing?

DORY. I have to audition for a concert-master from Philadelphia.

NICO. Does that have to be in the evening?

DORY. Apparently.

NICO. When would it be, that tour?

DORY. Not a tour, a job.

NICO. A job?

DORY. Yes.

NICO. Permanent?

DORY. Yes.

NICO. No!

*

ALEXANDER *and* ZWART.

Meanwhile ZWART *has become adept at throwing cubes of cheese up in the air and catching them in his mouth. He now moves freely among the guests demonstrating his skill. Because he is always looking up he keeps bumping into things and people.*

ALEXANDER *is phoning the operator.*

ALEXANDER (*on the phone*). I just wanted to check if there was anything wrong with the line. I've been calling all evening you see – yes yes yes yes. Thank you.

ZWART. Yes yes yes yes. Thank you. Chin up, man.

*

ADA *and* JANNA.

ADA. I think it's marvellous, this new freedom, everyone getting on with everyone else's exes, no jealousy, nice and easy, so you don't lose people the way you used to when things went wrong, and had to replace them in your affections, and get attached to the new ones, even though you still loved the old ones, not that you wanted it to be that way, or anything. Because, of course, with the old ones, you have 'more years to love them with'.

*

LEA *and* NICO.

LEA. If I really really loved you, you'd die, I'm absolutely sure you would.

NICO. Then it's better this way. Shall we go to bed? Just one more time, one last time?

LEA. Could you talk to Dory?

NICO. I can't talk to anyone, you know that. People talk to me. Come on.

LEA *is unwilling.*

*

DANIEL *and* ADA.

DANIEL. I understand you perfectly. I understand why you're doing it, I see the necessity of your decision and I think you're very brave. You're giving up everything, your house, your whole existence, in order to prepare – you're seeking peace of mind in order to be able to face old age – and death.

ADA. What on earth are you talking about? How do you know I'm going away?

DANIEL. My dear Ada, the whole wedding party is buzzing with it.

ADA. The only one who knows is my husband. And Lea. And Nico, of course.

DANIEL. And me.

ADA. Apparently you eavesdrop on conversations which are not meant for your ears. I hadn't expected this. You didn't seem the nosey type. If I had known, I would never have taken you into my house. We have many guests but I've never had anything like this.

DANIEL. You're afraid of me, while I am your greatest friend. I am the only one here who isn't going to leave you alone.

ADA (*first taking it literally*). While I so long to be alone for a moment.

DANIEL. I'm not talking about this evening. I'm talking about life as a whole.

ADA. But leave me alone now, will you?

DANIEL. Just as you wish. (*About to leave.*)

ADA. What do you mean: 'I'm not going to leave you alone'?

DANIEL. I'm coming with you. It's that simple.

ADA. With me?

DANIEL. I've cancelled my ticket. I'm coming with you.

ADA. I don't understand.

DANIEL. You'll see me appear every visiting time.

ADA. No, that's not possible.

DANIEL. That is possible, there's a youth hostel quite nearby. I've done my homework!

ADA. Look, it's terribly nice of you but it would be better if you just went back to Israel – that's where your home is –

DANIEL (*interrupting*). I don't have a home!

ADA. In any case, that's where, where, where – (*She keeps herself from saying: where your heart is.*) – where you were planning to go back to.

DANIEL. Yes, but I have no home there and nobody is waiting for me, whereas here I have a job to do.

ADA. Let me make one thing quite clear: I want to be alone.

DANIEL. I'm no psychologist, but it's as clear as day to me that a strong desire 'to be alone' usually means the opposite. There is no stronger cry for help than this very 'leave me alone'. But this plea is never understood, and that's the cause of all loneliness, all misery and isolation.

ADA. Then how can I make you understand that I really couldn't stand it?

DANIEL. I knew you would protest, I was prepared for that. But I am absolutely determined to carry out my plan, and I'll tell you where I get my enormous determination from, for once – I thought: if Ada were my own mother I would not leave her alone now.

*

DUIFJE *and* ALEXANDER.

ALEXANDER *is sketching* DUIFJE.

DUIFJE. Mind you don't take the bloom off the rose!

ALEXANDER. Just go on.

DUIFJE. Yes, what I wanted to say was, I always like it when the pattern of the tiles is repeated in the toilet paper. Don't you?

ALEXANDER. Yes.

DUIFJE. I always start itching on the bits that are being drawn.

You know what I don't understand?

ALEXANDER. No, what?

DUIFJE. Why choose me? There are far more beautiful people here.

ALEXANDER. Where?

DUIFJE. I used to draw as well. Rabbits. And dancers. Only in profile, the rabbits, I mean. Full face is very difficult with a rabbit, and from behind – well, who wants to see a rabbit from behind, but in profile it's very easy, with those ears, and those paws, lying down. (*Gesturing.*) I sometimes drew them on pieces of material as well and then embroidered them. Nico liked that when he was little, above his cot, but later he got so terribly critical I threw away all my drawing gear. Now he's become tolerant again, but what good is that, you could also call it indifferent. You're pretty aloof yourself. What is it you see in me?

ALEXANDER. Wait till it's finished.

DUIFJE. It'll never be anything special.

ALEXANDER. Why not?

DUIFJE. Because I'm so dead ordinary!

*

RIET *and* LEA.

RIET. Darling, I've had a wonderful time.

LEA. I'm so glad.

RIET. It was just as if I belonged this time.

LEA. But you do belong.

RIET. Do you think so?

LEA. Of course. Whenever there's something important –

RIET. Yes, whenever there's something important.

Silence.

RIET. Where is your father? I wanted to say goodbye to your father.

LEA. My father?

RIET. See you soon then. A promise is a promise.

LEA. Yes.

*

LEA *and* NICO.

LEA. Think how it will be when we come back and everything is different. My mother in a home, my father gone. Of course, he won't go and visit her there. Do you realise this may be the last time I'll be with my parents in this house? No, I can't go away with you, I can't leave now.

NICO. Do you realise what you're saying?

LEA. Do *you* realise what you're *doing*? Forcing me to go away when I want to stay here.

NICO. You won't be able to keep them together.

LEA. Who knows?

NICO. My God you can't even save your own marriage.

*

LEA*'s song.*

I know
It was far worse than I am able to imagine
But do you know
How far I go in my mind's eye
It doesn't stop at the facts
In my mind I see the bloodied axe
Make it stop! Make it stop!
The more I'm unable to imagine
The more I'm able to imagine
It doesn't stop! It doesn't stop!
It cuts, it bleeds, it putrifies
It never stops in my mind's eye
Until they're chopped up fine
The best, the softest, the most kind
I know it's only in my mind
Make it stop! Make it stop!
It never ever stops.

*

ZWART *and* NICO, *later* ADA.

ZWART. I was made a great proposition yesterday.

NICO. The only thing you need to get started is a little loan.

ZWART. How did you guess?

NICO. I'd love to help but –

ZWART. The fact that my son is a doctor is already a kind of guarantee –

NICO. Me, a doctor? Get away!

ZWART. It's a medical instruments company.

NICO. Don't know a thing about that.

ZWART. Come on, Nico, a reputable firm. Nico, stop being funny.

NICO. A reputable firm. That sounds suspect. Just leave me out of it.

ZWART. But your name was mentioned. They're checking you out.

NICO. But I'm not a doctor! I'm just going through the motions. My God, as if you didn't understand. You should be the first to understand!

ZWART. Nico, don't throw away those years I scrimped and saved for you!

NICO. Ha! And I studied just as hard as you scrimped and saved! Oh yes, I write out prescriptions, I do my rounds, and everyone falls for it. It's incredible! I hum my little songs, I make an impression. It's much easier playing at being a doctor than playing at being a businessman, it's true, that's why I'm respected and you're not.

ZWART. Nico, you're going too far!

NICO. I'm not going nearly far enough. Senior medical officer. I should give my certificate back. Humbly request to be released from responsibility, haven't cured a soul. And they can have my subscription to the concert hall while they're at it, because I've no ear for music either. Look at me. Can't you see I'm not a doctor! I'm nothing at all, and that's how it should be. But if I ask you to look at me you can't even do it. You squint a bit this way and that, to make it look convincing, but you don't dare really look, you've misbehaved too much and you're afraid it will show. You can't even look your own son in the eye to see if he's a doctor or not, or if he loves his wife or not, or if he's as big a phoney as you are.

ZWART. Someone's coming.

NICO. Lucky for you.

ADA. Nico, could you come, Simon doesn't feel well.

*

NICO *and* ADA.

NICO *is the perfect doctor once more.*

ADA. He's gone up to his room and locked the door. He doesn't answer when I knock. That's why I wanted to ask you to knock.

NICO. Does he do that often?

ADA. Never. Never at all. Yes, well, once, a long long time ago.

NICO. Marrying is exhausting.

ADA. Do you think that's what it is.

NICO. Let him rest a while, that's normal isn't it, just wanting to be alone.

ADA. But I immediately start to worry.

*

ALEXANDER *and* DUIFJE, DORY *joins them later.*

DORY (*a little more drunk*). Why am I so calm? Can you tell me why I'm so calm? I've been calm for years now, I can't seem to snap out of it. When I have to play, a terrible calm comes over me, even if it's important, like that solo last Wednesday for two thousand people, but today really beats everything! I've never been so calm in my whole life.

DUIFJE (*to* ALEXANDER). Turkey, now that's a nice destination.

*

HANS, NICO *and* LEA.

HANS. It still doesn't beat being engaged. I'd like to be engaged to life.

NICO. Nonsense. You've had too much to drink. You're much too serious for that. You're not at all the type for a fiancée. If you ever meet anyone who is good enough for you –

LEA. What do you mean?

NICO. Exactly what I say, that Hans hasn't found the right woman yet. That he doesn't experiment. That if she ever does appear, Hans will fall for her like a ton of bricks. Engagement my foot!

Marriage! Rubenesque arms and legs, in eiderdown forever.
Unity. Stability. Peace, quiet and safety. Capitulation.
Surrender. Totality, no more adventures, a home, a lamp . . .

LEA (*to* HANS) Do you know what he's on about?

HANS. I do know what he's on about, but I can't say it appeals to
me. I'd still prefer to remain single. Or engaged, from time to
time.

*

ZWART *and* JANNA.

ZWART. With my wife I could dance! I don't do that now, with
my step-wife, as I call her. I don't like this modern dancing
(*Imitates.*) It makes you feel so silly. We should have fucked
that one last time. She didn't want to. We knew she was going.
One last time, I said. But she didn't want to. Didn't want to
have one particular time to remember. Do you still remember
your last time with someone? I think one should. What else is
life about? She thought otherwise. She was a romantic. I was an
opportunist. I'm not an opportunist any more, or I wouldn't still
love her. If I were an opportunist, I'd – I'd – I'd –

But I'm still in love with her. Even though she's dead and
buried. Or not buried. There's no way of knowing. Now, Dory I
liked. I really liked Dory. She's like my wife. Nico finds it hard
to believe, but she is, she really is.

*

LEA *and* ADA.

LEA *has her coat on.*

ADA. What, are you cold too?

LEA. I'm going. But I just wanted to say goodbye. And good luck.
I hope you go through with it. And that it helps.

ADA. But I don't understand –

LEA. It's all too much for me.

ADA. Calm yourself, child, don't exaggerate. Come. (*Tries to get
LEA to take her coat off.*)

LEA. He's looking for something I haven't got to offer! Safety!
Security!

ADA. You just found that out today?

LEA. No, of course not. Don't be like that –

ADA. And why haven't you got that to offer? Safety, security?

LEA. Hark who's talking!!

ADA. I'm not mad!

LEA. You're mad enough if you start going on about safety and
security.

You know it's all nonsense, illusions, where do you get it from?
God, you must be mad, the whole world is busy planning the
third world war and you suddenly start going on about safety
and security.

ADA. No, you started.

LEA. So what?

ADA. If I'm not mistaken that's exactly what you were looking for
with him. And if we dare to be serious for two minutes –

LEA. Serious! That's the limit! I think you understand me and then
you start preaching!

ADA. On the contrary. You're the one who's preaching, with your
third world war, and your world problems. I'm down to earth,
I'm trying to tell you something very simple.

LEA. Which is?

ADA. Give it to him.

LEA. And you're going to the madhouse tomorrow.

ADA. Also something that needs courage.

LEA. Please forgive me. Oh darling please forgive me.

*

ALEXANDER *and* DUIFJE.

ALEXANDER. Living is what they used to do.

*

ZWART.

ZWART. Let's agree that from now on everybody stays with his or
her present partner.

*

DUIFJE.

DUIFJE. Hey, isn't that a willow warbler?

*

HANS and PIEN.

HANS (*locked in an embrace of mutual surrender with* PIEN).
Fantastic, fully automatic, with a lock on the lock, don't ask me
how. And if I forget to switch it off, a little bell goes
dingelingelingelingeling!

HANS *and* PIEN *act out great passion.*

DRUMMERS

by Arne Sierens

Translated by Nadine Malfait
with thanks to Paul Clark

Arne Sierens was born in 1959 in the Brugse Poort, a working-class neighbourhood to the west of Ghent city centre, where he also grew up. After secondary school, he studied stage directing in Brussels. He began his directing career working with the existing repertoire, classical and modern. Then he began writing and directing his own plays. In 1981 he set up his own company, 'Sluipende Armoede' (Sneeking Poverty), in Ghent, which provided the framework for the production of several of his plays: e.g. *De Soldaat-Facteur en Rachel* (*The Soldier-Postman and Rachel*).

From 1992 to 1994 he was the resident writer for one of the leading Flemish theatre groups, De Blauwe Maandag Compagnie (The Blue Monday Company), for whom he wrote *Boste* (which received the Drama Prize of the Flemish Community, 1994) and *Drummers*.

He now works freelance. His latest successes have been *Moeder en Kind* (*Mother and Child*) and *Bernadetje*, performance-based productions which he created together with the choreographer Alain Platel. The former production was chosen for the 1995 Theaterfestival in Amsterdam and was the Hans Snoeck Prize Winner. It toured in the Netherlands, France and Germany. *Bernadetje* too will be touring extensively.

Sierens' background is still very important in his work. This is the world of the little people, the downtrodden who nevertheless refuse to lie down and give in. 'To me, the Brugse Poort means the same as Rimini to Fellini or Little Italy to Scorsese: a place where the human condition is made visible. No gods live there, only poor souls; you don't see tragedies, only melodrama. That's why it's not fate that oppresses the characters in my plays, but fatality.'

He writes in a Flemish dialect of his own creation. Typical of his work is the simplicity and musicality of the language, the sparseness of the story, the minimal amount of action and a sensivity to the social problems in which his characters are enveloped. This austerity, paradoxically, provides directors and actors with enormous scope. His plays are also permeated by a wry and often bitter humour. They are not 'realistic' in a conventional sense, depending as most of them do on injections of music, dancing and other performance phenomena, but they are realistic in their faithful depiction of the raw energy and indomitable resourcefulness of those generally regarded as socially disadvantaged.

He is regarded as one of the leading Flemish playwrights.

Drummers is a two-hander with a much larger cast of unseen characters. Paola lives a rather sad life, arranging dried flowers to make a living for herself and her teenage son. Drummer Ray turns up at her house in answer to an advertisement for a drum teacher for Paola's son. It turns out he is the younger brother of Sean, who had been the great love of Paola's youth. During the subsequent drum lessons, heard off-stage, Paola is reminded of Sean, also a drummer. Gradually, in snatched conversations with Ray, their former lives are revealed, seen through a rosy glow of nostalgia for a freer, more carefree time. The dried flowers are a powerful metaphor.

As with all Sierens' work, the text is the framework on which the performance is hung, but much much more goes on in performance. 'Poetry of the commonplace, that is what Sierens creates', wrote one reviewer of the 1994 premiere in Flanders. 'It is precisely by omitting things that he creates a world that excites the imagination.'

PAOLA *is in her living room.*

The doorbell rings. She goes to the hallway.

PAOLA. Nick. You stay up there!

> *She opens the door.* RAY *is standing there with his nose in plaster.*

RAY. Mrs Tumble?

PAOLA. Do come in.

RAY. I'm a little early.

PAOLA. No problem. You find it all right?

RAY. Sort of.

> But I always allow myself plenty of time.

> *They go inside.*

PAOLA. My son will be down in a minute.

> Take a seat. Wait. Let me move those boxes for you.

> Please don't mind the house. It's such a mess.

> I've not had a moment to myself all week.

> My cleaning lady's ill.

> My son's upstairs studying.

> That was one of the conditions

> for letting him take drum lessons.

> That he should study more.

> Him and studying don't mix

> Sports? Forget it. Music!

> You should see his room. Posters all over the place.

> And now he's caught the marker bug.

> He's scribbling all over my walls.

> 'Are you going to redecorate the room?'

> I had all the upstairs rooms done last summer.

> Washable. Or so they said in the shop.

I've stopped looking.

(*Checks her watch.*) Another five minutes.

RAY (*laughs*). My nose.

It's a bit scary.

PAOLA. Did you walk into something?

RAY. No.

I had a crash last month.

Nothing spectacular. I wasn't even going fast.

Even so. No seatbelt.

PAOLA. I often forget to wear mine.

RAY. A split second.

Whammed into the steering wheel. Broken.

(*Pointing at the plaster.*) Two more weeks.

PAOLA. You really have to be careful these days.

Anyway.

You told me on the phone that you could make it

Thursdays and Saturdays. But Saturdays –

RAY. – were impossible.

PAOLA. So are Sundays.

They're with their father every weekend. My two sons.

Mondays and Tuesdays were out for you.

RAY. No. No Mondays.

PAOLA. No Tuesdays either.

RAY. My mother needs a driver then.

PAOLA. Wednesdays.

RAY. Are possible. At a push.

PAOLA. But that means changing your schedule.

RAY. I could. It's possible.

If it's really necessary. There's always a way.

If that's more convenient.

PAOLA. No no. Thursdays are OK.

RAY. Wednesdays are possible.

PAOLA. No no. Thursdays.

> As we arranged.

> If we go ahead with it.

> You both have to want it.

RAY. Of course.

PAOLA (*sighs*). I must sit down for a moment.

> I'm swamped with work at the moment.

> God knows how many orders I've got.

> Nothing for weeks and then everything at once.

> It's always the same.

> I'm in the flower business.

RAY. I see.

PAOLA. Dried flowers mainly.

> I make bunches. Ikebana and stuff.

> I do my own designs.

> Doesn't ring a bell does it ikebana?

RAY. I've heard of it.

PAOLA. It's going very well.

> Can't complain.

> You play in a band?

RAY. Not at the moment.

> I'm in the middle of negotiations.

> Yesterday. They phoned me again.

> Asked me to join. But I don't think I'll do it.

PAOLA. No.

RAY. They're so young.

> No. I've played with several bands.

PAOLA. Rock?

RAY. You name it. Reggae. Funk. Salsa. The lot.

PAOLA (*suddenly*). That drum kit!

> I want you to take a look.

> My son and I can't agree.

He says it's too small.

We went and got it last week.

He says there's a lot missing.

There should be woodblocks. He says.

A cowbell. More cymbals.

And those hanging tubes.

RAY. Angel dust.

PAOLA. 'Later' I said.

If you really need more things,

you can always get them later.

Start with the basics.

Learn to hold the sticks.

Now he's got a bass drum. A snare.

Two tom-toms. And two cymbals.

To start with. That must be enough. Surely.

RAY. Of course.

PAOLA. Those displays in the shops.

You know. Big enough to fill half a stage.

Talk about whetting a man's appetite.

'Start with playing tight' I said.

'Start with the basics.

Make sure you can keep the beat.'

(*Checks her watch.*) Time to go.

I'm warning you. He's got a mind of his own. My boy.

You'll have to keep him in check.

He's stubborn. My son.

He thinks he's got everything sussed.

Oh. He is so pleased with himself. That boy.

They move to the back.

PAOLA. Nick! We're going out the back!

Sound of bootsteps on the stairs.

PAOLA. It's right out the back.

We've got this shed in the garden.

I tried to insulate it with egg boxes.

To muffle the noise.

The neighbours.

RAY. You're telling me.

They leave. Drumming. When the drumming stops, we hear a telephone ringing.

PAOLA (*enters and anwers it*). Hello? Tumble's.

. . . Ah, Vivienne . . . Yes . . . Eight? . . . Yes. No problem

. . . By Monday. OK . . . Green and blue . . . Makes no difference.

. . . OK. No problem. Eight by Monday . . . Bye Vivienne.

Hard pounding on the bass drum. She stands stock still. When the drumming stops she goes to the back.

Later.

RAY *and* PAOLA *enter.*

PAOLA. I get the idea he's interested.

So if it's OK with you.

RAY. Then it's a deal.

PAOLA. Perfect.

You reckon the drums will do? It's enough?

RAY. Sure.

They're a bit new of course.

They have to be played in.

Need adjusting.

But it'll certainly do.

PAOLA. It cost me an arm and a leg.

Well, it's Christmas. Birthday and Christmas all in one.

RAY *looks steadily at her.*

PAOLA. . . .

RAY. You don't remember me. Do you?

PAOLA. Thingie. Isn't it?

RAY. Raymond.

PAOLA. Raymond. The brother –

RAY. Half brother.

PAOLA. Of –

RAY. Sean. That's right.

PAOLA. When you walked in.

I knew it. I had this feeling.

'I know this guy,' I thought.

RAY. The nose can't have been much help either.

PAOLA. No.

And you had the light behind you.

Well. Raymond.

RAY. It's been a while.

PAOLA. Ages.

How's life then?

RAY. Good.

Apart from . . . (*Points at his nose.*)

Fine. How about you?

PAOLA. I'm fine too. As you can see.

RAY. So you've got kids then?

PAOLA. Yes. Two.

One is thirteen. Nick. Short for Nicholas.

And the other's eleven. Peter.

RAY. I can hardly believe this.

Must be donkey's years.

When did we last see each other?

You were still with him then.

So you're teaching your son to play the drums?

PAOLA. Yes.

RAY. No stopping him.

But you said: 'If you want to play drums. OK.

But you're going to take lessons.'

PAOLA. Yes.

RAY. Hence your ad in the paper.

PAOLA. 'DRUM TEACHER WANTED.' Yes.

　　To be absolutely honest

　　I can't be sure that it's going to go through.

　　That you'll be the one.

　　There's this other candidate you see.

RAY. Right then.

PAOLA. A young chap.

　　From the music academy.

　　He's very eager and I more or less said yes.

　　He said he'd ring me sometime this week.

　　There was a slight chance you see

　　that he might not be able to do it after all.

　　He's got exams. Which is why I let you come.

　　In case he cancels. So I won't be left stranded.

　　I hope you don't mind.

　　You must understand, he said he'd do it.

　　He gets number one priority.

RAY. Of course.

PAOLA. He could only make Tuesdays.

　　(*Suddenly.*) Tuesdays?!

　　What was it we agreed on just now?

　　Tuesdays or Thursdays?

RAY. Thursdays.

PAOLA. Oh dear! I clean forgot.

　　He's got computer on Thursdays!

　　With that new school it got moved.

　　It's my fault. I got muddled up.

　　I'm sorry. It's been changed.

　　We're talking about Tuesdays. Not Thursdays!

RAY. Tuesdays.

PAOLA. That's right!

Tuesdays were out for you!

It'll have to be Wednesdays.

RAY. Wednesdays.

I could always move a few things about.

PAOLA. But you'd rather not.

So you can't do it.

Oh dear. So I've brought you here for nothing.

RAY. It doesn't matter.

PAOLA. You don't mind too much?

RAY. No. It was a pleasure to see you again.

PAOLA. I'm sorry.

I'm so absent-minded sometimes.

RAY. Can't be helped.

OK. I'll be off then.

Well. I guess I'll be seeing you.

PAOLA. Wait. I'll see you to the door.

It's a stubborn lock.

Exit to hall.

Wednesday afternoon.

RAY *is standing with a glass of water in his hand.*

We hear drumming in the distance.

PAOLA *comes in wearing her coat.*

PAOLA. I couldn't make it home on time.

Someone was telling me his life-story.

My car wouldn't start.

My son let you in?

RAY. Yes.

We've just finished.

PAOLA. I'm so sorry to have missed it.

So you actually started?

RAY. Yes.

The first lesson that is. Posture.

Learning to hold the sticks. Tightening the skins.

From scratch. The start.

PAOLA. And?

RAY. He's doing OK.

PAOLA. I take it he does listen to you?

He's got to listen. He can be so hard-headed our Nick.

RAY. We're doing fine together.

PAOLA. You mustn't be afraid to have a go at him.

Tell him the minute he does something wrong.

Can I get you anything to drink?

RAY. I helped myself to a glass of water.

PAOLA. Care for anything else? A beer?

RAY. No thanks. Doctor's orders.

PAOLA. Take a seat.

They sit down.

PAOLA. So it worked out after all.

RAY. Yes.

You're lucky about those Wednesdays.

The other one couldn't make it?

PAOLA. No.

RAY. All those Wednesdays that happened to come free so that I could do it.

PAOLA. I'm glad.

Lessons are important.

At first he was against it.

'No lessons Mum.'

But I told him: 'Listen here. No failure.

If you want to play drums. You're going to take lessons.

No failure. I've seen enough failures in my life.

No son of mine will turn into one.'

At first they told me to send him to the music academy.

Percussion. But well. That's four years.

And they have to sight-read.

He didn't like the idea.

He did solfeggio. And two years of piano on top. But no.

'Sight-reading?! Mum, please!' No.

RAY. I take it you no longer see Sean?

PAOLA. No.

I ran into him a couple of years ago.

On the street somewhere.

RAY. He rang me last week actually.

He's in Dakar.

PAOLA. Really.

RAY. A year already.

(– Don't talk about it. Please. –)

PAOLA. Do you teach a lot?

RAY. I've got my own studio at home.

Sixteen track.

The teaching is just a sideline. I enjoy it.

With the kids and everything.

It's enough for me if I can manage to get it

into their little heads that drumming is more

than just banging away in four-four

I do a lot of session work.

PAOLA. Do you?

RAY. I've made records.

PAOLA. Really?

You should bring them along.

RAY. I will.

I'll have to check my archives.

Records. Yes.

There wasn't much session work for a while.

With those drum machines.

But that's over. Thank God.

Those machines have had their day.

No soul. Too cold.

Crying out for real drummers again!

. . . We were talking about you yesterday. Mum and me.

My mum. She saw your mum. She said. Last month in the street.

She says she still looks great your mum.

Poor soul. She always was poorly.

Is she still around with that kidney of hers?

Your mum. She only had one kidney. Right?

PAOLA. Yes.

RAY. I still remember. In her shop.

She was always going on about it.

That kidney of hers.

MRS LOLLIPOP. And –

PAOLA. I was LITTLE LOLLIPOP. I know.

RAY. Yes.

How long were you together, you and my brother?

PAOLA. About two years. Isn't it?

RAY. That long?

PAOLA. Yeah. Sure. I don't remember exactly.

It's been such a long time ago.

RAY. Ages.

How old was I then? Fourteen.

How odd. One year older than your son now.

He was twenty-one. And you –

PAOLA. Nineteen. Going on twenty. I guess.

Yes.

RAY. Just now. In there with your son.

I said to myself: 'If he were to walk in

and see me sitting with Paola's son.

He wouldn't believe his eyes. My brother.'

PAOLA. Yes.

Pause.

RAY. You're divorced aren't you?

PAOLA. Yes.

RAY. Long?

PAOLA. Almost eight years. Must be.

RAY. It wasn't working?

PAOLA. We'd reached a point when we said 'Stop'. Got into a rut. I guess.

He was a workaholic.

Sixteen hours a day. Seven days a week.

He was in vases and antiques.

Buying and selling things.

Imports from Taiwan.

RAY. I'm still living at home.

With my mother.

PAOLA. Really?

RAY. It's convenient.

PAOLA. Any plans?

RAY. None. I'm too busy drumming.

I became a drummer too.

PAOLA. Like your brother.

RAY. Yes.

PAOLA. I never knew you drummed.

RAY. No.

My parents said I had to finish school first.

I started drumming later.

. . . You really had no idea it was me

when I rang you about the ad?

PAOLA. No.

RAY. I didn't know it was you either.

'Mrs Tumble.'

I remember you as Paola.

CRAZY PAOLA.

. . . 'Ray Fields' It didn't ring a bell with you?

PAOLA. No

RAY. Of course. Sean had his dad's surname.

PAOLA. It took me months to find out his first name.

RAY. Sean's?

PAOLA. He didn't want a name.

RAY. So how did you refer to him?

PAOLA. I didn't.

HE.

HIM.

RAY. He was in the Congo for a while.

PAOLA. The Congo?

RAY. Yes. He spent two years there.

In the interior. In the jungle.

Recording groups. For a record company in Paris.

He was in Morocco too. For quite some time.

PAOLA. In the mountains.

RAY. So you knew?

PAOLA. I remember once. It was all set up.

We were going to go to Morocco. For a year.

To go and see those drummers in the mountains.

The mountain drummers.

RAY. Nothing came of it then.

PAOLA. Everything was ready.

I wanted to go. I'd even dropped out of school.

But then all of a sudden he couldn't any more.

RAY. He claimed you didn't want to.

(– What? –)

PAOLA. He was the one who didn't want to.

Said he couldn't drop the group just like that.

RAY. You couldn't take the sun.

It would have been too much.

That was the reason all of a sudden.

The climate would bother you.

PAOLA. No way.

RAY. That's what I remember at least.

PAOLA. Crap.

RAY. I'll check with my mum.

She may remember.

. . . Was it long before the bust?

PAOLA. I forgot.

RAY. If you two had left.

They wouldn't have got him?

PAOLA. No.

RAY. Two years in gaol.

A real bitch.

Always extreme.

Never anything in between.

Good luck.

That record contract.

The French tour.

And bad luck.

Really bad.

. . . That bust.

That really finished him off.

Don't you reckon?

My mum had a hard time dealing with it at the time.

Her eldest son in gaol. Plus all those debts.

. . . All those opportunities.

My brother the opportunities he had!

And missed!

(– Enough. –)

PAOLA. Look. If you don't mind

I should be getting dinner.

Do you mind letting yourself out?

See you next week.

Blackout.

Next session.

PAOLA. One of the first evenings.

There was this heatwave.

We'd just left this party.

First ID Check.

RAY (*interjects*). 'Where are you off to then?'

'Haven't decided yet. Sir.'

'That's no answer. Shithead.'

It happened to me once.

PAOLA. I was shaking like a leaf.

It was all new to me. I didn't know a thing.

I'd been to a Catholic school. You see.

Like in his room. The first time.

RAY. Yes.

PAOLA. 'Just hang your jacket in the cupboard.'

RAY. Yes.

PAOLA. I opened the door.

RAY. Bertha.

PAOLA. Bertha.

RAY. His snake.

POALA. Yes.

RAY. He's had that a long time.

PAOLA. Always that sort of thing.

Anyway. They let us go.

The heat hit us.

He took off his shirt and trousers.

In his Y-fonts.

You know. By the big graveyard.

They've got this wall with sloping stones.

He climbs up and starts to walk along the top.

It's really high. I'm scared of course.

'Watch out! You're going to fall!'

Him: 'No. I won't'

Against the sky. A tight-ropewalker on a wire.

Suddenly I saw he was losing his balance.

He fell off. On the graveyard side.

Me: 'Hey. Did you hurt yourself?'

No reply. Me again:

'Hey man. Say something. Please.'

Nothing.

Panic.

He must have hit his head on a gravestone.

I dash for the fence. It was locked.

Stood on a dustbin. Tried to climb over.

No luck.

And then I heard banging on the other side.

I said: 'Hey. Is that you?'

Nothing.

'Hey. Say something'

Then suddenly: 'Hang on. One second'

One second. It was five minutes.

And then he jumped over the wall

He'd just written a new song!

That banging was him trying out the rhythm.

RAY. At times he really did have a screw loose.

No stopping him.

PAOLA. You're telling me.

That drumming. He was obsessed with it.

RAY. It's in our blood. Drumming.

PAOLA. His blood.

RAY. Ours.

His and mine.

'MUSIC IS NOT SOMETHING YOU CHOOSE.

IT CHOOSES YOU.'

My dad. His stepfather.

Music. Always been against it.

'NOT IN MY HOUSE.'

Sean always used to tell him:

'MY FATHER WOULD HAVE SAID YES.'

Sean's dad I mean.

Sean's dad –

PAOLA. He used to play in the orchestras.

RAY. You knew?

Yes. The trumpet.

PAOLA. Cornet.

RAY. Was it?

PAOLA. I'm sure it was the cornet.

RAY. My dad was going to put him in a reform school.

The fuss he kicked up when he got his first drums.

My dad broke the sticks in two.

Stuck a knife in the skins.

Dumped the drums in the garage.

With a whacking great lock on it.

Sean didn't let him get away with it.

Went at it with this crowbar until the lock broke!

A real madman. When he got started.

So he went and practised in the basement of the paintworks.

In winter. Froze his butt off.

He was playing with six bands at one stage.

He could play with everyone.

None of these bands were any good.

Most of those guys had held a guitar maybe twice in their lives.

Six bands.

He was constantly lugging those drums around.

He didn't have a car at the time.

On his pushcart. On the train.

Mind you. I used to carry mine on my bike.

Can you imagine?

I remember one night it froze over.

Jesus Christ. The things you do.

I couldn't now. Not any more.

Back then you did.

Why? You're asking me.

He was hell-bent.

Once he nearly drowned.

Because of his drums.

They were coming back from this gig in Scotland.

In two cars. One car and a van.

That van. The musicians were behind.

It suddenly started veering across the road.

Into a canal!

I don't know if it's true.

That's what I heard.

That van. All the gear was inside. It was sinking.

Sean dived into the water. After his drumkit.

He'd had one stolen the month before.

He was determined to save those drums.

In the end they had to dive in to get him out.

Apparently.

Could be.

PAOLA. He told me exactly the same story.

He nearly drowned.

RAY. It may only have been a ditch.

Over the years it became a canal.

Pause.

PAOLA. Music.

RAY. 'MUSIC.

ONCE YOU'VE CAUGHT THE BUG.

THERE'S NO WAY OUT.

EVEN IF IT MEANS THE END OF YOU.'

PAOLA. He went too far sometimes.

RAY. Sean was a nutcase.

You too for that matter.

A raving nutcase.

PAOLA. Me?

RAY. In those days?

You certainly were.

'THE MADWOMAN.' My mother still says.

'THE NUTCASE.'

'THE COW.'

'THE BEANPOLE.'

Your name was mud with my mother.

'BAG OF BONES.' The children on the street called you.

PAOLA. Skinny? Me?

RAY. Fat wasn't really the word for you either.

'A STICK WITH TWO FLEABITES.

THROW A SPUD AGAINST IT AND YOU GET CHIPS.'

About you.

You were quite a success on our street.

With those short skirts of yours. And those boots.

PAOLA. They were the in-thing.

RAY. You caught the eye.

You with your wig and Sean with his black leggings.

The way the two of you were sometimes decked out.

Hats. Scarves.

PAOLA. Those were the days.

RAY. He collected crazy dames my brother.

PAOLA. You were impossible sometimes.

You'd come to our place and insist on leaving straight away.

Nothing was ever any good. Nothing.

Always complaining. And then you'd run off.

With him following you.

Sean could be very gloomy at times.

My mum: 'YOU'D THINK YOU ENJOY BEING
UNHAPPY.'

You certainly weren't easy.

PAOLA. He wasn't exactly easy either.

That period. We were living together.

In that little house on Sugar Street.

RAY. THE CAVE.

Jesus. What a dump.

PAOLA. He needed the workshop for his drumkit.

We should never have gone there.

'FORGET THE GUY.' My sister.

'DROP HIM. HE'LL MAKE YOUR LIFE A MISERY.'

We were stuck.

Stuck to each other like glue.

We were hooked.

RAY. On the needle.

PAOLA. On each other.

RAY. On the needle too.

PAOLA. Not me. I wasn't.

RAY. Sean was. Everyone in the band.

They were all tripping. Any old thing.

The way they went on about it.

You'd swear they were a bunch of doctors and chemists.

Sniffing and blowing.

The things they shoved up their noses.

A Harley Davidson. They snorted and smoked a small fortune.

PAOLA. Sean didn't smoke.

RAY. No. Not Sean. But Francis and Patrick.

And not just a little. Mega-joints.

Always before gigs. Blowing their minds.

Snorting. Smoking. You name it.

PAOLA. And Francis the needle.

RAY. No.

PAOLA. He was mainlining. I tell you.

RAY. Because he was diabetic.

PAOLA. He told you that too?

Mainlining he was.

RAY. No he wasn't!

PAOLA. You should have been there when he was desperate.

He would have stuck a knitting needle in his arm.

RAY. No way! I would have known.

PAOLA. His arms were blue.

Red. Purple.

His arms were already covered in those horrible tattoos.

Daggers with blood. Snakes. LOVE. HATE.

Francis. He just loved needles.

RAY. He wasn't a junkie.

PAOLA. Junkies always deny they're hooked.

A lot of groups broke up that way.

RAY. Chicks are worse!

The minute they get themselves a girlfriend you can forget it.

Needs to have her say about everything.

That's when the nagging and misery start.

And once they get married that's it.

PAOLA. I never stopped him playing music.

RAY. That's not what I said.

I'm talking about other groups.

Girlfriend. The joker in the pack.

Impossible to combine.

Like doing gigs and working.

Plus trying to do some decent rehearsing to boot.

Only a few strike the right balance.

Sean didn't manage either.

It's harder for a drummer for a start.

Drumming is more physical than playing the guitar.

I lose up to two kilos a gig.

But it's more than just doing a gig.

It's the whole caboodle.

Setting things up and taking them down.

And you have to do it on your own.

Let anyone help you and you lose stuff.

PAOLA. Plus they can't go straight to bed afterwards.

RAY. 'AFTER A GIG. YOU HAVE TO WIND DOWN.'

PAOLA. And the hanging around.

RAY. It's not just the hanging around.

PAOLA. It's the booze.

RAY. It's not the booze.

PAOLA. It's wanting to drive afterwards.

RAY. You bet. You've been there.

It's not the driving either. It's being stopped.

A drummer without a driving licence. Disaster.

PAOLA. Once you start you know how it'll end . . .

The way things fuck up! . . .

We loved each other to death.

RAY. You were always fighting!

PAOLA. No.

RAY. You had an affair with fat Patrick too didn't you?

PAOLA. No.

RAY. No affair. But you did sleep with him all right.

PAOLA. I don't know. Maybe.

RAY. I do. You'd broken up with Sean.

Or he'd dumped you.

PAOLA. We were forever dumping each other.

Pause.

RAY. I remember spying on you.

You and Sean. Did you know that?

Once you came to our place. Mum was out.

You were lying on his bed.

I could see you from the attic.

Only your legs.

You didn't know?

PAOLA. 'THE SPROG'S SPYING ON US.' I told him.

'THE SNOTNOSE.' Who sat wailing in the attic when his mother wouldn't buy him flares!

RAY. . . . You're not exactly a raving beauty.

PAOLA. I'll have to throw you out I'm afraid.

RAY. Yes. It's getting late.

Those boots.

I still can remember them.

I used to love them.

Blackout.

PAOLA*'s living room.*

PAOLA. Do you remember?

Sugar street. The woman who got killed?

RAY. Vaguely.

PAOLA. We'd been living there a month.

She lived next door with her husband.

I saw her in the newsagents with her four-year-old daughter.

Only the day before.

They'd been telling us they never fought.

She'd been seen in a pub in the afternoon.

She drank. But nobody'd ever seen her drunk or anything.

It was a Sunday.

Sean was in the workshop drumming.

I was there too. Reading.

It happened around eight in the evening.

The woman stuck a breadknife in her husband's arm.

He went and got his gun and shot her.

When they heard the shot everyone came out on the street.

They tried to break down the door.

He fired another two shots.

Sean was keeping this strict rhythm.

Those shots must have coincided with his beats.

We didn't hear a thing.

Only when we heard the ambulance siren.

Then we went out and they told us.

What had happened next door.

'Why do you think they did it?'

RAY. Did what?

PAOLA. Sean refused to talk about it.

He didn't want me to even think about it.

'Don't think about it. It's no good.'

It's hard

not to think about it.

He could drum it out of his system.

Pause.

PAOLA. So he's getting there is he?

RAY. He'll learn in no time.

He's dead keen. That's obvious.

He bangs away much too hard of course.

Youthful energy. They're all the same.

I've given him a few triplets to do.

What he needs is practice. Every day.

Pause.

RAY. Sean's group.

I've still got recordings of some of their gigs.

When you listen to them now –

PAOLA. – They were good.

RAY. Not that good.

PAOLA. What do you mean not that good?

Come on.

RAY. Musically.

PAOLA. They were out of this world.

RAY. Patrick was lousy on bass!

Had no idea how to keep the beat. On those tapes.

PAOLA. Patrick sure.

RAY. Sean too.

In some places he's really just banging away.

PAOLA. Musically I wouldn't know about that.

RAY. Forever missing the first beat.

Out of rhythm. Playing sloppy.

Useless songs too. Just listen to them. Useless!

Especially –

PAOLA. – Francis's.

RAY. No. Those were all right.

I mean the ones they used to write together.

Those half-baked attempts. Those experiments.

PAOLA. Underground.

RAY. BULLSHIT. That's what I call it.

Listening to those tapes. I keep thinking:

'What on earth were they doing?'

PAOLA. Derby for example never really got going.

No atmosphere. That was a lousy gig.

But Nottingham.

The gig in Birmingham.

The one in Manchester.

In Leeds.

Edinburgh. Glasgow.

That entire period before –

Before –

RAY. The period before France.

PAOLA. – Was great.

So full of energy.

Sparks flying off the stage.

You didn't see them all did you?

RAY. No.

PAOLA. The public went beserk.

Not just one time. Every time.

RAY. I'm sorry but those recordings.

All I hear are guys playing offbeat.

That they managed to get themselves a record deal.

And a tour to boot. That's beyond me.

I really don't get it.

PAOLA. Because –

They were completely original.

RAY. Original?

PAOLA. Bass. Sax. Drums.

Nobody was doing that.

RAY. Loads of them were.

PAOLA. Later on yes. But not at the time.

RAY. In America.

PAOLA. No.

RAY. I can name the bands if you like. Dozens of them.

PAOLA. Not even in America.

> Not in Ireland. Not in Germany. Nowhere.

RAY. All I can tell you is what I think.

> When I listen to those tapes I just don't get it.
>
> The success.

PAOLA. They worked bloody hard to get it.

RAY. Those guys?

PAOLA. They rehearsed all the time.

RAY. Rehearsed? Bullshit around you mean!

> Francis could never get them all together.

PAOLA. Sean rehearsed a lot.

RAY. Practising on his own. Ego-tripping!

> Rehearsing that's practising to play together.
>
> You hear it the minute you put those tapes on.
>
> That band never rehearses!
>
> Anyway. As if you'd know.
>
> You weren't even allowed inside their den.
>
> That was no-go territory.

PAOLA. Because I didn't want to disturb them.

RAY. No. Because Francis wouldn't let you.

> You couldn't keep your hands off Sean.

PAOLA. No. Because the man was jealous.

> Sean was his. All Sean had to do was look at me and Sir got on his high horse.
>
> I don't have anything against queers –

RAY. Francis wasn't queer.

PAOLA. Oh no?

> He used to fondle Sean while I was standing next to him!
>
> Not that I cared. I knew he didn't pose a real threat.
>
> But that eternal hatred.

RAY. Francis was a transvestite. Not queer!

PAOLA. He should have thrown Francis out at the beginning.

RAY. Without Francis Sean was nothing!

PAOLA. Without Sean Francis was nothing!

RAY. You're no musician.

You have to have played in a band to know.

PAOLA. They were always fighting.

RAY. They were. But they made it up.

PAOLA. Towards the end they threatened to split every day.

RAY. If they were any good it's because Francis was good.

PAOLA. Provided he didn't fall off the stage.

RAY. And Sean didn't tumble over his drums.

PAOLA. Just the once.

RAY. Three times.

Pause.

PAOLA. After the gigs.

When everyone had been dropped off

and the van had been taken back.

Those were wonderful moments.

Going for a fry-up at Martha's.

He only had two hours before he went to work.

Then we'd stroll through town. Along the new canal.

In summer it would already be light.

In the docks. By the warehouses.

Him on a crate as if behind his drums.

Me on him.

Slowly.

Superb.

Surrounded by yellow-and-green BP oil drums.

On that crate. The first time.

Tense.

Taut.

Doing nothing. Giving nothing.

'How long have we been at it?'

'Did anyone else keep going so long?'

His hand on my buttocks.

'Those drums. On the Antilles they used to emboss them and play music on them.'

Even then. Drumming.

I was lucky. In that respect.

He was good at sex.

RAY. Any chance your son could be his?!

PAOLA. No.

RAY. I wouldn't be surprised.

Couples who don't get on any more.

They have a kid to make up.

(*Laughs.*) In which case I'd be an uncle now.

Pause.

I asked my mum.

You did have an affair with fat Patrick she says.

PAOLA. No.

RAY. She claims that Sean suffered terribly when he found out. He even followed you once.

That's how he found out that you were two-timing.

She claims.

PAOLA. That was something else. That was nothing.

When you're young you do silly things.

You 'd do anything to hang on to each other.

Anything.

RAY. Like going to bed with another guy?

PAOLA. Yes.

What do you know about that anyway?

You have to have had a relationship to know what it is . . .

You know what my sister used to call me at that time?

THE CORPSE.

Pause.

RAY. Remember that tour through France?

It never happened!

Toulon. Bordeaux. Paris. Cancelled.

Remember the hassle about that article in MUSIC MAKER?

That said they were so fantastic?

No one has ever seen it!

The band that was going to conquer Europe.

Off the boat. Road to Paris.

Not used to driving that van.

On another planet themselves.

Stoned out of their minds.

Got lost. Left the road. Into a transformer. BANG.

Amplifiers not tied down of course.

Everything thrown to the front.

Sean dislocated two vertebrae.

Patrick's guitar in pieces.

Francis missing one tooth.

They meant to call a breakdown van but they couldn't.

Singing in French. Yes.

But speaking it? Oh no!

And bragging to everyone that they played in France.

To my mum.

PAOLA. Your mum.

She never went to see Sean not once

when he was in hospital with his back.

RAY. She didn't want to! Because of you!

Pause.

PAOLA. Yesterday. You know what my son said?

That he was a better drummer than you are!

RAY. They think they know everything. These kids.

Drumming's more than hitting a dustbin with a crowbar!

Blackout.

RAYMOND's *studio.*

RAY *is sitting behind his drums. Immobile.*

The bell rings. He gets up and opens the door.

PAOLA. Ah.

I've come to tell you there's no need to come tomorrow.

My son. He's been punished.

He came home with a terrible report last week.

So no drum lesson.

RAY. I was about to ring you myself.

Tomorrow would have been impossible for me anyway.

This band have asked me. I want to go and check them out.

I know their bass player.

I think I might do it this time.

Yes. These next few weeks . . .

They've got a gig next month already.

I'll have to learn all the numbers.

I'll have to see if I can still combine it.

Rehearsing and teaching.

Blackout.

Another day.

RAYMOND's *studio.* RAY *is standing at the back.*

PAOLA (*standing by the door*). I don't know what to do.

My son didn't come home last night.

Who else can I ask?

I know he spends a lot of time in those discos by the station.

Would you mind checking whether he's there? Would you?

Blackout.

PAOLA's *living room.*

RAY *and* PAOLA *are sitting at the table.*

We can hear drums.

PAOLA. I'm not quite sure.

   But I may have reported him to the police.

RAY. Reported him?

PAOLA. I don't think I did.

   But I may have done it.

RAY. Have you gone out of your mind?

PAOLA. If two dogs are locked together.

   They get a bucket of water thrown over them.

   Someone had to separate us.

   We were killing each other.

   We were dead.

   'THE CORPSE.'

   That's what my sister used to call me.

RAY. Report him.

PAOLA. To save us.

   His life and my life.

   'THE CORPSE.'

   I was transparent.

   I was so thin-skinned.

   I was a bundle of nerves.

   Look anyone in the eye and I'd start to cry.

   One evening I started this letter.

   I wrote his name with letters cut out of the newspaper and an arrow. DRUGS.

   They're going to force us apart.

   We were addicted.

   Cold Turkey.

   That's the only solution.

RAY. Did you send it to the police that letter?

PAOLA. I put it in an envelope.

I went outside. I was going to post it.

I lost it on the way.

RAY. Are you sure?

PAOLA. I lost it.

RAY. Nice story.

It makes sense. Musicians and stupid women.

What on earth gave you that idea?

PAOLA. I don't think I did though.

Report him. I don't think so.

The bust was months later.

RAY. Nice ending. Well done.

Like a Johnny Cash song. Country and Western.

THE BALLAD OF SEAN AND CRAZY PAOLA.

He goes away.

(*Comes back.*) I've been thinking.

That son of yours – It really isn't his fault is it.

I'll come after all.

PAOLA. You mustn't come any more.

RAY. I want to.

PAOLA. If you're doing it for Nick.

I'd rather you didn't. He claims you can't keep your paws off him.

RAY. He'll say anything that comes into his head.

By the way. About reporting him.

There was never any need to report him!

They'd been onto him for ages.

He'd done four months probation.

Mind you. He never got picked for the stuff

but for those stolen radios!

There was no need to report him.

He took care of that himself!

PAOLA. Out.

RAY. I'm out.

Pause.

PAOLA. When I was pregnant and he started kicking.

It would wake me up at night.

I'd drum on my belly with my fingers.

Sometimes I dreamt he was his.

There was a beat to those kicks.

Finding a rhythm in everything.

Putting a rhythm into everything too.

We were always doing it.

Along the new canal out for a stroll.

When he was little. Nick.

I'd walk around with him in his pushchair.

He used to love it. Going for walks every day.

Two to three hours. All over town.

When he started walking.

It got on my husband's nerves.

The walking.

The stopping.

Falling.

Staggering to his feet.

Walking on.

Stopping.

Walking.

Falling.

'EVERYTHING HAS A RHYTHM AND A BEAT.'

End.

BURYING THE DOG

by Karst Woudstra

translated by Della Couling

Karst Woudstra was born in Leiden in 1947. After wide-ranging studies – comparative literature, Italian, Russian and Scandinavian languages – he gravitated to the theatre. (He had written a lot of plays and novels as a teenager, so in a sense this marked a return.)

Since the end of the 1970s Woudstra has been very active in the theatre world as dramaturg, director and author. He has worked not only in the Netherlands, with some of the top companies, but also in Flanders and Sweden.

During the 1980s he became the leading director of the Dutch theatre company Het Publiekstheater in Amsterdam, and is today considered one of the Netherlands' leading playwrights. His work has been translated into German, French and Spanish. Woudstra also translates from several European languages and is an authority on the works of Henrik Ibsen, August Strindberg and Lars Norén.

In Woudstra's work the characters are frequently marked by the past, a consciously repressed past that eventually surfaces and causes disruption and – ultimately – liberation. His work is also shot through with a black humour.

In *Burying the Dog*, premiered in The Hague in 1989 by Het Nationale Toneel, we find again a metaphor for past and present Dutch concerns. The air is heavy with unfinished business: the tortured relationship between the two brothers, Peter and Bart, and between them and their parents, whom they perceive in widely different ways. Peter's relationship with his girlfriend, Muriel, full of fears and unfulfilled expectations, is also echoed, in a very different idiom, by Bart's barren relationship with his wife.

In one hilarious night, the various tensions between the characters pass breaking point, and the resultant disasters, symbolised by the dog, who had started the evening by following Bart and is then run over and killed (and is the unwitting instrument to bring the two brothers together after a long absence), are finally resolved by a symbolic burying of the dog, a deeply cathartic act for all three characters.

'In well-written dialogue the language flows like water', wrote *Vrij Nederland*. 'The words . . . do their real work under the surface. The actual past, what really happened, is taboo, and Karst Woudstra has used that taboo in his play. Here the unprocessed, hidden past lies like a sinister threat behind the words of the characters who carry on a flowing dialogue in ordinary contemporary language – words which, even in the presence of the tragic, never lose their light tone and comic aspect.' 'Again and again,' wrote the daily *Trouw*, 'Woudstra dismantles the realistic value of the situation by means of a bizarre symbolism, whose comic effect must both reinforce the trio's tragedy and at the same time serve to unmask it.'

Cast

PETER

BART, *his elder brother*

MURIEL, *a friend of Peter*

Peter's half-converted apartment on the Herengracht in Amsterdam. On the left, doors to the bedroom and bathroom, on the right a door to the stairway and lift. Upstage right an open kitchen. The conversion of the apartment is not yet complete and the partly visible wall of the kitchen section consists of a row of porcelain urinals.

PETER (*in the kitchen, invisible to the audience, with the telephone on his knees in front of the cooker*). Yes, yes, now it's rising, but very slowly, very slowly.

(MURIEL'S VOICE. That's how it should be.)

That slow?

(MURIEL. You're sure the oven's not set too high?)

No, just like you said. I wrote it all down very carefully.

(MURIEL. What colour is it now?)

Pale. Really pale. But it's gradually getting a bit darker. Very very little.

(MURIEL. And nothing is running over the edge of the tray?)

No, nothing, yes, maybe just the odd drop.

(MURIEL. That doesn't matter.)

How much longer?

(MURIEL. Just be patient.)

The bell rings, the intercom, beside the door.

That's the doorbell.

(MURIEL. You can't leave it now.)

But the doorbell's ringing. I'll have to go and see who it is. Just stay there, don't hang up, I'll be right back.

PETER *comes out of the kitchen with the telephone, lays it down with the receiver next to it on the sofa. The doorbell rings again. Urgently.*

OK, OK, I'm coming. (*Picks up the intercom receiver.*) Who is it?

(BART. It's me, Bart.)

Bart, Bart, Jesus, you, Bart? What on earth are you doing in Amsterdam?

(BART. I'll explain right away.)

You've come at a bad time. I'm sorry. I didn't know you were coming. Someone's just coming for a meal. And right now I've got a soufflé in the oven. A work of art in white chocolate. Can you hang on a minute? (*Goes back to the telephone.*) It's my brother, Bart.

(MURIEL. I didn't know you had a brother.)

Yes, I do. One. Haven't seen him for years. Since my father's funeral. I can't imagine why he's suddenly turned up out of the blue.

(MURIEL. Then ask him.)

I have. He said he'd explain right away.

(MURIEL. Is he coming up now?)

No, I didn't open the door for him. He's still standing in the hall downstairs, I suppose. I said you were on your way here to eat.

(MURIEL. Let's do it some other time.)

And that I had a soufflé in the oven.

(MURIEL. You can forget that.)

Do you think so? (*Goes with the telephone into the kitchen.*) Shit! It's running all over the place. It's completely black on top.

(MURIEL. Turn the oven off quick and open the door.)

Noise of the oven.

And it stinks! It's completely burned!

(MURIEL. Next time, don't leave it.)

He comes back with the telephone to the intercom receiver.

Can you come up?

(BART. Yes, of course, if that's OK.)

But why? I mean, what are you doing here in Amsterdam? I thought you couldn't stand Amsterdam. Pickpockets, coloureds and dogshit. So what are you doing here?

(BART. I'll explain it to you straight away.)

OK, just come up. Take the lift at the end of the hall and go up to the fourth floor and it's the first door on the left. I'll open the door for you now. (*He presses the button to open the door downstairs. Barking through the intercom receiver.*)

(*To* MURIEL) Can you hear that?

(MURIEL. What?)

That dog. You must be able to hear it! (*He holds the two receivers together. Calls.*) You must hear that racket! (*In the telephone receiver again.*) Did you hear it? If he's got a dog with him I'm getting rid of him straight away. I can't have a dog here.

(MURIEL. First take the soufflé out of the oven.)

OK. (*He opens the door and goes back into the kitchen with the telephone.*) Ouch!

(MURIEL. Put oven gloves on, idiot. What do you think I gave you the things for?)

Too late. What oven gloves do you mean anyway? I've never had any oven gloves from you. It must have been someone else. Ouch!

(MURIEL. Under the cold tap.)

God, that was hot.

Sound of running tap.

Ow, Ow! I'll try again.

Tap is turned off.

I'll use the teatowel. Ow! (*Drops the dish.*) That's all I need. What a mess. It was still all runny inside. (*Into the telephone.*) I've even dropped it on the floor, damn it!

Sound of the lift door. BART *enters the apartment, looks around, then goes in the direction of the kitchen where* PETER, *swearing, is cleaning up the awful mess. Stops, surprised, when he sees the urinals.*

BART. Is this where you live? In a urinal?

PETER. No, it's called a casco – it used to be offices and I got it cheap because I have to do the conversion myself. This is going to be the kitchen. Ran out of money. (*Into the telephone.*) I'll hang up now. Ring back again a bit later. Then I'll know more. See you.

(MURIEL. In about fifteen minutes?)

Yes, that's fine. Sorry Bart, don't come any further. Stop there. You can see what a mess there is here.

BART. It doesn't matter, you can mop it up. On a tiled floor like that.

PETER. What a shame! This was supposed to be a soufflé.

BART. So you said.

PETER. White chocolate.

BART. Just clear it up. I'll amuse myself. (*Goes back into the room.*)

PETER (*cleaning up in the kitchen*). Was that your dog making all that noise?

BART. No. But that's why I'm here. It's been following me ever since the station. And I couldn't get rid of it. Even slipped onto the tram with me. I was thrown off because the dog wasn't on a lead. It was running round the tram barking. It's not my dog, I said. Nobody believed me. I lured it out, and jumped back in again quick. Then the dog went and stood in front of the tram barking. You'll have to get off again, sir. I wouldn't like to run over him just because you want to get rid of him. So I got off the tram again. (*Picks things up and puts them down again. Carelessly. Not exactly in the same place.*) Then I thought, I know, I'll drop in on my little brother. Then the dog will give up. He'll just start following someone else. (*Listens through the intercom.*) I can't hear anything any more.

PETER. What did you say?

BART. That I can't hear anything any more.

PETER. So you can go away again right now.

BART (*listens*). No, he's still there. I can hear him panting.

PETER. Sure it's not a wanker?

BART. A what?

PETER. A heavy breather. Someone who stands there jerking off. I had one last week. He thought he had a woman on the line, I think.

BART. Through the telephone.

PETER. Yes.

BART. But this isn't the telephone.

PETER (*comes out of the kitchen with sleeves rolled up*). No. Oh, no. Of course not. Sorry. Misunderstood. Has he gone now, do you think?

BART. Just listen for yourself.

PETER *takes the intercom receiver. The dog barks, loudly.*

PETER. Just lucky a dog like that can't talk. I've had enough trouble with the Association.

BART. Association?

PETER. Of owners. They decided only last week they didn't want any dogs in the building. I was against it. If that dog could tell them now he was supposed to be here there'd never be an end to the uproar. And I was only against it out of principle. Any moment and they'll be saying they don't want any small children or old people or immigrants. Who knows. Though I'd never get a dog myself. Dogs don't like me anyway. They sense I'm afraid of them.

BART. I've never exercised much of an attraction for dogs before either. Just for those dogs that try to fuck your leg. Poodles.

PETER (*still with the receiver in his hand*). He's still there. You should hear. Somebody's trying to get him outside!

BART *listens.*

Can you hear. That's that woman from the second floor. Pissed. Can you hear? She's always pissed.

BART. That's what you get when you live in the big city.

PETER. Keep your voice down. Or she'll hear us. She'll get even more paranoid. She thinks she hears voices. That she's being laughed at.

BART. Can you hear it downstairs if we're talking to one another?

PETER. You heard me, didn't you?

BART. Yes. Because you were talking into the receiver.

PETER. That's what we're doing now. Sssh. You should hear her carrying on! She's so vulgar, that woman. Like our neighbours at home. Do you remember, that woman could kick up an awful stink too. And if she gets the chance she nicks my newspaper in the morning. I'm positive it's her.

BART. And you don't do anything about it?

PETER. What can I do. Get up an hour earlier? Anyway I get enough of them at the newspaper office, ten if I wanted.

BART. You could hide somewhere, in that alcove opposite the lift and then when she gets into the lift with your paper . . . Why don't you just stop your subscription?

PETER. She's always naked under her dressing gown . . . Because I like reading the paper at breakfast.

BART. Then wait for her in the lift . . .

PETER. Sooner you than me. Do you know what she looks like?

BART. No, of course not.

PETER. Late forties. Sooner you than me. But maybe you

wouldn't even notice that.

BART. How are things at the paper, by the way? Still any firms that want to advertise in it? I never read it. Just can't manage. Far too small print for a morning paper. The *Telegraaf* at least takes into account that most people's eyes are still half shut in the morning.

PETER. There's no one who doesn't advertise with us.

BART. But the *Telegraaf* has more. More death notices, anyway. How do you get them, by the way?

PETER. You ring them up and ask if they want to advertise. But that's not what I do. I develop contacts with the big advertisers. With the Giro Bank and the insurance companies and KLM and so on. (*Listens.*) She's given up. I can't hear anything any more.

BART. Who knows, maybe he's bitten her to death.

PETER. And what have you come here for actually?

BART. I told you. I had to try to get rid of that dog. And as I knew you didn't live very far from the station, although I didn't know exactly how far, you just said it wasn't far from the station . . .

PETER. When?

BART. At Dad's funeral.

PETER. I wasn't even living here at that time. I've only been here a year, no, nearly two.

BART. So I was in luck. Where were you living then?

PETER (*points*). There. In Hartenstraat. Over what was then still a . . .

BART. Not far from the station either, then . . .

PETER. . . . ceramics gallery. Now it's a pizzeria. Muriel's living there now.

BART. And who's Muriel? A girlfriend? Your girlfriend?

PETER. Sort of. Someone I know. She's coming here for a meal this evening.

BART. So she's not French?

PETER. No. Why?

BART. But that's a French name, isn't it, Muriel?

PETER. Yes. She was named after someone out of a nouvelle vague film. Her parents are real cinephiles.

BART. Oh.

PETER. People who love films.

BART. I'm not that out of touch. There was a film club in Delft too, you know.

PETER. But you weren't a member, were you?

BART. No.

PETER. Here you have the Film Museum and cinemas that only show art films.

BART. We have that in Leiden too.

PETER. Before, you only had that peculiar place on the Breestraat. I saw a Bergman film there once, I was only fifteen then, you took me to see it, about those lesbians.

BART. No idea.

PETER. Doesn't matter anyway. But what have you come here for? To Amsterdam?

BART. I was just going to tell you. Maybe. Do you have anything to drink? Shouldn't you offer me something now I'm here?

PETER. Were you planning on staying? Or do you think that dog's gone now?

BART. Well, I'm here now. Couldn't we have a beer together? Or don't you have any? Doesn't that agree with your leftwing principles? Frightful working-class stuff, beer, don't you know.

PETER. It's even in fashion, beer. Belgian beer.

BART. Grolsch? No, that's Dutch. What's it called?

PETER. Duvel, Dentergems. Stella.

BART. I know that. Stella. You can get legless on that. It's got more alcohol in than Dutch beer.

PETER. And all sorts of chemical muck. But never mind, that can't matter much to you, of course. That tap-water you produce is full of crap too.

BART. Not enough to harm anybody. It's just that lately they keep changing the standards. Where yesterday nobody had ever died of it, today suddenly apparently everyone gets cancer from it. And we're doing our best.

PETER. Are you still an assistant?

BART. I could have been director years ago somewhere else, but Em didn't want to leave Leiden. Because her parents are in Noordwijkerhout. Because of the kids. They can come and look after them now and then. And it's right by the sea. Em's with the kids at her parents this weekend.

PETER. And you?

BART. I'm in Amsterdam, as you see. Now do you have a beer or do I have to go to a bar and get one?

PETER. No, sorry, I'll get it. (*Goes to the kitchen, opens the fridge, takes two glasses, comes back with two bottles of Brandpils and the glasses.*)

BART (*sitting down*). Belgian?

PETER. No, from Limburg. That seems still to be made with relatively pure water.

BART. Still at it! It's a wonder you don't go mad with all that worrying. As long as it tastes good. That's why I don't ever read that newspaper either. Worrying about everything. Straight away at breakfast your day's ruined. Cheers!

PETER (*pours for himself*). And?

BART. You didn't fall for it? Pity. Before, I could always really get you wound up. I just had to wave my old college tie under your nose. Got a reaction straight away. Still no plans to start studying?

PETER. No, not really. They don't exactly make it attractive for you, do they?

BART. You had your chance, matey. All you had to do was get your A-levels. Dad would have paid. But no, you had to leave school and go off to the big city. Because his little lordship couldn't stand it any more at home. And now it's too late. Now your old man's pushing up the daisies.

PETER. Do you know that for sure? Whether he is or not?

BART. Who?

PETER. That man standing behind you.

BART *looks behind him.*

Can't you see!

BART. What?

PETER. That's what I mean. We'll never get him under the ground, dead or alive. Even if we got a crane and plonked a granite slab down over his grave. Just like a jack-in-the-box. Although just once I did manage to respect him.

BART. When?

PETER. When he hit you. In the face. Over and over. And then when he hit your ears you yelled out, 'I'm deaf, I'm deaf', and then he stopped, just like that.

BART. He never hit you.

PETER. He didn't dare.

BART. He didn't think you were worth it. He expected something from me. He only beat me when I disappointed him.

PETER. And did you ever disappoint him?

BART. Only once. I think. When they kicked me out as captain of the hockey team.

PETER. Because you'd embezzled the cash.

BART. Not even three hundred guilders. I could have earned it back in four Saturdays. Nobody would have been any the wiser.

PETER. If that Van der Klei hadn't been such a little sneak. I know. Jesus. I know. I know everything. I don't have to go through another refresher course on your life, this evening, OK. So, you'd better clear off straight away.

BART. Have I ever asked you to forgive me for it?

PETER. For what?

BART. Selling your stamp collection. I thought I'd get enough for it to make up the shortfall.

PETER. You've only just asked for it.

BART. That's true. But you were thirteen then. And I was four years older.

PETER. I didn't care anyway. Those stamps. After that old man had died – can you still remember his name, by the way?

BART. Vist or something like that. Something like that.

PETER. I thought you had a good memory for names.

BART. I do. I could still tell you the names of everybody in the street. Ranselaar, Kok . . .

PETER. Stop it. But you can't remember the name of that old man.

BART. Yes I can. I do know. Vlist, van der Vlist.

PETER. Dammit, yes. Van der Vlist. Nice man. I felt safe there. That's why I saved stamps, because he collected stamps. I went with him to the stamp exchange. There were letters there that had been brought out of Paris when it was under siege by the Germans in the 70-71 war, 1870.

BART. Did they have postage stamps then?

PETER. What do you think?

BART. No, I didn't know then. Stupid of me. I should have known. I should have had a good look at them before I sold them.

PETER. Or you should have asked me how much they were worth. Those two letters alone would have been enough. But you slept with a knife under your mattress and said you'd slit my throat if I said anything about it to Mum or Dad. Scared stiff. So scared you daren't even ask me how much the collection was worth. How did you get hold of that knife, by the way?

BART. It wasn't a knife, it was a bayonet.

PETER. A bayonet? Where did you get it from?

BART. One bottle of beer. Is that all?

PETER. No, I've got another one, I'm sure. But I don't want any more. I'll be having wine in a minute with the meal. Will you stay and eat? I mean, everything's ready. I just have to warm it up.

BART (*looks at his watch*). I don't know. And what about that girl of yours?

PETER. Muriel? I'll just ring and call it off. Or did you have other plans?

BART. I don't know. Sorry. No. I don't know. Not yet. I'd have to ring up first. But I suppose . . . Although.

Pause.

PETER. Although what?

BART. Yes, well it's like this . . . Em doesn't know I'm here. She thinks I had a lot of work and just wanted some peace and quiet this evening and tomorrow. And then on Sunday I'd just go to Noordwijkerhout. To go to church with her. And then go to the beach with the kids. If this good weather keeps up.

PETER. Oh.

BART. That's how it is.

PETER. OK. Then just stay and eat.

BART. But no more questions, all right? Or I'm going right now.

PETER. No, no more questions. But wouldn't you rather have a glass of wine now?

BART. No, I'd rather drink beer.

PETER. OK. Then I'll just go and get another lager for you and then I'll ring Muriel. OK? (*He does that. With the telephone in his hand.*) She's used to it. Not that I do it very often, ringing up to cancel, I mean, but she does. Why isn't she answering now? Under the shower or something, probably. I'll try again in a minute. Would you like to eat straight away? It'll take about fifteen minutes at most.

BART. What?

PETER. Warming up and so on.

BART. I'm not hungry yet.

PETER. Then we can wait a bit.

Pause.

Well, if I can't ask any more questions and you don't say anything, it's going to be difficult, isn't it? Shall I read you something from the paper?

BART. I can read for myself.

PETER. I thought you had a bit of trouble with the small print.

BART. I can manage.

PETER. Shall I put a record on?

BART. As long as it's something classical. Something peaceful. I can't stand pop music. It drives me crazy. All that droning. Em has the radio on all the time, in the kitchen. But you can hear it all over the house. One of those local stations with stupid commercials for local traders. Everything in a flat Leiden accent. The butcher's wife: 'This week we have some lovely beef steaks on special offer.'

PETER. What would you like to hear, then? Wagner?

BART. Wagner? I said peaceful. That's not peaceful.

PETER. There are some really peaceful bits. The Siegfried Idyll. He wrote more than the Ride of the Valkyries. Though I've only learned that since I left home. That was the only thing Dad every played by that man. When we were in bed. At full volume. We had to go downstairs . . .

BART. I did.

PETER. . . . . to ask if he couldn't turn it down a bit. You did, yes. Or one of those marches. As long as it was German.

BART. Yes.

PETER (*after a short pause*). The Horst Wessel song.

BART. I thought you said you didn't want any refresher courses.

PETER. We never talked about that before.

BART. Much too often.

PETER. When?

BART. Oh, cut it out, please. I really don't feel like talking about it now. Can't we talk about something else?

PETER. What then?

BART. I can think of lots of things. About that girl of yours. That Muriel. What does she do?

PETER. She does a fresh fruit juice campaign. She stands in a stall and sells fresh fruit juice. In department stores and big self-service shops and so on.

BART. Is that her profession?

PETER. At the moment. She works for a temping agency. She wants to be a stewardess but she can't at the moment. But she's doing all sorts of language courses and stuff.

BART. Have you known her long?

PETER. One or two years. Since I moved here. She heard I'd left the Hartenstraat and she didn't have anywhere to live then. And so. But that ceramics shop was still there then. Now it's a pizzeria.

BART. You've already told me that.

PETER. And it comes up through the floor. The stink. I can't stand it there even for an hour. It makes me feel really sick. I'm glad I got out.

BART. What do you expect. That's what you get with all those Italians and Turks. Those little takeaways everywhere.

PETER. As though sauerkraut doesn't stink if you live over it.

The bell rings.

Yes. Hello. Hello. Who's there?

(MURIEL. It's me. Muriel. Why don't you open the door?)

I've just tried to ring you.

(MURIEL. Yes, I was already on the way here. I've just bought something really nice.)

Something nice?

(MURIEL. Yes, for you, sweets, at Leonidas.)

Oh, yes, nice of you. Is that dog still there?

(MURIEL. What dog?)

A dog that was following my brother.

(MURIEL. Your brother. Is he still there?)

Yes, he's still here.

BART. I don't believe it.

PETER. No, not you, that dog. Is he still there?

(MURIEL. How am I supposed to know?)

No, that dog. Whether he's still there. In the hall.

(MURIEL. No, there's no dog here.)

He's gone, that dog.

(MURIEL. But why don't you open the door?)

Yes, that's what I was just trying to phone you about. My brother's still here.

(MURIEL. I know that. Just open the door.)

OK. I'll open it. (*Presses the button and puts the intercom back. To* BART.) Muriel.

BART. So she wasn't under the shower after all.

PETER. No, she was on her way here. With something nice. She'd gone to buy something nice. Sweets.

BART. Kind.

PETER. That she'll scoff all on her own if I . . . Oh yes, there's something else I have to explain to you.

BART. Oh?

PETER. Yes, I mean, when you meet her now, no questions. OK? I mean . . . Of course you can ask her ordinary things. But not, not . . . Not about her condition. She's got a belly on her, if you get me.

BART. Yes, you always did fall for the chubby ones. What was the name of that one again you were going out with just before you left school . . . A funny name, Friesian name, what was it?

PETER. Baukje. But it's not that. Muriel's not chubby. She just has a fat belly.

BART. A fat belly . . .

PETER. Yes, as though she's pregnant . . .

BART. By you?

PETER. No, not by me. Are you crazy? By nobody. In fact she's not even . . .

A knock on the door.

I'll explain in a minute. (*Opens the door.*) Hello. (*Kisses* MURIEL. *She kisses him, on the cheek.*) Come on in. This is my brother Bart, this is Muriel.

MURIEL. Hi. (*She shakes hands with* BART.) Jesus. He looks just like Clark Gable, Peter. In that Hitchcock film. You know. Where he nearly falls off the roof. No, Cary Grant, that's the one I mean. I'd never have thought that, Peter. With which one of you was your mother having a bit on the side, Peter. Come on, tell me.

PETER. Muriel always plunges straight in.

BART. The understatement of the year.

MURIEL. Although at the moment somebody has plunged in on me. It has advantages. (*Taps her stomach.*) Before I would have got a glass of beer in my face, but not any more. Little smile. Oh well. Poor thing. Bit mixed up, is she? Then they ask: Is it your first one? But your glasses are empty, I see. I wouldn't mind one either, a small lager.

BART. Do you think you ought . . . ?

MURIEL. Why not? I smoke and drink where I can. Who knows, maybe it helps. Has Peter told you?

PETER. Sort of. (*He goes to get beer.*) What did your doctor say this morning, by the way. I completely forgot. What did he say?

MURIEL (*looking at* BART *in frank admiration*). Sorry, I'm just standing here staring with my jaw on the ground. I'm rather frank. In your face, that's me. But it'll pass. When my jaw starts to hurt.

PETER (*comes back*). Well, what did he say?

MURIEL. Nothing. Gave me another load of tranquillisers. And asked if I really wouldn't like to go and have a little talk with a psychiatrist. No thanks. I'd rather let someone take away the whole shooting match than let anybody go rooting around in my mind. Strange hands are only allowed to touch the material bits. (*To* BART.) Are you staying to eat?

BART. Yes. No.

PETER. That's what I was trying to ring you about. Just now. But you'd already left.

MURIEL. That your brother's staying to eat? You didn't have to ring up about that. Or should I have brought something more? Don't you have enough? Let me have a look. I can fix something. I get that from home. From my mother. Cottage in France. People who just drop in. Always at meal-times. Improvise. Nothing in the cupboard but conjuring up a complete meal. You must have a packet of rice or something?

PETER. Rice?

MURIEL. Rice, yes. Bitter rice. Anna Magnani if I remember right. With one tit hanging out of her dress. In the Calypso cinema. Before they redecorated it, of course, do you remember, on the left, right at the top of the stairs. *Bicycle Thieves*, Buster Keaton . . .

PETER (*who meanwhile has gone to look*). No.

MURIEL. Chaplin . . . How come you haven't? I'm sure you have.

PETER. No rice.

MURIEL. Then go and borrow some from somebody. From one of your neighbours.

PETER. From that woman on the second floor, maybe? I can go and see whether she's taken pity on that dog.

BART. Or the dog on her.

MURIEL. What dog?

BART. The one that was following me.

MURIEL. I can just imagine. You turning up here with a whole string of women trotting along behind you.

BART. No, a dog, he followed me from the station . . .

MURIEL. A dog? Oh well. Why not? Pedigree dog?

BART. No idea.

MURIEL. Those two gays next door then? They hoard stuff like crazy, if you ask me. The stuff they're always carting in. The two of them can't possibly use all that. And they get it all from the health food shop. Whole grain rice. You can make fantastic risottos with that. Shall I go?

PETER. No, please don't, or they'll be in here like a shot, eating with us, just like last week . . .

MURIEL. It was a pleasant evening, wasn't it?

PETER. Pleasant? Pleasant? Christ, Muriel, they spent the whole evening talking of nothing but Aids.

MURIEL. Well, what do you expect. They're worried. Though

those two don't know what having a bit on the side is, if you ask me. I do, on the other hand. So. I mean, so we talked about it. (*To* BART.) But you look as though you never leave home without your condoms!

BART (*embarrassed*). Well, I . . . No . . . Yes . . .

PETER. I'll go. And if you don't mind, Muriel. He comes from Leiden. Leiden! And you don't read about things like that in the *Telegraaf*.

BART. You don't need the *Telegraaf* to read about that. Even if you just go to the post office they stop you and shove one of those leaflets under your nose.

PETER. OK. So you know what Muriel's on about.

BART. Yes. And long before you did.

PETER. I'll be right back.

MURIEL. Festina lente.

PETER. Which means?

MURIEL. Hurry up slowly.

PETER. I'm not setting foot inside there without you.

MURIEL. They won't jump on you. Sorry.

PETER. That's all right then.

PETER *goes. He leaves the door ajar.*

BART (*after a short pause in which* PETER *is heard ringing the neighbours' doorbell. Looking at* MURIEL's *belly*). Congratulations.

MURIEL. What for? O, for that? That really landed me in it. The fresh fruit juice people were furious. In one week two new dresses. They have all sorts of fruit printed on them, you see. Pineapples and pomegranates. On the material. And then I have a sort of cap on. Totally insane. With little apples and pears and kiwis and lemons all round the brim. You see. But the dress I've got now you could get two Michelin men in.

(PETER'S VOICE. I just wondered if you might have a packet of rice you could lend me. You'll get it back tomorrow.)

The answer is unintelligible.

No, I'll just wait.)

MURIEL. He daren't go in. The coward. As if they could rape him on their Italian furniture. Break the little legs off straight away.

BART. But it's not Peter's then?

MURIEL. Peter's. This? No, if I only knew who I had to thank for it. Then I'd have got rid of it straight away.

BART. Do you want to then?

MURIEL. Yes, what do you think. I'll miss another selection procedure, damn it. I want to be a stewardess, you see. But now I read this morning in the paper . . .

(PETER'S VOICE. Thanks very much. No, you'll get it back tomorrow.)

MURIEL (*to* PETER *too as he comes back*). Did you read that? Air France are looking for Dutch stewardesses. Stewards too.

PETER. I'm frightened of flying.

MURIEL. Because we speak languages so well. And they don't bother about your height either. What did I say. (*Takes the packet of rice.*) Wholegrain rice. You'll just see what a fantastic risotto I'm going to make out of this. That fills your stomach. Then we'll have plenty left of the rest for the three of us.

BART. Yes, I don't know . . . Perhaps I . . . Do you have a phone, Peter?

PETER. Yes, of course. There it is.

BART. Maybe I'd better ring up first.

MURIEL. It's my fault. Is that my fault? Oh God, I'll go. I'll go.

BART. No, it's not that. It's just. You see, I'm here in Amsterdam . . .

PETER. Yes, why ARE you here?

BART. I really didn't feel like telling. Because Peter has always had these strange prejudices. Leftwing, but full of prejudices. Moral.

PETER. I know what you're on about, but that had nothing to do with politics. You think that, but that's where you're mistaken.

BART. Moral prejudices then. But seeing you have a girlfriend now who seems to be less bothered about it . . .

PETER. I've never spoken to her about it.

BART. Then you should sometime. Who knows, it might be a relief. I'd just like to say I'm here in Amsterdam and Em doesn't know.

PETER. So you said.

MURIEL. Who's Em?

PETER. Emmy, his wife and the mother of his two sweet little kiddywinks.

MURIEL. And I've been thinking the whole time he's married to Marilyn Monroe, if he's married, though I hope he isn't married, as if isn't married yet, there's still hope . . .

PETER. That jacket's from C & A, I presume . . .

BART. Burton's. And Em doesn't know that, I mean, I didn't tell her because I had planned, because a few weeks ago I met a woman, while we were on holiday, Normandy, just like last year, yes, God, yes. Em and the kids had gone to the beach, and I hadn't, because I had got badly burned the day before, so I went off to a town, Rouen, and I met her there, and she lives here in Amsterdam and I said . . .

PETER. You can't do that.

MURIEL. Why not?

PETER. Simply cheat on your wife, with a cheap excuse like that . . .

BART. Do you know a better one?

PETER. I didn't expect anything else actually. And I still thought, he'll drop in sometime, in the end, to have a talk, because he's got a problem, because he suddenly remembered he still had a brother . . .

MURIEL. How sentimental, Peter. What's up with you. I've never known you like this. Sorry. I don't want to get mixed up in it, OK.

BART. But seeing you asked me to stay and eat and I was still hesitating . . . I mean, she has no idea I'm here. Maybe she has other plans. For this evening. Maybe she has a friend. But when Muriel came and you started on about eating, then I thought, I must just ring her up first, and if she's not in, then I'd like to stay here and eat, and then I'll just go back by train. Em's got the car. She's so used to the car she just doesn't realise any more that there are still trains.

PETER. I presume this isn't the first time.

BART. What?

PETER. That you've cheated on her.

BART. What did I say. Every inch the little bourgeois. No, this isn't the first time. No.

PETER. It's something I can't understand.

BART. No, you don't understand that.

PETE. My father did that too. He went to the whores in The Hague while Mum was slaving away trying to make ends meet. Altering your clothes so I could wear them.

BART. The wife of a city surveyor doesn't have to slave away. She was just thrifty. She thought it a sin to throw clothes away. I grew out of everything.

PETER. I never had anything of my own. Only when I had to go to dancing lessons, then finally I got a jacket all of my own. And shoes you hadn't worn down on one side.

BART. Then I'd just like to ring up now.

PETER. Forget it. You can go to a phone box. There's a whole building full of telephone boxes in the Raadhuisstraat.

MURIEL. Or you can come home with me, you can ring up from my place.

PETER. Christ, Muriel. Don't you understand . . .

MURIEL. No, I don't understand anything about it. Really not. I don't understand why you've got so excited about it. What business is it of yours who your brother has it off with?

PETER. OK. Do what you want. Do you have her number?

BART. No. But I do have her name and address. Have you got a telephone book?

PETER. Of course I've got a telephone book. What's her name? I'll look it up for you.

BART. Her name's Marianne Goudsmit and she lives in . . . (*Looks in his wallet for the scrap of paper with her name and address.*)

PETER. There can't be that many with that name. There are about thirty here, three, no four, with an M. Where does she live?

BART. Cartesiusplantsoen.

PETER. Then it's this one. (*Dials the number, waits till the telephone is answered.*) Here you go. (*Gives the receiver to* BART.)

MURIEL. Shouldn't we start on the meal now?

PETER. While we still don't know if he's going to . . .

BART. Hallo? Is that Marianne Goudsmit? Then may I speak to her? (*To* PETER *and* MURIEL.) A girl. Not a kid's voice. (*Into the receiver.*) Marianne. It's me, Bart.

(MARIANNE'S VOICE. Bart? Bart? You?)

Yes, I just happened to be in Amsterdam . . .

PETER. Just happened!

MURIEL. You just keep your mouth shut.

BART. And I thought I'd give you a ring, I thought maybe you'd completely forgotten . . .

(MARIANNE. Me? What gave you that idea? Are you in Amsterdam now, did you say?)

Yes, I'm in Amsterdam and I've . . .

(MARIANNE. Have you eaten yet?)

No, not yet. But if you've already got something lined up . . .

(MARIANNE. No, that was my niece who picked up the phone, I'm helping her a bit with her homework.)

Her homework?

(MARIANNE. Yes, she's got her final exams coming up, but she was just leaving, weren't you, Lottie?)

Well, in that case . . .

(MARIANNE. Shall we go somewhere for a meal? I know a fantastic fish restaurant. Not as good as that one in Rouen, but still. Want to come here first for a drink? Then we can go out and eat afterwards and then see how things go.)

That sounds wonderful to me.

(MARIANNE. Do you know how to get here?)

I'll find it OK.

(MARIANNE. You got my address?)

Yes, I've got that.

(MARIANNE. You coming straight away then?)

Yes.

(MARIANNE. Then I'll get changed in the meantime. Jesus, Bart, what a surprise. What a pleasant surprise. I thought I'd never see you again.)

Lo and behold.

(MARIANNE. Yes, lo and behold.)

If you're going to get changed, why don't you put that dress on . . .

(MARIANNE. But that's a summer dress.)

Doesn't matter, does it? Just put a thick coat on.

(MARIANNE. OK, OK, if that makes you happy.)

Yes.

(MARIANNE. See you in a minute, then.)

Yes, in a minute. In a minute.

(*Hangs up. To* MURIEL.) She was wearing a dress in the summer, something Em would never dare wear, really thin, with loads of folds . . .

MURIEL. Pleats.

BART. It was just like sinking into a cloud. That sort of feeling. Groping around in a cloud with something really soft inside it.

MURIEL. Just like those sweets you used to be able to get, with a soft filling.

BART. Something like that. I think Em gets harder and harder. I get that feeling. A sort of chemical process. As though slowly but surely she's changing into a sort of reptile. Just as though she's getting scales.

PETER. I've never noticed it.

BART. No, you don't see that. I mean scales on her soul. Anyway you don't see her that often. When did you see her last, by the way?

PETER. At Dad's funeral. Where I saw you last as well, as it happens. But Mum sees her often. And she rings me up often.

BART. Because she's got nothing else to do. When she's not trundling her little book trolley round the university clinic of course.

PETER. But it's good she does that, isn't it?

BART. It would be a relief if she'd behave a bit less self-sacrificing just for once. Did something she enjoyed. That you could see she was enjoying. But never mind. So I'm going to eat out with her.

PETER. With Marianne Goudsmit.

MURIEL. I think that's a nice name. I had a girlfriend at boarding school called Marianne. She already had breasts in the second grade. Although I got my periods a few months before she did. But you couldn't impress any boys with that. Quite the opposite. But you could with those breasts.

BART. She hasn't got very big breasts though.

MURIEL. That Marianne wasn't called Goudsmit either, but . . .
God, I can never remember names . . . Stupid but impressive.
Raquel Welch. Something along those lines. I was more the
Meryl Streep type.

BART. Do you have a map of Amsterdam, Peter, or do you know
where it is, Cartesiusplantsoen?

PETER. No idea. And I don't have a map either. But you can get
one anywhere.

MURIEL. You'll take a taxi, won't you?

BART. But what if it's right on the other side of town?

PETER. Just like my mother. Thrifty. He gets that from my
mother.

MURIEL. I'd take a taxi.

BART. You're right. If I go by tram or bus it'll take me hours to
get there.

PETER. Shall I call for one?

BART. Isn't there a taxi stand near here?

PETER. You can choose between the Dam and the Westermarkt.

MURIEL. The Dam is safer.

BART. Then I'll do that. I'll go to the Dam. On the way I can buy
some flowers or something. Maybe that would make too much
of a calculated impression. No, I won't take anything. And you
know what, Peter, tomorrow morning I'll drop in here again.

PETER. But not too early.

BART. No, not too early, or even this evening again, but I
wouldn't reckon on that too much.

PETER. But you can't sleep here.

BART. I wouldn't have to. There are night trains. Don't worry.
Who knows, I might change my mind. I might be disappointed
in Amsterdam, I mean. Compared with Rouen. In spite of that
dress. It happened to me once before.

MURIEL. Oh yes?

BART. Yes. The reality doesn't come up to the memory. If
anything like that happens, then everything inside you just
wants to scream and run.

MURIEL. Then you don't see the difference any more between fleecy clouds and thunder clouds.

BART. Something like that. God, Peter, don't look so glum. Peter Glum. You haven't changed much either. I couldn't do anything about it that my girlfriends didn't fall for you. He sat there on the beach, with that face on, Muriel, you should have seen it. And thought I ought to lie on my belly if I got an erection.

MURIEL (to PETER). Didn't you get them then?

PETER. Not from his girlfriends. The ones Bart knocked around with. My mother even threw one out once. She worked in Hema, in the cosmetics department. She couldn't get rid of the stink. It used to give my mother asthma. A ghastly cheap smell. Know what I mean?

MURIEL. I know exactly what you mean. I stink too every evening of fresh fruit juice when I'm finished. Especially that pomegranate smell, once you get that in your hair.

PETER. But that's completely different.

BART. Peter, do you mind if I leave my wedding ring here for the time being. I'm scared I might lose it if I just stick it in my pocket.

PETER. Of course not. Would you like to fuck her here sometimes as well? Only I don't have a bidet in the bathroom.

MURIEL. That's very thoughtless of you.

BART. Then I'll just put it here, OK? Now I'm going.

MURIEL. Have fun.

BART. Yes.

PETER. Yes.

BART. I'll ring before I come back.

PETER. You see. I'm home. Does she like dogs, by the way?

BART. Who?

PETER. Marianne.

BART. Why? Oh. No, he's gone. You didn't see a dog, did you? When you came in?

MURIEL. No. No, definitely not.

BART. So it's gone. OK, then I'll be off.

PETER. So you keep saying.

MURIEL. You're doing well for yourself. Poor you, having to play the virtuous family man, and the whole time women are queueing up to throw themselves at you.

BART. Till tomorrow then.

PETER. Yes.

BART (*shakes hands with* MURIEL). If I don't see you again. All the best. Good luck.

MURIEL. What for?

BART *nods in the direction of her belly.*

MURIEL. Oh, I'll manage. A question of patience.

BART *laughs and leaves.*

MURIEL. He's walking over a carpet of women to his taxi. Jesus, what a man. And thank God I'm not as prudish as you, matey.

PETER (*stung*). Prudish? Me?

MURIEL. Puts on the outraged virtue act when his brother has a bit on the side, doesn't fuck pregnant women . . .

PETER. Apparently pregnant. No. I find that a disgusting idea.

MURIEL. OK, apparently pregnant. You didn't tell him, did you?

PETER. What?

MURIEL. About the phantom pregnancy.

PETER. No, I didn't get round to it.

MURIEL. Because you found it more important to rake up youthful memories.

PETER. I'd really rather not have done that either. But if you knew how he terrorised me all the time. He thought I was asleep and lay there jerking himself off. And groaning and gasping and making weird noises. And then I thought, he's ill, he's going to die, and put the light on. I asked him, what's up? And he pretended nothing at all was up. He never told me what he was doing. That's the kind of person he is.

MURIEL. Is he a lot older than you?

PETER. Only four years. We slept in the same room. Also a crazy idea, of course. In the attic. A semi attic. Because Mum and Dad didn't want us to be able to hear them. Or the other way round. They were dead scared we might hear. In the night. Music blaring out so we couldn't hear what they were saying. Until Bart went downstairs to say we couldn't sleep. Terrible. And Bart's just like my father. Nothing but sex on his mind.

And as right-wing as stink. Just like my father again.

MURIEL. Well, look, sorry, I don't know . . .

PETER. No, you don't know at all. He slept with a knife, a
bayonet under his mattress, so I didn't tell my parents
everything he got up to. He pinched money, he pinched drink,
broke into cigarette machines. Threatened me with that knife.
At night he crept in the dark to my bed, pressed my head in the
pillow, put that knife to my throat. I still have nightmares about
it sometimes.

MURIEL. I don't have any brothers or sisters. I was an only child.
A little mistake. I think they didn't even know that's where
babies came from. How old were they? Eighteen, nineteen. But
they managed well. The films made them a lot wiser and
brought them closer together. Andy Warhol, in the City
Museum. Mum can still wax quite lyrical about it. Flesh and
Trash. They came from Den Bosch after all. So I don't know
what that is, a brother. I've probably missed something.

PETER. Nothing at all. Take my word for it.

MURIEL. A younger brother, that would have been nice, I think.
Older, no, I don't know. I'd rather have been the eldest, I think.

PETER. The elder always has it easier.

MURIEL. Always?

PETER. Not always perhaps. It depends. But it's certainly no fun
being the youngest. Certainly not if your older brother's a
fascist like Bart. Muriel, would you do something for me?

MURIEL. Depends what it is.

PETER. Would you ring up that Marianne and pretend you're
Bart's wife.

MURIEL. Pretend what?

PETER. That you're Bart's wife. To spite him. To be able to get
my own back on him for once.

MURIEL. Why?

PETER. Everything I've just told you. Don't you get it. I'd do
anything if I could finally get my revenge. Just once. What do
you care about that Marianne. I'm sure he'll never find out.
And it's not that I feel sorry for Emmy or anything. Just to be
able to put a spoke in his wheel. Leaving his wedding ring here.
What a man.

MURIEL. What must I say then?

PETER. That you're his wife and that you'd like to speak to him. That's all.

MURIEL. OK. If you'll go with me tomorrow evening to Elsje and Jonathan's party.

PETER. Who are they? Do I know them?

MURIEL. I've told you all about it. They are the only friends of my parents who really have something to do with films. Jonathan anyway. And so I have to go. And I always feel a bit daft on my own. In that crowd. If I have to depend on my parents. And I won't say anything else. I'm not going to tell her I'm against Bart having a bit on the side or anything. But if the woman has a brain in her head and not sawdust then she won't mind. 'If you need me, just whistle. You know how to whistle, don't you? Just put your lips together and blow.' To have or to have not, Humphrey Bogart and Lauren Bacall. That's what my mother sounds like even now, but she smokes at least two packets of Gauloises a day too.

PETER. Please. We haven't got much time.

MURIEL. OK. Hand it over. What's the number?

PETER *hands her the phone book.*

Only that I'm his wife. Nothing else.

PETER. No.

MURIEL. She must be still under the shower . . . Hello. Yes, this is Emmy van der Gaag. I'd like to speak to my husband please.

(MARIANNE'S VOICE. Your husband?)

Yes, my husband. Isn't he with you? Then he must be still on the way. Yes, then I'll ring back again in a minute.

(MARIANNE. Is it something special? Can I give him a message?)

No, nothing special. I just wanted to speak to him. Don't put yourself out. Thank you very much. (*Hangs up.*) Happy?

PETER. Yes.

*

PETER *and* MURIEL *are at table, after the meal. They are drinking coffee and eating the sweets* MURIEL *brought with her. They have both drunk a lot, during the meal.*

MURIEL (*offers the box of sweets to* PETER). Another one?

PETER. No, thanks.

MURIEL. Don't you like them?

PETER. Yes I do.

MURIEL. Since I've had this stupid fat belly I've just had a terrible craving for sweet things as well. Though normally I don't fancy them at all. When I was a kid I went through a period like that too. When I was about fourteen. When I realised my parents were in a film no one would ever want to see. My father would go and stand in the garden, under the chestnut tree, cigarette, French cigarette dangling from the corner of his mouth. Belmondo in one of those Duras films. My mother would put some Brahms on, and she was completely convinced that any moment Antony Perkins could walk in. God, were they mixed up. And then suddenly one day my grandparents turned up. Out of nowhere. Petit bourgeois, crumpled little people with rough workers' hands. Said grace before meals.

PETER. And you'd never seen them.

MURIEL. I swear to you. Never. Two or three times a year they went to Den Bosch. On birthdays. I slept at Elsje and Jonathan's. So that's little Mooreel, said my Gran when I came home from school. She'd had a grandchild for fourteen years called Muriel and no one had ever bothered to tell her how my name was pronounced.

PETER. Nor did you.

MURIEL. No, I didn't dare. She seemed so tiny. I sort of felt that if you said anything to her she'd just disappear. Little Mrs Thumbelina living with that little husband of hers in a thimble. Forget about Shalimar, that my mother always wore – 4711 on a handkerchief in a bag with a clasp. If you live in Amsterdam you forget so quickly that thirty kilometres away they're still running round in black stockings. Suddenly I realised my parents had learned their whole way of living from the nouvelle vague. From the subtitles anyway. Because, in spite of those Alliance Française courses and that cottage in the Dordogne, they never learned enough French to be able to follow a film they didn't already know.

PETER. I went through something like that myself. When I was fourteen too. Just. Almost fifteen. Bart was in his first year in Delft.

MURIEL. He must have really suffered there.

PETER. How do you mean?

MURIEL. All those budding Madame Curies wouldn't have been

much like large white summer clouds. Rather the scaly sort I'd say. I did find that weird. I could immediately see it in front of me. The sort of woman who in the evenings creeps out of her old shell when she goes upstairs and when you get in bed next to her the new one has already gone hard.

PETER. Don't forget the nurses in the Dijkzicht.

MURIEL. The what?

PETER. The Dijkzicht hospital. In Rotterdam. All those Zeelanders. He likes the redheads.

MURIEL. Since when do all Zeelanders have red hair?

PETER. That's what my father always said. He was full of that kind of generalising. That's the sort of values Bart has inherited.

MURIEL. Prejudices.

PETER. Exactly. But what I wanted to tell you. Hand me another one. (*Takes a sweet.*) Do you want any more coffee?

MURIEL. No thanks. I'd never be able to get to sleep. But it's odd he hasn't rung up. Do you think he could be on his way back to Leiden?

PETER. To Leiden?

MURIEL. To make it up. With Em. And the poor cow will know nothing about it.

PETER. I don't think so. He'll be having it off with her in bed.

MURIEL. Drifting happily along on his fluffy cloud nine.

PETER. Something like that. (*Pours himself another cup of coffee.*) Then tomorrow morning he'll come and get his wedding ring and then I'll try to make it clear to him yet again why I haven't got anywhere in life. Why I'm happy I can keep my head above water with that stupid job.

MURIEL. And why is that?

PETER. And I'll never get very far in life. Why I was glad I left school. Relieved. Because I was crawling with shame. And he knows that, but he pooh-poohs it. He has always pooh-poohed it.

MURIEL. Sorry.

PETER. That's because my father went wrong in the war.

MURIEL. Wrong?

PETER. Yes. A fascist. A Nazi.

MURIEL. Really?

PETER. Yes. Not a Dutch Nazi party member and stuff. And he didn't fight for the Germans or anything. He couldn't have done. He was twelve when the war broke out. But then you're old enough to know what's what. Although Bart swears that's not so. But I have proof. I found it. Up in the attic. Very well stashed away. A whole pile of German soldiers' magazines. 'Signal', it was called. German magazines from the Nazi time.

MURIEL. Well, I . . .

PETER. That's why.

MURIEL. That's why what?

PETER. I've never got anywhere. Because I was ashamed. Because I've been ashamed my whole life, you understand. In front of everybody. Only not with you. Because you're not ordinary either. Like Bart I mean. He's ordinary. He sleepwalks. Does what he feels like. Is blind and deaf to everything happening around him in the world. He only comes to life when he sees a skirt fluttering.

MURIEL. He doesn't look that ordinary. Or do you think Harrison Ford looks ordinary as well?

PETER. Yes.

MURIEL. Or Liam Neeson?

PETER. Yes. Just the same as I think Cary Grant looks really ordinary. If they didn't look ordinary they wouldn't get anybody to watch their films. They'd only be shown in art cinemas.

MURIEL. But when you found that out, about your father, what did you do then?

PETER. Nothing. At first I did nothing. Then I told Bart about it once.

MURIEL. But he knew, didn't he?

PETER. How come? He knew it? He wouldn't have believed it.

MURIEL. But did you show him those magazines then?

PETER. Of course I did.

MURIEL. And he still didn't believe it?

PETER. No. He said I didn't understand anything about it. That I should put those things back where I'd found them. That I was exaggerating wildly. The way I always did. That it didn't mean anything. A few of those old magazines. That it wasn't at all certain he had bought them in the war. That perhaps they didn't belong to him at all. That I should stop nosing around in other people's lives. That he didn't want to hear about it either.

MURIEL. So he knew but didn't want it to be true.

PETER. Do you think so?

MURIEL. That's what you said, that he was the sort who just doesn't know what he doesn't want to know, who believes what he likes, who didn't want to ruin his relationship with his father. Did he get on well with your father?

PETER. Yes. He did. They went out together sometimes. To the café. He never did that with me. They had long talks together. About politics. About technical things.

MURIEL. Then it must have been something like that. Maybe they had talked it all out with one another long ago.

PETER. Then, a few months after I had discovered that, we had Commemoration of the Dead at school . . .

MURIEL. Commemoration of the Dead?

PETER. Yes, fourth of May, flags at half mast, two minutes' silence, and instead of the last lesson a gathering in the school hall with pupils playing music, solemn music, of course, and poems read out, about resistance heroes and stuff, Jan Campert, 'The I-don't-remember-how-many dead', that sort of thing, and a speech by the headmaster and then we all filed giggling and sniggering past the memorial plaque of old boys in the hall and then we went home . . .

MURIEL. We didn't have that. Not that I can remember. Just lessons. And my parents always – quote – 'forgot' that two minutes' silence. Because they refused to turn on the radio or TV. Because it made my mother so depressed. All those clanging bells. The fourth of May we always skipped. The fifth of May as well, come to that.

PETER. I felt excluded from it all, that I didn't belong. I just felt so ashamed. So instead of going to the commemoration of the dead I just went home. I just get home, creak, creak, Dad, at lunchtime. He probably did that often when I was at school for the whole day. He came home. To fuck.

MURIEL. Really?

PETER. I've just said that, that he was just as fixated on sex as Bart. If only you knew how similar those two are.

MURIEL. But how did you know that?

PETER. Because Mum asked me once not to come home when I had no lesson for the last hour. She said I was to go home with one of my friends. Because she and Dad wanted to be alone for a bit. With no children in the house.

MURIEL. To fuck?

PETER. No, to do the things adults do with one another when they are alone. Like fucking.

MURIEL. Not exactly discreet of her.

PETER. She thought she was, though. And now makes out she doesn't understand what I mean when I try to talk to her about it. The walls people put up. But anyway, creak, creak. Dad. What are you doing home? I didn't go to the Commemoration for the Dead. I don't think it's got anything to do with me. Why not? First I try to skirt round the difficult point, because they are commemorating the old boys who died in police actions and in the Resistance, but not those from the concentration camps. Nonsense. As though you don't know they do that every year. I couldn't get the words out. Well, finally he hauled me by the ear out into the street, across the square, into the school. We lived close to the school. I only needed to leave home when the bell started ringing. Jumped over the hedge and through the bushes and there I was right on time. Holding my ear through the school, past the porter, into the school hall and in front of the whole school right up to the headmaster. I wanted to sink through the floor. My father said something about assuming the headmaster would punish me and disappeared. Whether I really did get punished I can't remember. I don't think I did actually. In any case that evening, when my mother called me and I came down to eat, Bart was in Delft by then . . .

MURIEL. So you said.

PETER. . . . I brought down those magazines and put them down next to his plate. Without saying anything. Not a word. He didn't and neither did she. After a while my mother took them away from the table. In fact I never spoke to my father ever again. Just brief communications.

MURIEL. And then you left school?

PETER. Yes. I was ashamed. I was so terribly ashamed. I couldn't think of anything else and didn't dare talk to anyone about it. Then they'd tell everybody and then I'd go mad, then I'd put an end to it, if everyone knew it. I've never told anyone about this before.

MURIEL. Except Bart.

PETER. Yes, Bart. But he didn't believe me. He still doesn't
believe me. I did talk to Bart about it. Often in fact. Too often,
he thinks. That's why he didn't want to see me any more.
Because I always started on about it again. Even at my father's
funeral. But I had to talk to someone about it. And I discovered
more and more, after I'd found those magazines. The whole
business. 'Mein Kampf', behind the encyclopedias, records of
German soldiers' songs, the Horst Wessel song in a slip-case
with 'The Blue Danube and other Strauss Waltzes' on it. I
thought, I've never heard those. I look in that slip-case, the
'Horst Wessel Song and Other Soldiers' Songs from the Third
Reich'. Ghastly. And then once, in the Greek lesson, someone
had to translate a sentence, I still remember it exactly, 'The
people who made fun of the Greeks, which was not in their
nature, as they were not so witty'. The teacher looks for his
cigarettes, suddenly asks what I think of that translation. I start
a long story, stuttering, that it depends what relation that people
had to the Greeks, what standpoint the writer occupies, we are
always inclined to take the side of the Greeks, but they were in
a certain sense the occupiers, if you think of Germans in the
place of the Greeks then you could also translate it as 'The
people who played a trick on the Greeks, something that did not
lay in their nature, as they were not underhand'. Teacher looks
up absent-mindedly and asks me to go and get his cigarettes
from the staff room. I think, he's rumbled it. Later it turned out
of course, that he really only wanted his cigarettes, that he even
found it brilliant, what I had said, that it just didn't fit in of
course, because that writer had been a Greek. I didn't go back,
after that Greek lesson, never again. To school. I went home
and told my parents I wanted to leave school. They agreed
straight away. First I spent a year with an aunt and uncle. I was
just fifteen. Tried another school. In Amersfoort. The same
agonies. Then Amsterdam. It took years before I got over the
feeling that I'd actually be better off dead.

MURIEL. And the only person you could talk to about it was Bart.

PETER. Who didn't want to talk about it.

MURIEL. Because he didn't want to know.

PETER. Something like that.

MURIEL. Do you have anything else to drink? The wine's all
gone. I think we should drink something more. I'm glad you've
told me all that, that you trust me. I'm glad about that. You
often get that feeling, that people are carrying all kinds of
secrets around with them, old hurts. Why don't you say anything, I often think, just get it out and don't go sitting there

night after night brooding about it. Or those lads who have a different girlfriend every weekend. Who turf you out when you reach the point where they would have to say something more than – I don't know – I'm feeling randy, or I'm not feeling randy, or I'm hungry or I'm not hungry. But of course they don't have anyone they can unload their secrets on either, like you do.

PETER (*from the kitchen*). I've still got half a bottle of brandy. Without a label. Have you seen by the way that Davidoff sells brandy now as well. Terribly expensive.

MURIEL. Gives people a safe feeling, brand names. That somehow they belong. That they've made it. That they won't slip down into the morass of the bottom thirty per cent. You have to belong somewhere. My parents were the only ones who drank Ricard. Foul. You know, on those ashtrays. And those disgusting goat cheeses brought back from holiday. If I hadn't had a phantom pregnancy, would you have gone to bed with me this evening?

PETER. Maybe I would.

MURIEL. Would you have fucked me up against the wall again, just like that first time in my place, I found that so exciting.

PETER. Just never again against that wall. That wasn't a wall at all. Just a piece of board. It bent right over. It's a wonder we didn't go right through it.

MURIEL. That's good, when a man is in such a hurry, the first time, then the second time he'll do it much more calmly. Do you think I'll pass it, that selection?

PETER. What selection?

MURIEL. Air France. That they'll take me. As a stewardess. I can speak French. Thanks to my parents. When they couldn't manage I had to do the talking. Est-ce-que vous avez deux chambres pour une nuit seulement, une pour mes parents and une pour moi? I hated it when I had to sleep in the same room as them. Bad beds. That sort of third bed in a room is always awful. So when I got the chance I always asked for my own room.

PETER. I never went on holiday with my parents. Never. I never slept in the same room with them. They always went off together. To do the things adults do with one another when there are no children around. I don't think Bart's coming back. What do you think?

MURIEL. No idea. I don't know him. Couldn't he be sitting somewhere getting pissed?

PETER. No. Definitely not. If anything he'll be in bed with some other woman now. Or he's trudging through the whole red light district looking for a whore who'll do it half price. In Rotterdam he sometimes got them for nothing, he told me once, when he said it was his first time. He managed to swing that one for a long time, apparently. So he says. Though he was fifteen the first time. With a certain Doreen. We were at home together one Sunday. My parents had gone to The Hague. Would I like to go for a bike ride. Doreen was coming to visit. She was in the sixth form. Two months from A-levels. The school whore. Went with anybody. Had a relationship with the gym instructor. The boys' one. The girls had a dyke.

MURIEL. So did we. 'Period? What's that.' Yes, I've got my period. 'I don't know what that is. Is that an illness?' No, not really. 'Only girls who are really ill don't have to go to gym lesson. Why don't you come and sit next to me?'

PETER. Sorry, but I really can't cope with that belly. What's in there actually?

MURIEL. How do I know. Air, I assume. It's not dangerous, the doctor says. Awkward, but not dangerous. Apparently it will pass. If I could only figure out why I want to be pregnant. But I don't want to be pregnant at all. Quacks. Why don't you come and sit next to me. Can you really not sit next to me. I just want to be able to lean against someone. Just for a bit. I'm going home in a minute, really. I promise you.

PETER. Yes, if you don't fall asleep again, like last week.

MURIEL. I still don't understand why you didn't simply go to bed then.

PETER. I thought, she'll wake up again in a minute.

MURIEL. It wasn't because you were afraid I'd creep into bed beside you?

PETER. That too.

MURIEL. Do you feel a bit better now?

PETER. Better? Why should I?

MURIEL. Now you've told me all that. About your brother and so on.

PETER. I don't know yet.

MURIEL. And because I rang up that Marianne Goudsmit?

PETER. I hope she really gave Bart hell. He still always thinks he can cadge a penny out of anyone for the roundabouts.

MURIEL. And he still can?

PETER. Yes, always.

MURIEL. I would have emptied my whole purse out for him. He certainly is good looking. I mean, you're nice, terribly nice, but not somebody you'd immediately fall for when you saw him. But you would when you got to know him better. Then certainly. And by now I have got to know you better. Which doesn't exclude the fact that of course it is nothing if once in your life you can go to bed with Sean Connery. I would have liked to have saved something for that. For the roundabouts. God dammit. I can't understand why you had to start on about roundabouts . . .

PETER. Because when Bart took me to the funfair . . .

MURIEL. I suddenly feel really terrible. Is there something wrong with that brandy. Are you sure it's brandy? A moment ago I felt terribly hungry, but now I feel really ill. I'm sorry but (*Staggers off to the bathroom.*) Could you just turn on the light for me? I can't see anything. I can't find it.

PETER *turns on the light.*

Thanks.

PETER *closes the door after her. Vomiting sounds.*

PETER (*sniffs the brandy*). It does smell a bit odd. Or am I just imagining that. (*Takes another sip.*) Doesn't taste funny.

The bell rings.

Jesus Christ. I don't believe it.

MURIEL (*in between sounds of vomiting*). You're more someone to get old with, to have children with . . .

PETER (*at the intercom. In the direction of the bathroom*). What did you say?

MURIEL. To have children . . .

PETER. Who is it?

(BART'S VOICE. Well, who do you think?)

Is that you, Bart? But you were supposed to phone first.

(BART. Yes, who else?)

I don't know, it could have been anybody.

(BART. No, it's me.)

MURIEL *falls down in the bathroom.*

PETER. Jesus, what are you doing back here? Have you passed out?

(BART. Who? Me?)

No, not you, Muriel.

(BART. Is she still there then?)

Yes, what did you think? Muriel? Muriel? Have you fainted?

MURIEL. No, slipped up. On my own puke. It's all over me, dammit. Peter! Do something!

PETER. She slipped up in the bathroom. Felt sick. Threw up.

(BART. Can't you just open the door.)

OK. I'll open it, but are you staying then?

(BART. I've just come back to get my ring and then I'm straight off again.)

Ring? Oh, of course, yes, it's still here. But you'll stay for a bit? Please, Bart. You won't leave again straight away.

(BART. OK. Just a very short time. A few minutes. Otherwise I'll miss the last train.)

There are night trains, aren't there? You said so yourself.

(BART. There are some awful people travelling at night.)

Bart. Please. Bart? Bart?

MURIEL. Peter! Do something! Help me up.

PETER (*goes to the door of the bathroom*). Jesus, Muriel. What are you doing?

MURIEL. I just told you. I slipped up. On my own puke. Yes, and now I've got it all over me. If you can just bring something I can put on, then I'll have a shower and clean it all up here. I can well understand you won't fancy clearing this up.

PETER. No. I'll just go and get something you can put on. (*Goes into the room. Hears the lift door. Picks up the ring. Picks up his glass and swallows the ring with the remainder of the brandy. Opens the door.*)

MURIEL. Peter?

PETER. Yes, I'm just coming. I'm just opening the door for Bart.

BART *enters.*

MURIEL. Bart?

PETER. Didn't you hear the bell just now?

MURIEL. No. Did he say anything about why he's come back now?

BART. No.

MURIEL. Is he up here now?

PETER. You can hear he is.

BART *goes to the door of the bathroom.* PETER *goes into the bedroom to get clean clothes for* MURIEL.

BART. What's happened to you then?

MURIEL. Nothing. I just suddenly felt terribly sick and then I had to throw up.

BART. For no reason at all?

MURIEL. No. Because Peter suddenly started wittering on about roundabouts. Because you always got a penny for the roundabout.

BART. That's true too. From total strangers.

MURIEL. But it can have been because of something else, that we were talking about before then. I've just forgotten what it was. Or simply because I've drunk too much. And have been eating sweets. I can't tolerate them so well at the moment, you know.

BART. I think the baby can only be grateful to you for that.

MURIEL. What baby?

PETER (*comes back with clothes*). She's not pregnant at all. Don't you realize that. It's all hysteria. (*Shouts.*) Hysterical. (*Normal voice again.*) Muriel is an hysteric. Aren't you, Muriel? Muriel wants to be overpowered. She only wants to go to bed with a man against her will. I don't want to go to bed with her that much. And she doesn't want to go to bed with me just casually. She doesn't want to want it. I have to want it. And then I have to impose my will on her.

MURIEL. Do we have to talk about that now? Can't you just leave me in peace for a bit. Both of you. Both. You both find that really pleasant, don't you? How I'm lying here.

PETER. Sitting.

MURIEL. OK. Sitting. In the puke. On the loo. No longer in a state to defend myself against you two. Out for the count. Gone. Go away, dammit. You dirty swine.

PETER (*taken aback, closes the door*). She's drunk.

BART. I can see that.

MURIEL (*from the bathroom*). Not any more. I'm stone cold sober again. (*Turns on the taps.*) And we'll talk about that, matey. Hysteric? You must mean your mother!

BART. She's certainly right there.

PETER. And how was it? With Marianne?

BART. I don't feel like talking about that now. I want to get home. You look after that Muriel for the moment. See she gets home safely. I don't know what it's all about. You could swear she's pregnant.

PETER. But she isn't. It's a phantom pregnancy. Something in her subconscious convinces her body she's pregnant. Do you get it? Though she definitely doesn't want children there's something in her that does want children. Mine. God save us. And I don't want children at all. Not with her. Not with anyone, for that matter. But certainly not with her. Not with her either, I mean. I don't want children. I've never understood it that you did dare to have children.

BART. The first one was an accident.

PETER. But you have abortion clinics and God knows what.

BART. But Em wanted to keep it and I did find her cute. So I felt sort of why not. Her or another one. You have to get married. You can't stay on your own. That's impossible. You have to have something that brings a bit of order and regularity into your life. Responsibilities. Otherwise you never become adult. Just like you. You just don't want to grow up.

PETER. No.

BART. You should try it, I think.

PETER. Why?

BART. Because then you'd start to look at a lot of things differently. At all those things you still cling on to. As excuses. Not to have to make decisions. Just vegetating on. An advertising tout. With your brain. No wonder a woman like Muriel feels attracted to you. She's exactly the same.

PETER. I don't know what you mean.

BART. No.

PETER. What's wrong with you? You've completely changed.

BART. Do you think so?

PETER. What happened there? Did you really go there?

BART. Where?

PETER. To that Marianne's.

BART. Where did you think I was?

PETER. I don't know. In a brothel.

BART. Me? In a brothel?

PETER. Yes.

BART. I haven't been with a whore for years. Years and years. No. That was only when I had just gone to Delft. Because I was still so damned unsure of myself then. All confused.

PETER. So you get confused sometimes too?

BART. What do you think?

PETER. I don't know.

BART. That's not anything special. It's never been that easy.

PETER. What?

BART. I told you I didn't feel like talking about it now.

PETER (*at the bathroom door*). You managing OK, Muriel?

MURIEL (*indistinctly*). Yes, fine. Don't worry about me. Can I take some of your shampoo?

PETER. The whole bottle as far as I'm concerned.

BART (*has gone to sit down*). God, what a fucking awful sight.

PETER. What?

BART. That dog. (*Still under the impression of the sight.*) A car had run over it. Here, right in front of the door. Not just one. Dozens. No one had stopped. I dragged him under a tree at the other side of the road. What was left of him. Then I couldn't get rid of it the whole evening. That sight. Do you have anything to drink . . .

PETER. A glass of brandy. Just a bit left. So you'll stay for a bit.

BART (*looks at his watch*). Just for a bit then.

PETER (*pours him half a glass of brandy*). Till she goes home.

BART. Why?

PETER. I don't want to be left here alone with her. Not now. Not this evening.

BART. Not afraid of her, are you?

PETER. I am now. A bit.

BART. But she's really scared of you. Can't you see that? Don't you realise? She's only got such a big mouth because she's dead scared you'll throw her out.

PETER. Her? Afraid of me? She was once maybe. Not any more.

BART. OK then. Sorry. It was just a shot. OK. You're afraid of her.

PETER. A bit.

BART. I don't understand that. If you run over an animal like that, that you don't even stop, get out to see what you've run over.

PETER. Maybe it was someone who thought it was a pigeon.

BART. A dog? A pigeon? It could have been a kid.

PETER. All the more reason to keep on driving for an awful lot of people, I should think.

BART. Then there'd be somebody now somewhere sitting watching television and in the back of his head the idea he's run over and killed a kid.

PETER. Who knows.

BART. Incredible.

MURIEL (*from the bathroom*). Do you really mean me to put this on?

PETER. What's wrong with it?

MURIEL. Nothing. But don't you have anything old?

PETER. No.

MURIEL. OK.

PETER (*more or less apologising in* BART's *direction*). I don't have any old clothes.

BART. Why not?

PETER. Because I always had to wear your cast-offs, I've become allergic to old clothes. Sometimes I throw them away after a few months. When I get the idea they're worn. Then I have the feeling someone else has worn them and then I just can't bring myself to put them on again.

BART. Because of that dog everything went completely differently from what I'd thought.

PETER. Oh.

BART. It really threw me. Just as though it had been my fault. So when I arrived at Marianne's I just sat and talked.

PETER. Did she say anything?

BART. Now and then. Yes, of course. Why? She said an awful lot. I talked about you too. About my guilt feelings.

PETER. Towards me?

BART. Yes. Towards you. I always did have. That I'd done my level best to protect you. But that I hadn't managed to. That I'd rather you had remained totally unaware. That you'd never known anything. That you'd always stayed my little brother. In your pyjamas, just out of the bath. Do you still remember. Then I used to read to you. Then you snuggled up really close to me. And you smelled so nice. Sometimes I still think of it, when my own kids snuggle up to me like that, at night, in front of the telly. I don't read to them. Em does that. They're not used to that from me. And then I always have to think of you. You had lovely sturdy little legs.

PETER. Oh.

BART. That all came out this evening. And a lot more. I just couldn't stop.

MURIEL (*comes out of the bathroom*). How do I look?

BART. Really nice. You can safely go out on the street like that.

PETER. Would the trousers do up?

MURIEL. No. (*Shows him.*) But they stay up with this belt and then I can pull the sweater down over them. Is there any brandy left?

PETER. Bart's had the last drop.

MURIEL. Oh.

PETER. But you can have a glass of mineral water.

MURIEL. Please. I have such an empty feeling in my stomach. A bit burning.

PETER. No wonder. (*Goes to get the water.*)

MURIEL (*calls after him*). Have you told him?

PETER. What?

MURIEL. That we rang up.

PETER. No. Jesus, Muriel.

MURIEL. Oh, sorry. I didn't say anything.

BART. What do you mean? Who did you ring up?

PETER. No, it's nothing.

MURIEL. Really nothing.

BART. Who did you ring up? Emmy?

PETER (*relieved*). No. Of course not. Why should I?

BART. Who then? (*Pause.*) Marianne. (*Pause.*) To ask if I was coming? Out of curiosity?

PETER. Yes.

BART. When then? (*Pause.*) After I'd left? Because when I was there no one rang.

PETER. Yes.

BART. So why did you pretend to be so surprised when I rang the bell just now?

PETER. Me? Surprised? Just confused. The whole business with Muriel.

MURIEL (*has drunk the whole glass of water*). So, I feel a bit better now. What do you think, boys? Shall we go out somewhere? To Doffer or Van Puffelen?

PETER. Don't you have to work tomorrow?

MURIEL. Yes. Of course. Why? Do you want to get rid of me?

PETER. Of course not.

BART. Yes.

MURIEL. You want to get rid of me?

BART. No. Not me. Peter.

PETER. Me?

BART. Then you don't. Sorry. I'm always getting mixed up with things that aren't my business.

MURIEL. So you think I should push off?

PETER. No. Of course not.

MURIEL. Then why would he say so? He wouldn't have thought that up himself. God, what a wimp you are. A measly little wimp.

BART. If you give me my ring now – where is it, by the way? Where did you put it? Then I'll go and then you can carry on fighting this out with her.

PETER. I have nothing to fight out with her. But what do you think of that idea? Of going out somewhere for a drink?

BART. No way.

PETER. Really not?

MURIEL. Did you think I'd still feel like going anywhere with you for a drink? Then you're mistaken. I've gone right off you. You want me to clear off? Then why don't you just say so?

BART. Just give me my ring, Peter.

MURIEL. Give the man his ring.

PETER. In a second. In a second. Yes. I would rather you went, Muriel. Not because. Nothing about us. But because Bart is here. Because I still have to ask him something.

BART. But I'm going straight back to Leiden, Peter. We can make a date.

PETER. We can do that. But you've missed that last train now anyway.

MURIEL. I get it. I'm going. You'll get these clothes back some time. I'll drop them off at those dear homo neighbours of yours. No, better not, they might infect them. I'll take them to the drunk woman downstairs.

PETER. What with?

MURIEL. With Aids, of course.

PETER. Jesus, Muriel. I really don't find that funny.

MURIEL. Oh no? It isn't either. You're right. It's not funny. But it wasn't meant to be. OK. Clark Gable. I'm going. You'll have your little brother all to yourself. Just try to explain to him. How you've done it. Who knows, some of it might be of use to him.

BART. What?

MURIEL. To become a man. A real man. A decent family man who rats on his wife and is too chicken to own up to it.

BART. I'm not. Not any more. I rang her up. I'm going to talk to her tomorrow. The kids are staying at her parents the whole day so we can talk.

PETER. So?

MURIEL. So that little phone call was worth it, Peter.

PETER. Get out. Now I've had enough. Get out. Go, Muriel. I want you out of here right now.

BART. What did you say to her then?

MURIEL. I . . .

PETER. Get out!

MURIEL. OK. I'm going. Sorry. That was not the intention. I'm sorry.

PETER. Get out.

BART. Shouldn't she have a jacket or something . . .

PETER. For a few hundred yards? In this weather. It's not raining or anything. Just make sure you don't break your neck.

MURIEL. Why should I?

PETER. Because there's a dead kid lying in the road. (*Shuts the door behind her.*) Run over.

BART. A dog. Not a kid. Look, just calm down a bit.

MURIEL (*thumping on the closed door*). What kid?

BART (*shouting*). Not a kid. A dog. That dog that was following me. It was run over right in front of the door here. But now it's lying against a tree on the other side.

MURIEL (*screaming*). What kid?

PETER (*shouting*). Go away. Please go away, Muriel. You must go away.

(A VOICE. What's going on here?)

MURIEL (*calming down*). Nothing. Really nothing. (*Calls.*) I'll get you yet, you swine. Peterkin. Little Peter Pan. I'll get you yet.

The sound of the lift door.

PETER. Thank God. She's gone.

BART. What was that about that phone call, Peter, that you were so shifty about?

PETER. We rang her up. Not just now but just after you'd left.

BART. Why?

Pause.

She didn't say anything about it.

PETER. All the better.

BART. But why did you ring her up?

PETER. Oh, nothing. I shouldn't have done it. But I was so annoyed. It's always the same. Whenever I finally do see you again, alone, you don't want to talk to me. And I can't talk to anybody else about it except you.

BART. OK. Have it your own way. We can talk that out sometime. But not now. Another time. I just want to know what you said to her.

PETER. To who?

BART. Marianne.

PETER. Muriel. Because I asked her to. She just pretended to be Emmy and asked to speak to you.

BART. She didn't say anything about it.

PETER. Sorry. I'm really sorry. Honest.

BART. Stupid. Really stupid. And then you thought, well, what?

PETER. I don't know. That she would slam the door in your face. That she didn't know you were married and that you would come back again. With your tail between your legs.

BART. Christ how childish.

PETER. That you'd come back. And that then we could finally have a talk together.

BART. With that Muriel there.

PETER. I would have sent her home.

BART. You?

PETER. Yes. She wasn't drunk then.

BART. But what about? What was it that it was so necessary to talk about?

PETER. About Dad, of course.

BART. Again?

PETER. That he went wrong in the war and how . . .

BART. He didn't. He was twelve when the war broke out, Peterkin.

PETER. You see. And not Peterkin, Bart. I'm really too old for that.

BART. OK, Peter then. But you really can't be a Nazi when you're twelve.

PETER. But you can at sixteen.

BART. Not yet. You have strange ideas perhaps, wrong ideas. You get fanatical about something you really have no idea about. But after the war he understood bloody well what sort of people they were who'd been throwing dust in his eyes. Really. You can take that from me.

PETER. Why should I?

BART. Because I talked to him about it. Because he came to me after that performance of yours with the magazines you'd found in the attic. Because he asked what he ought to do.

PETER. And what did you say?

BART. That he shouldn't do anything. That he should let you get on with it. That anything he might say would only make you more suspicious. I shouldn't have done that, of course. I should have said to him that he ought to go and talk to you. But as I said, I always tried to protect you. I said I'd talk you out of it. That I'd go and talk to you. But I didn't dare.

PETER. But now you do.

BART. Yes, now I do. But not now. I want to go home. I have to talk to Emmy. Because I've rung her up. She's sitting at home now waiting for me. Next weekend. OK?

PETER. No, no. NOW! Now!

BART. Jesus, Peter. Just think of me for once. Just for once. I don't feel like it now. I've got other things on my mind. I sat talking to Marianne for hours. I cried for the first time since, since, well, I don't know, since I had my wisdom teeth pulled out. And there's a hell of a lot I have to talk to Emmy about. That it can't go on like this. That our marriage isn't a marriage. Never was. Because all that time I kept everything from her.

PETER. About Dad.

BART. That as well. But that's not the most important thing. OK. I don't feel like standing here whingeing on any longer. Just give me my ring and I promise I'll come to Amsterdam next weekend.

PETER. I can't.

BART. Why not? You must have Saturdays off.

PETER. Your ring.

BART. Why not?

PETER. Because I've swallowed it.

BART. You've what?

PETER. I've swallowed it. Eaten it.

BART (*starts off by laughing heartily, then becomes terribly angry*). You've done what? What? Swallowed it? Are you out

of your mind. Ye gods! What kind of a sneaking, underhand . . .
God Almighty! But now I can't. You just make sure I get it
back.

PETER. How can I?

BART. You just make sure I get it back! You just make sure you
get the trots. I don't know. Castor-oil. You go to the chemist's
and get a laxative.

PETER. A chemist's.

BART. Yes, a chemist's, dammit. You bugger. (*Hits him a few
times.*) Bugger. You bloody sod. God almighty. Yes, a
chemist's. And I'm going with you. Come on. Get your coat on.

PETER. Right now?

BART. Yes, right now. Jesus Christ. What possessed you to do
such a thing?

PETER. Because I didn't want you to go home straight away.

BART. You've got your own way. Because I'm not going home
before I get that ring back. But we're not going to sit around
waiting for nature to take its course. Just don't think we are.
Your coat, come on. (*Opens the door.*) Come on then.

*

The same night. PETER *is sitting on the loo, the door to the
bathroom is open.* BART *is sitting in a chair with the newspaper.*

BART. Having any luck?

Pause.

I said, are you having any luck?

PETER. I've just got terrible cramps. Do I really have to stay on
here?

BART. I don't care. As far as I'm concerned you can shit all over
the place. Or take another swig of castor-oil.

PETER. Then I'll have to throw up again. That won't do any good
any more. I'd just puke up those laxative pills again.

BART. And that suppository? Is that still in there?

PETER. I think so, though I can't feel it any more.

BART. That's because it's dissolved now.

PETER (*in the doorway in a bathrobe*). Can I have a bit of the
paper?

BART. Here. (*Gives him a section of the paper.*) Shall I turn the radio on? Who knows, it might help, a bit of distraction. Not holding on to it, are you?

PETER. Leave it off. Just don't turn it on too loud.

BART *turns the radio on.* PETER *goes back into the bathroom.*

OWWWW!

BART. What's up? Is it coming?

PETER. Cramp. Jesus. I'm dying of cramp. No, I don't think so.

BART. If I were you I'd go and sit quietly on the loo. It's not my business, but it seems a pity about the floor.

PETER (*after a pause*). You must listen to this. Have you read this?

BART. What?

PETER. This. (*Reads aloud.*) 'The court of appeal in the French city of Rennes has this week upheld a judgment which had earlier been pronounced by a juvenile court judge in that city, pursuant to which a four-year-old girl was removed from parental custody.' We could have done with a judge like that.

BART. What are you saying?

PETER. Turn the radio down a bit. (*Waits.*)

BART *turns the radio down a little.*

PETER (*reads on*). 'Not an everyday case, not everyday grounds: the parents hold neo-Nazi views which have led them to indoctrinate the child to such an extent that she has become disturbed. In November 1987 a GP had first drawn the attention of the health and social services of Rennes to "the case", in which a little girl was being brought up "according to fascist principles which were putting her upbringing at risk". The local court later ascertained that there was also a question of "deviant sexual education" and the court of appeal has now affirmed that the child's development was being seriously endangered "by the family environment". For example, the girl was forced to burn a doll representing someone of "an impure race".'

BART. You don't mean to say Mum and Dad ever did anything like that?

PETER. Not with that sort of crude means maybe. (*Comes back in his bathrobe.*) But in a much more subtle way, yes. Don't you ever have that, that feeling that you're polluted, right into the farthest corners of your brain, poisoned, as though just like the witch in 'Hansel and Gretel' they fattened us up with all those ghastly ideas and prejudices of theirs, that they stuffed us full of all sorts of impossible nonsense, from blacks who love dancing to Italians who'd rather be lazing around, from the Jews who've got control of the American film industry to the KGB agents who've infiltrated everywhere. And we're not the only ones, Bart. Even at my newspaper you're not safe. It's called positive discrimination there, but it's the same dirty prejudices.

BART. What sort of ideas are you on about, for God's sake, Peter? Stop it. That's all rubbish.

PETER. No, that's not true. Sometimes I have days when I sort of silently monitor my own words to catch myself out again and again at the most impossible nonsense, the unemployed who've got no backbone, that a strong chin has got something to do with willpower, I don't know, someone with black hair is not a real Dutchman but maybe had a Spanish grandmother, and it drives me crazy. Because they are all little seeds, and in an unguarded moment, with my monitor off duty, the same ghastly misconceptions can grow that they fell victim to themselves. Our whole culture is full of them. Everything you see and hear all around you. I don't know anyone who's totally free of it and there's nobody left who notices or is really ashamed of it. The door is standing wide open again, as it were.

BART. For what?

PETER. For such terrible things to happen again as happened during the second world war. That again some sort of people or other will be wiped out and nobody will react.

BART. That happens anyway, every day.

PETER. But I'm sure there are people who are sort of inoculated against it by their parents. Who didn't have a mother who said 'what a lovely little Jewess' or a father who said, 'now that's a genuine Germanic head'.

BART. But they didn't mean anything by it. That's the way they'd grown up. Everyone said things like that when they were little. That doesn't mean . . .

PETER. It does, it does, it's exactly the same. OOWWW.

BART. What's the matter?

PETER. Cramp, cramp, terrible cramp. (*Goes back into the bathroom.*) I think it's happening. At last.

BART (*turns the radio up again*). Close the bathroom door behind you, if you don't mind!

PETER. I can't reach it. You do it. OOWWW!

BART (*closes the bathroom door*). I'll make you a cup of tea. And do you have any dry biscuits around?

PETER *makes indistinct noises.*

BART. OK. I'll have a look for myself. You can consider yourself
lucky if it doesn't get stuck in your appendix. It's your own
stupid fault. Whoever does such a thing. Whoever swallows
somebody else's wedding ring. Emmy couldn't understand it at
all. How am I going to explain all this? I said I'd come back
next weekend.

PETER. But that was only afterwards.

BART. No, before, before you told me.

PETER. No, after I'd swallowed it.

BART. Is it hurting a lot?

PETER. Yes, what do you think, dammit, with all that muck I've
swallowed?

BART. I'm sorry. I didn't mean that to happen. But I was so
angry, at first. Not any more. As far as I'm concerned you can
flush it all away. You can save yourself the bother of
rummaging through it all. I don't need it any more. It's all
nonsense anyway.

PETER. What?

BART. I don't want that ring back at all.

PETER. Couldn't you have decided that a bit earlier?

BART. No. I've only sorted it out now. I mean, my marriage is not
that ring. If that were the case we could just as well split up
right now.

PETER. Don't go away.

BART. No, I'm not going away.

PETER (*in the doorway*). What must I do now then? Do you have
to have it or not?

BART. No. Flush it away. I don't need to have it back. I don't
fancy the idea, to tell the truth.

PETER. Dammit, Bart, couldn't you have decided that earlier . . .

BART. No, I just said.

PETER. So I can just flush it away?

BART. Yes.

PETER. OK. (*Flushes the lavatory.*) Oh no. Again. Again.
OOWWW!

BART (*closes the bathroom door again. Rather worried*). Is there more coming?

PETER. No, yes, Oh, these cramps. It's terrible. It's so painful. OOWWW! Shit, I think it's whatsitsname – dysentery, isn't that what it's called?

BART. Diarrhoea?

PETER. Is that what it's called?

BART. Shall I turn the radio off?

PETER. No, please don't. It's just too embarrassing.

BART. Sorry. Sorry. I really didn't do this on purpose.

PETER, *after he has flushed the lavatory again, goes and sits in a chair.*

BART. Tea's nearly ready.

PETER. I just couldn't.

BART. Just a few sips. To calm your stomach down a bit.

PETER. No, I really couldn't. You have some. OOWW!

BART. Is it still hurting?

PETER. Yes, but it's not quite so bad. Jesus Christ, what a nightmare. And you're just standing there.

BART. Well, what else can I do?

PETER. I don't know. Say something to me. Tell me something. Read something to me.

BART. What?

PETER. I don't know. A fairy story. You always used to read fairy stories to me. What was that one called, the one . . .

BART. The little woman of Stavoren?

PETER. No, that one about the little prince . . .

BART. What little prince?

PETER. I can't remember. OOWWW! I can't think for the moment. You'll have to.

BART. Something about a little prince? What sort of little prince? (*Turns the radio off.*) A real prince?

PETER. Yes, I think so. Look, there, in that bookcase. Right down the bottom, that's where our children's books are.

BART. Have you got them?

PETER. Not all of them. Only the little brown books of Grandma and Grandad, that one about the man who catches birds, do you remember that one? And a few fairy tale books. Andersen. You never asked for them. Yes, right at the bottom.

BART. And the others? Where are they?

PETER. What others?

BART. 'The Living Brooms', for one. I found that sort of thing creepy. And exciting. About those kids who were forced through the chimneys like living brooms. Who were bought in Italy and then all died of TB. And 'Alone in the World'.

PETER. They're all with Mum. Did you think I'd carted all that misery here as well. We only liked those books because we felt just as alone as that little boy in 'Alone in the World'. And I cried at the death of Mr Van der Vlist, that one about the postage stamps, or about the old man in that book, nobody cared about him. It's getting a bit better, I think. No. Jesus. Sorry. (*Goes back to the bathroom.*) Look for that story. About the prince.

BART (*looks through the Tales of Mother Goose*). Was it one of the Mother Goose tales or the Brothers Grimm?

PETER. Mother Goose.

BART (*looks in the contents list*). 'Prince Riket with the crest'?

PETER. It could be that one. OOOWWW!

Immediately after, the sound of the lavatory flushing is heard again. BART *has gone to sit on the sofa with the open book beside him.*

PETER. Have you got it?

BART. I don't know.

PETER. Read it out.

BART. Peter. It wasn't at all the way you think.

PETER (*in the doorway*). What?

BART. That Dad went wrong in the war and all that.

PETER. Yes, according to you, I know. Do we have to go through all that again.

BART. It was quite different. I never spoke to anyone about it. Nobody.

PETER. No.

BART. Only this evening. For the first time. With Marianne.

Because you had started on about it again. And because of that
dog or something or other. I've never dared to talk about it
before to anyone.

PETER. Did you know there was a boy in our school who
committed suicide because of it?

BART. Why?

PETER. Because his parents had gone wrong in the war. Diederik.
Still remember him? He was in the next year down to you.

BART. Diederik ten Holt?

PETER. Yes, that's the one. Everyone knew. And everyone gave
him the cold shoulder. He was always doing really strange
things. To impress. In the middle of winter he swam across the
canal for a guilder. And once at a school party he climbed up
the tower and put a flag or something on the weather vane.
Drunk. He died in a crash. Went into a tree. On his motor bike.
Once he'd cobbled a motor bike together. Without a driving
licence. He was only seventeen. A Harley Davidson. He had
that sort of spiky blond hair. That he pulled out in tufts.

BART. With Mum and Dad it was something else, Peter.
Something much more banal. Sex.

PETER. Sex?

BART. Yes. Sex. A game. Fantasising. When I went downstairs to
ask them to turn the music down a bit, I stood listening for a bit
at the door first. Nosy. I heard Dad saying things to Mum. And
Mum to Dad. Telling stories. At first I couldn't understand
anything, but later I did. That he was a German soldier and that
he was on patrol somewhere in Poland and searching through a
deserted house to see if there were people hidden there, in the
cellar, that he found a Polish girl there, in the coal cellar. That
sort of story. Other things. Much worse. That with a girl like
that, he . . . At first I didn't understand what it was about. But
in the end. And after a time I even went downstairs to listen to
it. Took part, in a way. And I always wanted to protect you
from that. As long as Peter never finds out anything about it,
I thought. That was the only thing. That you weren't to know
anything.

PETER. That's true. I never knew anything about that.

BART. No. Because I. It started when they went to sex counselling
because they couldn't have sex any more. And then they joined
a group. And after that they did wife-swapping and sex week-
ends and I don't know what else. And they talked to people
who said you don't have to be ashamed of your fantasies. That

they were only fantasies. And they tried that. Of course they were ashamed of themselves. Mum most of all. She would never talk to anyone about it. She would firmly deny the whole thing.

PETER. But not Dad?

BART. Not Dad. That time you found the magazines I talked to him about it. The following weekend. He asked me what he ought to do. I said it was better if he let you go on thinking he'd bought them as a boy of fourteen, fifteen.

PETER. But wasn't that true?

BART. No, it wasn't. He'd bought them in Amsterdam, on the Waterlooplein. Because he thought it might help. In fantasizing. But it didn't. So he'd put them up in the attic.

PETER. Why didn't he throw them away?

BART. I don't know. Frightened someone might find them in the dustbin or something.

PETER. He could have burned them.

BART. Where? In the back garden. With all those neighbours mowing lawns day and night? Or in the boiler. Of course he did mean to get rid of them but just never got round to it.

PETER. Why didn't you tell me this before?

BART. I told you. Because I was mixed up in it as well. Without their knowing. Because I was also going around with that sort of image in my head. And because no one dared to talk to anyone about it. And because I was running from one woman to the next because I was always made keen to be doing it. And not just talk about it. And I had the feeling that if I started to talk about it I'd want to do it myself. And I was afraid I wouldn't be able to stop. That it would end in murder and mayhem.

PETER. I can understand that.

BART. Really?

PETER. Yes.

BART. Do you have that too then?

PETER. No. Not to that extent. But what I said just now, about fascist images, that's the same kind of thing. You say something, you don't reflect on what you say, you even believe it yourself. Someone else says it too. You're in agreement on it. You become a member of something, a postage stamp club or something innocent like that, and there you meet even more people who say the same and before you know it . . .

BART. But I'm not afraid of that any more. Since this evening. Since this evening I really know for certain I never want to cause anyone real pain, I mean, not really hurt them. I was talking to Marianne about it. Because it all suddenly looked much less dramatic. Because she reacted so normally to it. And that's why I decided now to talk to Emmy about it. Though I don't find it bad that I've just postponed it now. Emmy . . .

There is a knock at the door.

PETER. Who is it?

(MURIEL'S VOICE. Me.)

PETER. How did you get in?

(MURIEL. When that man from the hunting clothes shop came out. He always leaves at around eight. I knew that. I've been waiting for him.)

PETER. But why?

(MURIEL. Can't I come in?)

PETER. Why? Are you bringing back the clothes? You can do that another time.

(MURIEL. Is Bart still there?)

BART. Yes.

PETER. Yes, he's still here.

(MURIEL. Can't I just come in for a bit? I've got to go to work. Just for a minute.)

PETER (*looks at* BART, *who nods*). Just for a minute then. (*Opens door.*)

MURIEL *enters with large plastic bag.*

PETER. I said the clothes could wait.

MURIEL. It's not the clothes. It's that dog.

PETER. That what?

MURIEL. That dog Bart ran over. (*She takes off her coat. Lays it over a chair. She is wearing her fresh fruit juice dress, she looks ludicrous and terribly pathetic.*)

BART. I didn't run it over. I didn't come by car. Em has it. I came by train.

MURIEL. Oh.

BART. Won't you sit down for a bit? You look as though you could collapse any minute.

MURIEL. That's true. I'm so tired. It's those tranquillisers. They make you so drowsy. But you don't sleep.

PETER. Haven't you been to bed at all. What's the time anyway?

BART. Nearly five o'clock.

PETER. But Muriel. That man from the hunting clothes shop doesn't open up his shop at five in the morning.

MURIEL. But it was him.

PETER. Are you quite sure he went out then?

MURIEL. No. But he let me in, I'm sure about that.

BART. Haven't you got a balcony or anything, Peter. That we can lay the dog out on. Maybe I'm just imagining it, but I keep thinking I can smell him.

PETER (*bursts out laughing*). Here? That dog? Jesus, Bart.

BART *also starts laughing*.

MURIEL (*very seriously*). There were two rats gnawing at it when I came out. I chased them away and then I went home.

PETER. Yes, and then you went out again.

MURIEL. When I got up. To go to work.

PETER. But it's five o'clock, Muriel.

MURIEL. What time?

PETER. Five o'clock. (*Shows her his watch.*) Five o'clock.

MURIEL. Oh, I thought it was much later. Funny, eh? And then I thought, when I got up, first I must bury that dog somewhere. So I got dressed and took some old newspapers and a plastic bag. I had a cat once; my parents just put it out with the rest of the rubbish. It upset me so much. That dog has to be buried. What do you two think?

BART. I'm easy. But does he have to stay here?

MURIEL. If you don't find it too bad?

PETER. I can put him in the freezer in the meantime.

BART. Are you out of your mind?

PETER. But it's empty. And he is in a plastic bag. What sort of dog was it, by the way?

BART. Small. Black and white patches.

MURIEL. With really sad eyes. Real dog's eyes.

PETER. My dear Muriel, every dog has got dog's eyes.

MURIEL. People sometimes too.

PETER. No, they've got human eyes.

MURIEL. But they can look really sad too.

PETER. What's up with you? Look at me.

MURIEL. Nothing. Nothing's up with me. But there is with the dog. He's dead. And he must have a decent burial. And not like now in a parcel of old newspapers. I wasn't thinking when I came out. He's pretty heavy too. I thought, maybe Peter will help me carry him.

PETER. Where to?

MURIEL. I thought near that violinist without a head, that little park on the Marnixstraat. What do you think?

PETER. Have you got a shovel or anything?

MURIEL. No. I haven't got a garden. But in any case he can't be buried in those old newspapers. Haven't you got an old sheet or something.

PETER. I don't have any old things. Nor any old sheets.

MURIEL. Something else? A piece of material or something. I'd love to have buried him in this dress. But I have to keep it for my work.

PETER. I still have a flag. I found it here in the house before they were finished with the partitioning.

BART. Partitioning?

PETER. Yes, before they made apartments here. There had been offices here before. These were the lavatories. Some kind of obscure trading concern, Rekom or something. And they left a torn flag here. There was all sorts of stuff here. Rubbish. Files. And this flag. It's a bit tattered and pretty dirty.

MURIEL. That doesn't matter.

PETER *goes to get the flag from a cupboard in the kitchen.*

BART (*when* PETER *comes back*). Is that it?

It's the Dutch flag.

PETER. Yes.

BART. And you want to bury the dog in that?

PETER. Yes, why not?

MURIEL. What's wrong with that?

BART. In the Dutch flag?

PETER. It was a Dutch dog, wasn't it?

MURIEL. Definitely.

BART. OK. I'm not saying any more.

PETER. Do you find that odd? I won't be using it anyway. I've been meaning to throw it out for a long time. Never got round to it. Do you have a flag at home?

BART. Me? No. No.

PETER. To put out on the Queen's birthday?

BART. No. No, of course not.

PETER. So why shouldn't we bury the dog in it?

BART. I told you, as far as I'm concerned, do what you want. But how are you going to bury him if you don't even have a shovel?

MURIEL. Can't we go and buy one somewhere? Right now, before I go off to work. It's always handy, a shovel, having one.

BART. But when does your work start then?

MURIEL. At nine. I have to be there at a quarter to.

BART. But it's just gone five.

MURIEL. Oh.

BART. There aren't any shops open now.

MURIEL. No.

PETER. You wouldn't wrap him in that flag here, Muriel, would you?

MURIEL. What? No. No. Where we bury him. Are you two going to help me? That's kind. He is a bit heavy, you know. And I have a lot to carry.

BART. Does that weigh anything?

MURIEL. What do you think? It's all juice. (*Yawns.*) God I'm so tired suddenly. And I've just had a sleep. It's so warm in here.

PETER. When, then?

MURIEL. I told you. When I came home. I went to bed straight away of course. And I fell asleep immediately. Till I got up again. To go to work.

PETER. But it's . . .

MURIEL. Five o'clock. You've already said that. I'm not daft. But what can we do now, all that time.

PETER. Bart was just going to read me a fairy story.

BART. But that wasn't serious . . .

PETER. Why not? What's so odd about it? Then we'll go and sit down, Muriel and I. On the sofa. Like this, next to one another, and then you read us 'Prince Riket with the Crest'.

MURIEL. I don't know that one.

PETER. I don't know what it's about any more either. Just read it.

BART. Can't we put that dog in the hall for the time being?

MURIEL. No, I'll keep him with me. (*She puts the plastic bag on her lap.*) If you don't find that too awful?

BART. OK. Do what you want.

BART *starts to read. After a little while* MURIEL *falls asleep, half over the plastic bag.*

BART. There was once a queen who bore a son, so ugly that for a long time people wondered whether he really was human. A fairy who was present at his birth, assured the queen that in spite of his defect he would be extremely attractive, because he was so intelligent; she added that as a result of the gift which she had given him, he would be able to give as much intelligence as he himself possessed to whoever he loved. This was an enormous comfort to the poor queen, who was very unhappy at having brought such a hideous creature into the world. I forgot to say that he had been born with a small tuft on his head, so that people called him Prince Riket with the crest, as Riket was the family name. (*Stops reading.*) Is she asleep?

PETER. What? Yes.

BART. Was this what you wanted?

PETER. What? That Muriel should fall asleep?

BART. No. The fairy story. That you remembered. That I always read to you?

PETER. I don't know. It's a long time ago now.

BART. Yes.

PETER. But did you like doing that, reading to me?

BART. Yes.

PETER. And then I'd come and sit with you?

BART. Yes.

PETER. On your lap?

BART. Yes. After you'd had your bath on Saturday night. Don't you remember any more?

PETER. No. I don't remember anything cosy like that and this sounds very cosy.

BART. Yes.

PETER. I must have felt terribly safe with you.

BART. Yes.

PETER. And with me you never had that sort of fantasies?

BART. What sort of fantasies?

PETER. That you have with sex?

BART. No, of course not. Not with you. I wouldn't have wanted sex with you, would I?

PETER. No.

BART. No. Not that I know.

PETER. What did you think then, when I was sitting on your lap like that?

BART. That I'd like to eat you up. Because you smelled so lovely and had those sturdy little legs.

PETER. Isn't that the same kind of thing?

BART. As what?

PETER. That you wanted to eat me. That's not so easy. Try it.

BART. No thank you. You haven't looked that appetising for a long while. Certainly not now.

PETER. Pity. I wouldn't find it bad at all to be eaten by you, I think.

BART. I'd shit you out again.

PETER. That's true. Read on for a bit.

BART. Seven or eight years later the queen of a neighbouring kingdom gave birth to two daughters. The first-born was more beautiful than the day; the queen was so happy that people were frightened she might die of joy. The same fairy who had been present at the birth of little Riket with the crest was also present here, and to temper the joy of the queen, declared that the little princess would remain particularly stupid, as stupid as she was beautiful. That upset the queen; but a little later she became even sadder because the second daughter was extraordinarily ugly. 'Do not worry too much, Madam,' said the fairy, 'your daughter will be compensated for her defect, and she will be so intelligent that no one will notice how ugly she is.' 'God has so willed it,' said the queen, 'but does no means exist to give some intelligence to the eldest, who is so beautiful?'

PETER. Bart?

BART. Yes.

PETER. You must have really loved me.

BART. Yes.

Pause.

'I can do nothing for her, Madam, where her intelligence is concerned, but I can do something about her beauty; and because there is nothing I wouldn't do to relieve your mind, I shall give her the gift of making anyone she loves beautiful, man or woman.'

And what shall we do with her now?

PETER. We'll lay her down on the sofa, like this. And then we'll wait till she wakes up. And then we'll go and bury the dog. Before it gets light. We'll think of something.

BART. OK.

PETER. And then we'll take you to the station. And then I'll take Muriel home. She can't possibly go to work like this. (*He lays* MURIEL *on the sofa. Turns off a few lamps.*) Carry on reading. (*He lies down on the floor.*)

BART. 'The two princesses grew up, the eldest becoming more and more beautiful and the youngest more and more intelligent. And their defects became more and more striking too. The youngest became daily more ugly and the eldest daily more stupid. The eldest could not put four plates on the mantelpiece without breaking at least one of them and not drink a glass of water without spilling half of it on her clothes. The queen could not avoid letting her read the lesson now and again, after which the poor princess just wanted to die. One day she had fled to the wood to weep alone when she saw a particularly ugly and unattractive man coming towards her, but splendidly attired. It was the young Prince Riket with the crest, who had fallen in love with her after seeing her portrait and had left his father's kingdom . . . '

Are you asleep, Peter? Peter? Are you asleep?

He closes the book and sits with the closed book on his lap.
It slowly gets lighter.

THE STENDHAL SYNDROME
by Frans Strijards

Translated by Della Couling

Frans Strijards was born in Rotterdam in 1952 and made his debut
as an actor at the beginning of the 1970s, then as director and
playwright. By 1974 he had already founded his first company, the
Projekttheater, which lasted until 1982. During this period Strijards
wrote his first plays, under the pseudonym Cees Cromwijck. After
a period working freelance with various companies, he founded his
second company, Art & Pro (Artikelen & Projekten) in 1985,
which he continues to direct today, from the old Mickery theatre
on the Rozengracht. In addition to his own work, which is
invariably premièred there under his direction, he has directed
works by writers as diverse as Pirandello, George Tabori, Peter
Handke and Chekhov.

Strijards has to date written some fifteen plays, and ranks as one of
the foremost contemporary playwrights. Like Feydeau, his work is
based initially on a particular situation, with the characters
bouncing off the basic set-up and at times manifestly out of
control. Like Chekhov, Strijards is a master at depicting how they
also bounce off one another, in a sadly comic inability to
communicate. The resultant mix is all Strijards' own, however, and
his distinctive style is absolutely unmistakable.

In *The Stendhal Syndrome* a funeral party with a difference is in
progress, in the new, still uninhabited home of the widow, Hilde.
Her husband, a rich but irresponsible financier, has committed
suicide. His motive is not clear, but there are strong indications of
stock market speculation. He ordered a festive meal to be served,
with music and dancing, in his memory.

This is the basic setting. What Strijards makes of it, with his usual
elegance and wit, is a complicated dance, the characters, alone or
with others, describing circles that intersect, merge, re-form,
change direction. There is constant, circular movement in which
everyone is doomed to participate. Their arguments are also
circular and self-contained. There is no real contact with reality or
one another. Deftly, Strijards lays bare a society where 'art for
art's sake' leads to a sterile vortex.

The stage directions given in the text are essential. This play is above all an ensemble play. The organisation of exits and entrances has been very carefully worked out. The constant coming and going of the actors must create the impression that 'life' at the side of or behind the stage is permanently going on. On the stage, besides the action of individuals, group movement is also of great importance. This must be directed in a choreographic way and show clear patterns. Movement dynamics must be very accurately worked out but seem natural. This gives the 'dance of the rumour' its shape.

As only one individual fate dominates the set for long periods, the audience must get an idea of the forces at work in a group or community. These forces ultimately give shape to something like a destiny. An inner unrest forces people to keep moving, to meet or avoid one another. Within this fact there is then suddenly a space absurd enough for emotional discharges. During the party scene the party-goers sometimes dart past the doorway on the stairs.

In the staircase a spiral movement is visible which is continued in the more mass movements – the use of the space proceeds from this. The actors must master the art of moving in an extremely natural way very unnaturally and stiltedly in that space. Details and gestures are important and revealing.

It has rightly been noted that the play shows similarities to a certain kind of absurdism. Let us describe it as apparent and simulated realism.

The names of the artists in the monologue can of course be altered.

The action takes place on the day of Hilde's husband's funeral.

Scene of the action is the house the deceased bought Hilde just before his death.

The family has not yet been able to move into this house, and now it is to get a new function.

The Set

A large room with pillars, to the right a curving staircase leading upward, to the left a flight of steps.

Rear right, at an angle, a long table. Otherwise the room is empty.

There are six entrances: two on the left, which lead resp. to the terrace and the entrance hall, four to the right: rear right leads to another, invisible part of the room, where the kitchen is. Under the staircase a second way of reaching this space, halfway up the staircase a door, behind which are private rooms, among them a bedroom, and at the top of the staircase an exit to the second floor.

NB. Words like 'kitchen' are used as technical indication of an area of activity, and by no means always have psychological implications.

Cast

HILDE, *the hostess, wife of the deceased*
HEDDA, *Hilde's sister*
NATASJA, *daughter of the deceased, Hilde's stepdaughter*
SONJA, *photographer, Natasja's friend*
MARTHA, *maid hired for the day*
GABY, *guest*
VICTOR, *son of the former accountant of the deceased, Gaby's
    ex-husband*
ALFRED, *solicitor of both the deceased and the deceased's wife
    Hilde*
JOSEPH, *friend of Natasja*
MAX, *psychiatrist and oldest friend of the deceased*
GEORGE, *old family acquaintance, antiques dealer*
PAUL, *private detective*

ACT I

Darkness. VICTOR *is sitting on the stairs. Enter* PAUL, *from the terrace.*

PAUL. Ceremony over yet?

Enter MARTHA, *from the kitchen, pushing a trolley.*

MARTHA. Ceremony? You're coming?

PAUL. The fact is . . .

VICTOR. . . . and then the sort of parties he organised. Six architects. Three athletes. Four murderers. Two princes. Once he got going his imagination really took off. You have to give him that.

MARTHA. The chairs. I'll have to go and look. There isn't a single one here.

PAUL. Before I can explain why I'm here, I have a question.

MARTHA. No, no. I can't go into that. I'm not in a position at all to . . . (*Exit to entrance hall.*)

VICTOR. A tsarist way of life, you know. One of those people who never worry about things, don't brood about the mortality of the soul, no, just love Italian opera. Regarded himself, quite shamelessly, as the pride of the collection. You would almost call shame a form of lucidity.

PAUL. What's your relationship to the owner of this place?

VICTOR. What do you actually want to know?

Enter MARTHA *from the entrance hall.*

MARTHA. O God, now we're going to get it. Watch out.

Enter HILDE *and* HEDDA *hastily, from the entrance hall.*

HILDE. They'll just have to wait. Exact arrangements have been made. I just need time. Maybe they'll just have to wait, yes.

HILDE *and* HEDDA *go up the stairs.* ALFRED, GABY, GEORGE, MAX, JOSEPH *and* SONJA *enter from the entrance hall, they stop,* NATASJA *enters from the terrace. She is crying.* HILDE *finally disappears completely upstairs.*

HEDDA *waits halfway up.*

GABY. I feel like some music. Or is that not appropriate on this occasion?

MARTHA. Why aren't there any chairs?

The sound of solemn music, for example Mozart's Requiem.

SONJA. Actually I had only wanted to send a card. You've seen the flowers?

MARTHA. Rolls and coffee? Relatives? Friends? Yes?

JOSEPH. Aren't there any chairs here at all?

MARTHA, ALFRED, GEORGE, GABY, SONJA *and* MAX *go through, to the kitchen. Behind the scenes the talk continues, clearly audible.*

MARTHA. I believe that, yes . . . if people can just wait a minute.

ALFRED. He was a style-setter. You have to give him that.

GEORGE. A cultured person ought to know how to handle his wealth.

HILDE *and* HEDDA *appear again meanwhile on the stairs. During their descent emotion again.*

HILDE. Don't say I organised it like that. It's all as though, how can I put it, I have no way to turn. It isn't as though . . . I can see that. It doesn't fit in. Whether I say wait now, or I say nothing. Explain it to me. Please. Is it my fault? Can I help it? What is it? That's what I wanted to ask.

HEDDA. Calm down now. Sssh.

HEDDA *grabs hold of* HILDE, *leads her up the stairs, they go through the door halfway up the stairs.* ALFRED, MAX, GEORGE, GABY *and* SONJA *enter from the kitchen.*

MAX. What he essentially lacked was discipline.

ALFRED. And faith.

GEORGE. I think more than anything he wanted . . .

VICTOR (*to the group of guests*). Yes, just come along. If we can just all go out here now. (*Points to the terrace.*) Is anything wrong?

ALFRED (*to* MAX). OK, what is there still to talk about?

MAX. After death, the slate is wiped clean, don't you think?

VICTOR. Come on. Is everybody here? Now, how about doing it this way.

HEDDA (*appears on the stairs*). Out of the question, just let me explain what's got to happen here.

PAUL (*to* HEDDA). What do you think? What shall I do? It doesn't seem the right time to me. I'll come back. Will you say it is urgent? Would you pass that on?

HEDDA. Just a minute. You are . . . yes, I think I get it. (*Runs back up the stairs, to warn* HILDE.)

JOSEPH (*to the visitors*). May I, shouldn't I introduce myself, by the way?

GABY. Is that necessary?

JOSEPH. But I'm . . .

GABY. I don't find it necessary, you know.

JOSEPH. Shall I just introduce myself?

SONJA. O God! Why? I mean, why?

JOSEPH. No, but . . .

SONJA. No, I said, no!

ALFRED. Ah, I know who you are. Of course, you're the friend of, eh, yes, now I see, listen . . . It looks as though nobody's told you about it.

JOSEPH. What?

ALFRED. A certain degree of discretion, if you get me.

JOSEPH. Ah!

ALFRED. So just drop it, OK? Leave it, you don't have to start asking questions straight away.

JOSEPH. Yes, yes, yes.

HILDE (*calmer, coming from the stairs, with* HEDDA *nearby*). I'm at your disposal. I've just got to settle a few urgent things. Just make yourselves comfortable. Martha here will look after you.

GEORGE. Yes, yes, certainly, yes, of course.

HILDE (*to* PAUL). Then perhaps we can . . .

PAUL. I'm sorry I've got to bother you with this, I know it's a very difficult time for you.

HILDE. Just come with me.

HILDE *and* PAUL *disappear again via the door halfway up the stairs.*

GABY. Perhaps the fine weather won't hold and it will cloud over again. Shall we . . .

ALFRED. Let's do that, let's go outside for a while.

GABY, SONJA *and* MAX *exeunt to terrace.*

HEDDA. Perhaps we can start in the meantime. Look on me as the contact person.

GEORGE. Of course you're the sister of, of . . . (*Gestures in the direction of* HILDE*'s room.*) We know one another . . .

HEDDA. Yes, I am her sister.

ALFRED (*to* GEORGE). Listen, I think we ought to have a little talk about the problems too.

Exit ALFRED *and* GEORGE, *talking, to the terrace.*

HEDDA (*to* VICTOR, *who wants to say something*). And I must request you to leave. There's no special reason for your presence here today. You have no function here, you weren't invited, and you are seen as a symbol of events which are not highly regarded here.

VICTOR. On whose authority are you saying that?

HEDDA. My statement is borne out by higher powers.

VICTOR. There are some things I'd like to discuss.

HEDDA. What is there to discuss?

VICTOR. Soft shoulders, follow the arrows, wet surface! You have to think about that, a hundred muscles in your face so you can talk, that demands care and attention, you shouldn't neglect that.

Enter SONJA, GEORGE *and* MAX *from the terrace.*

SONJA. Tell me, did you all find it an incredible . . . (*She notices that she is interrupting a conversation.*) Oh, sorry.

JOSEPH (*to* VICTOR). Well, maybe you can tell me who they are.

SONJA (*to* HEDDA). Or was it really the way you . . .

HEDDA. Here in the house we've prepared everything well. If anything's needed, you know, Martha's there.

VICTOR (*to* JOSEPH). Those two are a couple of dilettanti who've admired one another all their lives, in the worst sense of the word. They dabble in art because they are victims of a sentimental sort of masochism. You could hardly call them run of the mill. Stunted growth, alcoholism, mongoloid tendency. Worth studying.

GABY *enters from terrace, immediately followed by* ALFRED, *obviously after a discussion.*

GABY. Really, some people just haven't the faintest idea of what's going on inside them.

In the background, MARTHA *pours out coffee.*

ALFRED (*to* MAX *and* GEORGE). Pity that because of the circumstances in recent years not so much has come out about it.

GEORGE. No, it's up to us now.

ALFRED. What do you think of her idea, then?

GEORGE. I'd be more in favour of a festival or a competition.

ALFRED. A forum? Readings? Guests?

GEORGE. We mustn't let ourselves get sat on just because of the circumstances.

ALFRED. Actually I don't find this place suitable at all.

NATASJA (*staggers, suddenly hangs on to something*). Typhus! Cancer!

MARTHA. Don't let it bother you. Just don't try to understand her today.

ALFRED. What's she saying? What does she mean?

VICTOR. This creature is known here under the name of Martha. The idea is that she makes herself indispensable. No further details are known. The one she was talking about, by the way, is the daughter of the house. (*Points.*)

SONJA. Oh, but we know one another, you know.

GABY. That coffee, is that for us now?

MAX. Opinions on that are somewhat divergent. (*Tries to comfort* NATASJA.)

SONJA, GABY, MARTHA, VICTOR, HEDDA *and* JOSEPH *go in the direction of the kitchen. In passing, they each take a cup of coffee.*

ALFRED (*about* MAX). Even in this sort of situation he manages to look like a tourist.

GEORGE. He has what's called a reputation.

ALFRED *and* GEORGE *also go off to the kitchen.*

MAX. Don't stare at me, don't laugh at me. You just have to look disapproving.

Exit MAX *to the kitchen, meanwhile* VICTOR *and* GABY *enter again, drinking coffee.*

VICTOR. That sort of transformation to the cultured lady, how do you manage that?

GABY. It doesn't surprise me at all that you've got your own problems here as well.

Enter SONJA *and* HEDDA, *with coffee.*

HEDDA. And then the whole time those telegrams. Actually I'm indispensable in the business.

SONJA. But didn't you all expect something traditional? Folklore type thing? Men and women separated. I brought my camera on purpose.

Enter MARTHA *with coffee, also* JOSEPH.

HEDDA. Are you crazy? Why should we? Just use your camera.

Enter MAX, *with coffee.*

MARTHA. I hope everything is satisfactory.

JOSEPH. It looks as though they're all expecting an official announcement.

MAX. But do we have the courage to keep to that promise?

MARTHA. Yes, usually you notice that straight away, don't you? If there are problems. Oh well, we're only human and always will be.

NATASJA (*to* SONJA). It's amazing how well she's behaving. She's even starting to enjoy it.

JOSEPH (*to* SONJA). Sorry? Who? Something going on between you two again?

SONJA. What are you on about? What are you driving at? Married couple? Lesbian? (*Enter* ALFRED *and* GEORGE.) You seem to be well informed. Show us. Explain.

JOSEPH. OK. To start with I'll just introduce myself. That's best. I am . . . I don't get it . . . Everyone knows everybody here, I've noticed. Is that right? OK, now I'll keep quiet.

SONJA. That one over there is very vicious. The other one is a bit on the quiet side. Shall I introduce you?

GABY. Different music. That's what we need.

NATASJA *runs to a central point.*

NATASJA. Talking, that was his forte. Could he talk. The way he talked! I don't want to talk for long. Not a speech. Just one word. Just to get it off my chest. Let's not forget one thing, he was a bad man. Hence the relief! I mean it! Relief! That you could let that get on top of you. (*In tears.*) The risk of being caught up and carried along in it. The excesses, the extravagant behaviour. The fear of being seen as an accomplice. Annihilating. The hatred that possessed that man. The merciless rage. The total coldness. The anxiety. The extravagance that marked us. Ruled our lives. Shaped the world. And so a toast. Let us drink to liberation. A glass. A toast.

On MARTHA*'s trolley there is champagne.* NATASJA *has grasped the bottle.* JOSEPH *takes it from her. They all put their empty coffee cups on the trolley.* MAX *now has the bottle, is trying to open it.* MARTHA *takes it from him.*

GABY (*about* NATASJA). Does she mean all that?

JOSEPH. No, she doesn't mean it.

GEORGE. Of course she doesn't mean it.

ALFRED (*about* MAX). You know, his relation to anything consumable is that of a shark to a tin of tuna? Once when he'd had a few, he reached into a bowl of coloured shells and somebody had to point out they were part of the decor.

MARTHA *has opened the bottle.*

MAX. I assume that . . .

HEDDA. Yes, of course, that's what it's there for.

MARTHA. Well, what did I say?

Enter PAUL, *rushing excitedly down the stairs.*

PAUL. Can someone perhaps . . . I just don't know what to do . . . has she . . . is she I mean . . . is she on anything or what?

HEDDA. No, wait. Just hold on. (*Runs up the stairs.*)

ALFRED (*to* PAUL). Can I help you at all?

PAUL. I had to warn her. That there are funny things going on in the background. I know that. That could cause even more unpleasant gossip.

HEDDA (*on the stairs*). A blackmail attempt?

PAUL. It's quite possible someone's got something like that in mind.

HEDDA. But just drop by some other day.

HEDDA *disappears through the door.* VICTOR *meanwhile is talking to* GABY.

VICTOR. In my view you're only safe once you've hit rock bottom.

GABY. That sounds to me like a destructive self-relativisation.

VICTOR. For me it is a concept that at least leaves you with the odd possibility.

SONJA *is talking to* MAX, MARTHA, GEORGE *and* NATASJA.

SONJA. A special way of looking at things? Yes! Voyeurism? No. Or perhaps, now I come to think about it, in that sense . . .

NATASJA *has meanwhile moved over to* JOSEPH.

NATASJA (*to* JOSEPH). Oh, superman, come on, do it to me, oh do it to me. The fact he came to get her. Whether she would go with him. That depended on what he looked like.

Enter HILDE *and* HEDDA, *down the stairs.*

HILDE (*to* HEDDA). Details, for the life of me I can't remember them. Impossible to imagine myself in that situation. It can be that he said if you do it like that it will go wrong and that I then said that he . . . yes, that's the way we seem to have discussed it. There even seem to have been witnesses. Ice-cold memories.

At this moment GABY *puts an ashtray into* ALFRED's *hand.*

ALFRED (*startled*). God, yesterday evening you were a quite different person.

GABY. Make me jealous then. I want you to.

VICTOR (*to* GABY). When I see you, I think just one pill and an optimistic end is possible.

GABY *runs to* GEORGE. *Together they go towards the terrace. They obviously have something to discuss.* PAUL *has gone to* NATASJA.

PAUL (*to* NATASJA). I've spoken to your mother.

NATASJA. To whom?

PAUL. To your mother. I've spoken to your stepmother.

MAX (*to* HILDE). I must say I'd find it lovely to have a good talk again soon at somewhat greater length.

GEORGE (*comes rushing back from his discussion with* GABY. *To* MAX). What do I hear? Is that true? I've just heard such a story here! The things I'm getting to hear now!

HILDE. He was found in his car at the side of the motorway with two deep cuts in his wrist. Far-reaching administrative corruption, they said. He recovered, but stabbed himself in the heart with a knife in the kitchen while he was talking on the phone to his psychiatrist.

NATASJA. But everybody knows that bloody story in this family, don't they? A woman with a guy who's twenty years older than she is. She expects him to be rolling in money. Crazy with greed she pushes it too far. She drives him loony. The guy becomes unpredictable, his whole business, his life's work is up the spout.

HEDDA. That's your story. God knows you've got a sick imagination.

HILDE. Basically, I've been terribly faithful.

NATASJA. Basically? What does that mean? (*Goes towards* HILDE, *who flees up the stairs.*)

HILDE. What I say. Precisely what I say.

NATASJA. Basically you've been terribly faithful!

HILDE *and* NATASJA *disappear through the door halfway up the stairs.* SONJA, MAX *and* GEORGE *have in the confusion meanwhile gone off towards the terrace.*

HEDDA (*to those remaining.* ALFRED, MARTHA, JOSEPH, VICTOR *and* PAUL). It runs in the family. It all goes fine for quite a time. Happiness, success, wealth. And then suddenly, for inexplicable reasons, it all goes rotten. As though everything that could previously have been called sensible was just a whim. Psychology has turned into pathology. It's really odd.

PAUL (*to* HEDDA, *who is following* HILDE *and* NATASJA). What I still wanted to say to her, maybe you can do that for me . . . the fact is . . . I've, and that was through her husband . . . she apparently had suicidal tendences. I had to shadow her, I was employed to do it. I know everything. Notebooks full. What a job. How am I supposed to explain that?

HEDDA *is baffled, exit. Meanwhile* SONJA *and* MAX *have entered from the terrace.* SONJA *is taking photos.*

SONJA. For me this is a sort of anthropology. And whatever comes in front of the lens you take.

JOSEPH (*to* SONJA *and* MAX). But what is this? Is this a clinic? An asylum? Or a health resort? (*He exits via the terrace.*)

MAX. This is a salon. Nineteenth-century. Here people converse. Here we tell stories.

ALFRED (*to* PAUL). What a very weird story. What do you know precisely?

PAUL. Alas, professional secrecy. Ethics of the job.

MAX (*to* SONJA). You know what I'd like? That we could talk in a strictly logical language. A language in which a sentence has only one meaning, in which the information given contains no secrets. A language in which no misunderstanding exists.

GABY (*entering from the terrace*). Misunderstanding? But that's the nicest thing there is.

HILDE *and* HEDDA *appear again on the stairs.*

MAX (*commanding silence*). The lady of the house.

ALFRED. With her sister.

Enter GEORGE *with* JOSEPH *and speaks to* MAX *and* SONJA *who are going towards the terrace.*

GEORGE. I've just heard about a suicide. And that the business went bankrupt. (*To* ALFRED.) Did that business go bankrupt?

Musical cross-fade. background music of jazz.

HILDE (*to* HEDDA). Just you go and sit down.Take deep breaths. Relax . . . Have a cigarette. Dust yourself down. Relax. (*To* JOSEPH, *who is looking for* NATASJA.) What's that on your lip?

HILDE, ALFRED, GABY, PAUL *and* GEORGE *go to the terrace.*

HEDDA (*to* JOSEPH, *in passing*). She was already like that when she was little. Telling her little friends what to wear and how to behave. It always ended in tears, scraps. Real reign of terror. (*Exit to terrace.*)

HILDE (*offstage, on the terrace*). The trips! The trips we've made. That hotel, fantastic.

VICTOR (*the whole time has been standing unobtrusively but attentively listening. To* JOSEPH, *vehemently*). The risks he took, with his business, irresponsible. Just not on, either. But assuming responsibility? Never entered his head. No, no. Sir thought of himself as an artist. He found his way of doing business unconventional. Now I ask you, how unconventional are you if you aren't successful? Oh no, then you're artistic. Works thirty years at a business, then it turns out that from one day to the next he's blown a fuse. (*Produces a notebook from his pocket and waves it.*) You should read it sometime. Bookkeeping dodges with fantastic profits. Wrong investments at the wrong times. (NATASJA *has meanwhile appeared at the top of the stairs.* JOSEPH *goes up to her.* VICTOR *keeps on talking without anyone listening to him.*) Prestigious expansion plans. And coupled with that some iffy manoeuvres on the stockmarket. Just one big dirty swindle.

JOSEPH (*interrupting* VICTOR, *to* NATASJA). We can't save it like that.

NATASJA. You can tell that to other people.

JOSEPH. But I'm falling? Doesn't that sound fantastic? I'm falling. I'm plunging down.

NATASJA. Go on, look for a new toy. Go on!

GEORGE *enters from the terrace, goes to* NATASJA.

JOSEPH. I'm not disappointed, I just have the feeling – I'm giving it all I've got and nobody takes me seriously.

NATASJA (*to* GEORGE). In exchange for one comforting word, really, just one word of comfort, I'd willingly give up the whole battle with that woman and her sister. It's a fight that's been going on for years! That a man can destroy, smash to bits (*Enter* HILDE *from the terrace,* NATASJA *throws herself crying into* GEORGE*'s arms.*) the last remaining scraps of his instinct for self-preservation . . . Then to turn out a villain, a monument of indecency. And then to have to say: Daddy, Daddy – Yes, my dove – Daddy, Daddy, what's this I'm hearing about you? That's no good. (HILDE *wants to take her over from* GEORGE.) Played on by a woman who can admire anything that's appalling. Who in the murk can only see one colour. Says only one word. Evil. Evil. And then to be accused of jealousy. No, no, no, no.

GEORGE. Today you're playing the part of the great survivor.

JOSEPH. The situation. Please.

HILDE. Day after day, every minute, every detail of his personal life was being discussed, analysed, slandered, interpreted, tarnished, rubbished. Who gained anything from it? I? You? She? Slander, smears, insinuations. This man just had to go under. And he knew it. Why, I ask you. Why in that way?

HEDDA *and* ALFRED *are watching from the terrace.* PAUL *is listening somewhere in the background and disappears again.*

HILDE. Property? He's supposed to have had property? And me, I know nothing. I know nothing and they're talking about property? You should go into that, property. And then that rubbish about fraudulent bankruptcy? Bribery? He didn't even declare his travel expenses, he told me. He couldn't avoid risks. He stopped realising he was gambling.

Exit NATASJA, *towards the entrance hall.*

HILDE. How glad I am you've all come. (*To* ALFRED.) Nice that you're here too. I haven't had time yet for a little talk. The situation! So much going on. Emotions. My God, lovely. Lovely that you're all here.

ALFRED. This whole business will be finally wound up any moment now.

HILDE. Over, yes. Then fewer worries for a while.

HEDDA *disappears at a signal from* HILDE *towards the terrace.*

ALFRED. I'm not sure how I should put it, but . . . it's an urgent question . . . How complicated have things turned out?

HILDE. I don't know what you're driving at. Are you hinting at anything?

ALFRED. I find that a rather peculiar individual is going around telling some rather peculiar stories.

SONJA *comes from the terrace to* JOSEPH.

HILDE (*to* ALFRED). Now you just sit down and relax and enjoy yourself.

SONJA (*to* JOSEPH). Tell me, would you like to pose for me in a minute?

JOSEPH. Who? Me?

SONJA. Yes. Of course.

JOSEPH. Very flattered, but . . .

SONJA. I've got something in my head. Something curious.

JOSEPH. Why me exactly?

SONJA. A bathroom, they must have one here?

JOSEPH. A what?

SONJA. I'll sort it out. Just show me the way.

SONJA *goes up the stairs, disappears through the door.* JOSEPH *stops somewhere lower down on the stairs.*

ALFRED (*to* HILDE). Anything bothering you. Need any help?

HILDE. Let's just go and sit somewhere else.

ALFRED. Fine.

HILDE. Tell me, how are things with you?

ALFRED. Actually for me everything has stayed the same.

HILDE. Oh, but, and . . . is that good or ultimately bad?

Enter HEDDA, *takes* HILDE *to one side.* GEORGE *watches.*

HEDDA (*to* HILDE). It looks, dammit, as though they've all come here for a bit of fun, I feel each one of them has come with the most peculiar expectations.

JOSEPH. If that expectation is aroused, that's not so surprising, is it?

HEDDA. What do you think, are we going to keep running around to the end?

HILDE (*to* GEORGE). You know how things were then. He loved it. Open house. Peculiar types. He enjoyed it.

JOSEPH. But I've had enough. I mean it, enough.

HEDDA (*to* JOSEPH). You just have to think, what do you as her lover and a turkey have in common?

JOSEPH. No idea.

HEDDA. Neither will make it to Christmas.

GEORGE (*to* JOSEPH). The question 'why' has long been replaced here by the question 'why not'.

HEDDA (*to* GEORGE). People who have too crazy a look in their eyes, we'll kick out.

Exit HEDDA, GABY *meanwhile is going in* VICTOR's *direction.*

GEORGE (*to* GABY, *about* VICTOR). But tell me, what's it like, seeing him again?

GABY (*suddenly firing up*). Can you keep your innuendoes to yourself? And not try to remind me of the most disastrous mistake of my life?

HILDE (*shivering*). O, death, that seals human destiny.

GEORGE. What?

HILDE. No, sorry. Nothing.

GEORGE. But you're certain to live to a ripe old age?

HILDE. Don't say that. You mustn't say that.

GEORGE. Well, I'd say you're likely to hang on for quite a time.

HILDE (*in sudden panic*). I'd rather you didn't say things like that about me.

GEORGE. Are you superstitious?

HILDE (*fleeing up the stairs*). Knock on wood. No, go on. Knock on wood.

GEORGE. I could almost believe you mean it.

HILDE. I do mean it. Go on, knock on wood. No, not like that. Yes, there. No, there.

HILDE *disappears, while* MARTHA *has watched the foregoing.*

GEORGE (*to* MARTHA). By the way, I'm George.

MARTHA. What?

GEORGE. I'm George.

MARTHA. Fancy that.

Silence.

GEORGE. Isn't it a bore, having to dash about like that?

MARTHA. What?

GEORGE. A bore?

MARTHA. Just fancy that.

GEORGE. What are you doing? Can I help you?

MARTHA. I'm standing here waiting for the first plate to get smashed. (*Exit to terrace.*)

VICTOR. What a madhouse. And what a hassle getting out of it.

GEORGE (*to* VICTOR). You've insulted me. You won't escape your fate.

VICTOR. What do you mean?

GEORGE. No, no. No excuse. It's all up for you, as you'll soon discover.

HILDE *enters with a toy peep-show,*

HILDE (*to* GEORGE). Have a look in here.

Enter MARTHA, *from the entrance hall,* GEORGE *looks into the peep-show.*

MARTHA. Everyone having fun?

VICTOR. Yes. No. Yes, we are, we are.

MARTHA. Because that's what's been paid for here. (*Exit to kitchen.*)

GEORGE. What is this?

HILDE. What can you see?

GEORGE. A stage set. No, an interior. No, a room. This house, I can see. Where we are now. It's amazingly similar anyway.

HILDE. I made this peep-show when I was six. I wanted to live in a place like that. My castle. Realising your fantasies, that's what it's all about.

GEORGE. Really! Incredible.

HILDE *goes with the peep-show to the terrace, where a group forms.* HILDE, ALFRED *and* MAX.

VICTOR. Just look on me as a critical intimidating authority.

GABY, HEDDA, GEORGE *and* JOSEPH *form another group.*

HEDDA. He just managed to buy it for her. She really had luck there.

Enter HILDE, ALFRED *and* MAX *from the terrace.* ALFRED *and* MAX *watch, while* HILDE *points around.*

HILDE. I was so set on it. I knew it was empty. Styled emptiness. Ideal for me, I said. For my plans. 'Do', he said. 'I'll help. I'll pay.' Ages old. A monument. And then the renovating I have in mind, just imagine – realising a dream. A fantasy. Enforcing your will. Realising the impossible.

ALFRED, GABY *and* MAX *listen, while the two groups try to join up.*

VICTOR (*to* JOSEPH). The position of my father was what you might call a confidential one, in that firm. I have the impression they were even good friends. The fact it ended like that with that firm, hurt him. Not an easy-going man, my father, and a fanatical diary-writer.

PAUL *appears during this speech from the entrance hall, as though he has been waiting for it.*

JOSEPH. God, how do such rumours come about.

HILDE (*to* HEDDA, *about* PAUL). Oh God, just look at that man. Is he still here?

HEDDA. Just wait, I'll see him off!

HILDE *walks round with* GABY, MAX, ALFRED *and* GEORGE *via the terrace. They appear shortly after in the entrance hall, when* HILDE *gives them a quick guided tour.*

PAUL (*to* HEDDA). Of course it all gradually got a bit difficult. What do you expect? Of course it did. A weird experience, believe you me. If I wanted to keep an eye on the target.

HEDDA. The what?

PAUL. An eye on the target. I mean with all due affection. With all due affection, it turned into a total obsession. A compulsion. As though we had spent months together.

Synchronized events. The guided tour round the house has begun.

HILDE. The original purpose? I think it was a dance-hall. Although it was a cinema for a time too. Auction rooms. Restaurant. And prostitution of course. And God knows what else. And art went on here too. I think there was something different every five years. Traces and remains everywhere. Imagine, you're an archaeologist here of your own times.

HILDE *walks up the stairs with* MAX, ALFRED, GABY *and* GEORGE, *they disappear through the door.* JOSEPH *remains listening to* PAUL.

PAUL (*to* HEDDA). You feel with it all, you become part of it. And then suddenly, inevitably of course, you wake up. You have to wake up. You see it as a job, at first. And the rest is quiet reflection.

JOSEPH. Watch out, there's a fool around who wants to swindle the firm. Watch out.

PAUL (*to* JOSEPH). The double catastrophe of too much, mate. (*To* HEDDA.) Ears this size, and then hearing everything. Then you're doubly handicapped, as my mother would say.

MARTHA (*goes from the kitchen to the terrace*). In my country, on holidays, court dwarfs performed. And dromedaries.

GEORGE *appears again.* PAUL *becomes furious.*

PAUL. So no notice at all is taken of me? I don't exist?

GEORGE (*to* JOSEPH). No, it's really too ridiculous staying around here after everything I've just heard.

HILDE, ALFRED *and* MAX *enter, at the top of the stairs.*

HILDE. Fine, talk if you must. As far as I'm concerned you can talk as much as you like. Just gossip on about anything you want. Gossip. I can't avoid it. And I don't want to take this load on. So just keep going. I'll take it on the chin.

PAUL. But I swear I'm not trying to trip you up.

HILDE. I've understood perfectly well what you're saying.

PAUL. There is someone here who –

HILDE. Who is trying to trying to cause trouble. I know him.

VICTOR (*to* HILDE). Listen, just wait a minute.

NATASJA (*enters from terrace. To* HILDE). Just listen. let's stop getting on one another's nerves. Maybe you are right in a few things.

HILDE. Then be my guest and stay.

NATASJA. Yes, yes, good, I'll try.

HILDE. Let's put a stop to it all. Maybe we can do that. Together. So let's do it.

GABY *comes down the stairs smirking.*

GABY (*to* JOSEPH). Would you just like to hop into the bathtub.

JOSEPH. What?

GABY. For the photo.

JOSEPH. I just can't believe this. (*Goes upstairs.*)

VICTOR (*exploding*). Now I'm convinced I – yes, God Almighty! Of course, my good intentions . . .

GABY (*about* VICTOR). What's got into him? What's he up to?

HEDDA. What's the matter with you?

VICTOR. Unfortunately I find I have to leave.

Enter MARTHA *from the terrace.*

MARTHA. Where are you thinking of sitting?

HILDE *points to the table, which will then be laid by* MARTHA. VICTOR *carries on talking, the others walk around him.*

VICTOR. In a few words. there's going to be an almighty flood of publicity, as soon as certain facts become known. They will unavoidably become known, if an inquiry is set up. The rumours going around are so persistent, and the way people are acting here is so obvious . . . What you are up to, everything! Everything that's being so cheerfully discussed now. Everything that's being planned in his name or allegedly in his memory, it will be wiped out if public opinion is mobilised. And it will be mobilised.

HILDE. Unless . . .

VICTOR. I don't know if there is an 'unless'.

HEDDA. Don't get me wrong, but how do you know that?

GABY. I just can't follow any of this.

ALFRED. What do you mean now exactly?

VICTOR. I mean that it would be better for you to reveal the facts on your own initiative than to plan something in all innocence which might attract attention in the wrong way.

HILDE. I know there are rumours going around. But there haven't been any grounds for a trial, let alone a judgment. And as you know, in a civilised country –

VICTOR. Public opinion passes judgment in its own way.

HILDE. You must be speaking from special experience.

VICTOR. I would be glad to be at your service in these circumstances with some sensible advice.

HILDE. Must that be right now? On a day like this?

ALFRED. I think the sensible thing would be for you to just explain to me precisely what you are driving at with those insinuations.

PAUL *is seized with panic.*

PAUL. Heh! Look at me! Just take a look at me! Just look at me! I can't help it! I've had it!

PAUL *stuffs a handkerchief in his mouth and goes off.* HEDDA *looks into the wings and sees him throwing up out of nervousness. Although the suggestion is given that the discussions are taking place off-stage, this need only be shown to a minor degree. Nor is the intention that other sounds in the wings should be disturbing.* ALFRED *goes to* PAUL.

HEDDA. Yes! Wow! God Almighty. Jesus! What's going on now? Just take a look at that. Not that as well. Yes! Wow! O God, at home we had such good taste. We played the recorder, and people came, I had, we got a lot of people, artists and . . . and . . . and . . .

HILDE (*to* MAX). My palais de dance. Do you like it?

MAX. Oh, you're certain to be the radiant centre of attention here. (*To* GABY.) Of the most wildly active couturiers.

Enter ALFRED *from the terrace.*

ALFRED (*to* HILDE). Appalling.

GABY. What?

ALFRED. Well, just appalling.

MARTHA *lays the table.*

HEDDA. That's why fashion became a form of art for me. Of course, you can only resist chaos with quality. Against chaos . . .

HILDE (*as a kind of little speech*). I wonder whether it is – I think it is how he would have wanted it. In his mind, you see?

NATASJA. If he could hear you.

HILDE. Who are you talking about? Oh! Your father? Ah, child.

NATASJA. Would you all go and take your seats please? Silence. Everybody ready? Is anybody there somewhere? Papa, are you there?

GEORGE *tries to interrupt her, she signals to him to remain silent.*

Quiet. Let's try again. Is anyone there? Tell us, who is trying to make contact? Who is it? Who are you? Give us your name.

HILDE (NATASJA *has disappeared on to the terrace.* HILDE *calls after her*). You're crazy! And I'm going the same way.

JOSEPH *appears at the top of the stairs with dripping wet hair and a towel.*

HEDDA (*calls after* NATASJA). How about it if you just try to be kind, for once.

MAX (*reciting*). 'Der Tod, die Menschheit und die Ewigkeit. Ein dreifaches Grausen, das betet um unsterbliches Leben und dies findet in den Gruften der Kunst.' That you can be so bowled over by the beauties of Italian art that you have to be admitted to hospital. That's what I call the Stendhal syndrome.

GEORGE. Pardon? Would you just repeat that?

MAX *and* GEORGE *go out on to the terrace.*

HEDDA (*to* HILDE). That scares me, really. I can't help it.

GABY (*to* VICTOR). What are you looking so miserable about? How do you find it?

VICTOR. The portents were all bad.

GABY. Is that an answer? Do you call that an answer? I thought you'd studied the philosophy of language.

VICTOR. I did, dammit. I did.

GABY. And they didn't teach you you don't have to shout?

VICTOR. Just leave me in peace.

GABY. No, why? I love you, don't I? Why don't you say honestly that you haven't studied the philosophy of language at all?

VICTOR. I didn't finish, dammit. Didn't finish.

GABY *drinks champagne.*

GABY. This tastes of anthropoid.

VICTOR. Anthropoid?

GABY. You taste like that sometimes too.

VICTOR. Oh God.

GABY. Yeah. Really.

VICTOR *gives a strange scream, while* NATASJA *appears from the terrace, looking for* SONJA, *who is now standing at the top of the stairs next to* JOSEPH.

HEDDA (*to* NATASJA). I know what has been said about you. You don't have yourself under control. I know that you don't know what you're doing. I'm scared of you. Does that give you a special feeling?

NATASJA *flees up the stairs.*

GABY (*to* VICTOR). God, can you imagine how I feel?

VICTOR. Then don't drink. Go away then.

SONJA *leads* NATASJA *through the door, comes back furious.* HILDE *goes terrified to* MAX.

SONJA (*to* HEDDA). Don't you go anywhere near her again, do you hear?

HEDDA. What do you mean?

SONJA. I don't have an answer for everything. Being with her has cost me sleepless nights. As soon as anyone at all reacts badly, she does too. There is a real danger of accidents happening, don't you realise that?

SONJA *goes off after* NATASJA.

HILDE (*to* MAX). I am so grateful to you for your farewell words at the burial.

MAX. They weren't the right words.

HILDE. But at least it was something.

HEDDA (*to* JOSEPH). You aren't keeping to the agreements. You're just going your own way, aren't you? What are you up to now?

JOSEPH. I just came here after the burial . . .

HEDDA. We had agreed that with her you would specially . . .

JOSEPH. Oh no we didn't. I wasn't told anything about that. Nobody ever told me what was happening.

HILDE (*about* MAX). This man and his fabulous knowledge. The knowledge of that man, you should get to know him. Do you all know his reputation as an art expert?

MAX. A hopeless case. With regard to art I'm a hopeless case.

HILDE. As a child art said nothing to me. I couldn't make contact with it at all.

MAX (*to* JOSEPH). You know it perhaps. My book. About the Stendhal syndrome.

JOSEPH (*to* HILDE). Wasn't that something to do with people who are so affected by art they have to have medical treatment?

HILDE (*in general*). Once in Rome my husband and I were having lunch with the great Manzoni. He offered to sign us. My husband had his shoes signed. I wasn't so clever and got a signature on my forehead. I felt myself turned into a work of art on the spot, didn't dare to wash for years. And you can still faintly see it.

MAX. Art-lovers perhaps by definition need psychiatric help. But anyway, I think we should slowly get on to the next item on the agenda.

JOSEPH. How about that, item on the agenda. There is an agenda, I take it? Is anything expected from me?

HEDDA. You should know that yourself. Why else are you here?

JOSEPH. I know nothing at all about the whole business.

MAX *taps a glass. People gather round to listen.* NATASJA *appears above.* SONJA *follows.*

MAX. May I have your attention? (*Music stops.*) We have just taken the decision to read a statement. This statement is, we feel, appropriate, in view of the recent course of events. I have been asked, as the oldest friend, to read this statement. As you know, I am also involved in the proceedings concerning the inheritance.

HILDE (*goes to stand next to* MAX). I had hoped that if I were to grit my teeth and face up to it, all the rumours would stop.

MAX. We think it better to let everyone know what's going on.

NATASJA *goes to stand with the others,* SONJA *follows.*

SONJA. Oh dear, here we go again.

VICTOR. But I would just like to ask one thing . . .

Hissing.

ALFRED. First let's just . . .

GEORGE. Listen!

MAX. Imagine, early in the morning last Thursday one of our dearest friends puts an end to his life. So far no satisfactory explanation of the motive seems to have been found. That we are dealing here with a controversial personality, is clear to us all. Investigations have been made extremely difficult because all clues have been carefully erased. Removed. Papers burned. We suspect, by himself. What is undeniable is, that strange things have happened in recent years. The evidence is contradictory at present. There are strong indications pointing in the direction, as is known, of . . .

HEDDA (*interrupting*). Stock exchange specula . . .

MAX. Stock exchange speculations. Other evidence is still inconclusive. There are a number of matters we want to have investigated by the police, but prosecution on the basis of any criminal offences has been made redundant by circumstances. So we can do nothing but keep the picture before us, call it up, of the man as we thought we knew him, and forget his wretched years. Let us think about the future.

HILDE. Now you have the chance to ask questions. On the other hand, you will have to be satisfied with my answers, and have to accept that no adequate version of the truth is available.

MARTHA (*to* HILDE, *softly*). I'm ready.

MAX. I suggest that, also in view of the time, we leave this point for the moment . . .

MARTHA (*louder*). It's almost ready.

MAX. . . . and that we keep as carefully as possible to our agenda.

HILDE. Then shall I –

MAX. Get on with it then.

HILDE (*goes up the stairs*). He really knew what hospitality was! He saw to everything. Composed the menu, wrote the programme, ordered the decorations. (*Goes right to the top.*)

MAX. Baffling and typical.

JOSEPH. Unbelievable. What are we supposed to do?

VICTOR. What do you mean by 'there is no adequate version of the truth available'? What does that mean?

SONJA. Can't we stop this? I really don't need all the details.

NATASJA *disappears suddenly through the exit under the stairs,* MARTHA *continues laying the table.*

VICTOR. Strange.

GEORGE. You know the truth is a matter for naive people.

VICTOR. In that case we shouldn't stop the stories for the time being.

GEORGE. Young man, the art of narration cannot be encouraged enough.

VICTOR. What is this performance supposed to convince me of? Is this really all prepared? Agenda? What sort of agenda?

GEORGE (*going up the stairs*). Tradition, forms, discussions, style.

GABY (*teasing* VICTOR). When he started at kindergarten, four years old, he wore a policeman's cap. A little notepad in his hand. Every time he didn't like something, he tore out a page and handed out a summons. He even booked Santa Claus. And he hasn't changed much.

VICTOR. Of course cynicism is not an intellectual attitude, it is a question of temperament. I don't define anything, I don't understand anything, I distrust every judgment, I investigate.

PAUL. The art of narration, that's it, I'm a great admirer of that. Stories, yes, I know a few of those.

GEORGE (*before exiting through the door*). Another time I'd be more than happy to listen to you the whole afternoon.

ALFRED. If everyone would just smarten up a bit, take time to get themselves together and ready, then we can all gather round again.

MAX (*to* VICTOR *and* PAUL). And may I then request you – the part that's starting now I'd like us to go through as a small circle. You will I presume understand why. You will allow us our privacy from now on.

VICTOR (*to* PAUL). Those stories of yours, I'm really interested in them.

Exeunt VICTOR *and* PAUL *to the terrace.*

HEDDA. Do you think that was sensible? Don't you think the two of them together . . .

MAX. Could do damage? (*Follows* VICTOR *and* PAUL)

ALFRED (*about* VICTOR *and* PAUL). We have no other choice.

Enter GEORGE, *at the top of the stairs.*

JOSEPH. To summarise again for latecomers, do I understand that a meal is now being served?

GEORGE *stops halfway down the stairs, with a brightly coloured tie, with which he waves to* JOSEPH.

GEORGE. A banquet. That's what he wanted. His express wish. Agreed on ages ago.

JOSEPH *goes to* GEORGE, *they disappear upstairs.*

HEDDA. What's happening here –

ALFRED. What?

HEDDA. I don't know. Strange. Hectic. I don't know where I am. This uncertainty. As though any moment something unexpected –

Enter MAX, *from the terrace.*

MAX (*to* ALFRED). I think we just have to have a little chat about it. We've simply got to ask them point blank.

MAX *and* ALFRED *discuss it.*

HEDDA. That's what I mean. Well, anything wrong?

MAX. No, nothing. Just a minute.

HEDDA. Nothing, You don't have to tell me anything, you know. I don't count.

HILDE *appears in a long robe on the stairs.*

HILDE (*to* HEDDA). Listen, haven't you changed yet?

MAX (*to* HILDE). There's a tiny problem.

ALFRED. I'd go further, there is a problem.

HILDE, MAX *and* ALFRED *disappear talking up the stairs.*

HEDDA (*puzzled*). 'Haven't you changed yet?' No, I I changed yet. (*Suddenly sobbing.*) No! No! No!

HEDDA *climbs the stairs and goes to listen at the top.* NATASJA *appears, from under the stairs, SC been sitting waiting somewhere the whole time.*

SONJA. Just tell me. What are we doing?

NATASJA. What do you want to do?

SONJA. No, you tell me.

NATASJA. But I'd like you to tell me.

SONJA. You're behaving like a –

NATASJA. I have a few things to sort out here.

SONJA. Good, then I'll have to amuse myself some other way.

NATASJA. Bitch.

SONJA. But I'm a nice girl.

NATASJA. I've got to face up to a boringly normal conflict, haven't I? Banal, yes, yes. (*Looking for help.*) And no, I haven't got over it yet, no. It gets to me, what's happening here. No, I can't be neutral. I'm sorry. I'm sorry if I'm disappointing you. If you had expected something different, then I'm sorry. I don't want to disappoint you. I'm not doing it on purpose, you know. Please listen, you're torturing me. You're trying to – I can – I want –

MARTHA *stops laying the table, wants to say something.*

NATASJA. I'm just what I am, you know. That's all. So why? Why so hard on me? So hard, so – I know what you think, how you see it. Disappointment. I disappoint. No, I must – Oh, no. Yet I must – Where are you going? Don't go away. You mustn't. (*Flops down.*) You've got to stay with me. You mustn't –

SONJA. Spontaneous? Spontaneous feelings? Don't make me laugh. It's something you've picked up. You heap of misery. Shall I act it for you? I can act it for you right now, you know.

JOSEPH *appears from under the stairs.*

MARTHA (*to* JOSEPH). She's a bit –

PAUL *and* VICTOR *enter from the terrace, and watch.*

JOSEPH. Yes, well, yes, in my view, I get the feeling – I'm gradually getting pissed off with it, flaming mad. What is this? A nut farm, I knew it. (*To* HEDDA.) What are you looking at?

Me, furious? You bet I am. Dammit, God dammit what's been going on here again?

While MARTHA, SONJA *and* NATASJA *go off towards the entrance hall,* PAUL *and* VICTOR *move downstage.*

PAUL (*to* VICTOR). Did you see that? Did you notice that? Finally a reaction. You can bet on it, he saw through her. She doesn't think so. She was too young for him. Too young. He, that wily old man. And full of mistrust. Steeped in suspicion. That's why I had to follow her. Everywhere, in the car. Gruesome. It wasn't driving it was . . . mayhem. Now I get like that very quickly, scared, I mean. When I was still with the police. Vertigo, that's why I had to get out. Well, that old man, her husband, comes up with an incredible story, about superstition.

ALFRED *and* HILDE *enter, at the top of the stairs.*

PAUL. Her superstition. Yes! That's a well-kept secret, but it seems she's as superstitious as hell. Interested in higher things.

VICTOR. And so?

ALFRED. Tell me, matey, have you finished?

PAUL. What?

ALFRED. Have you finished?

PAUL. Oh well, there you go.

ALFRED. Stop it. Shut up. That's enough.

PAUL (*goes to* VICTOR). Whether that man saw through her. It made me sit up. Says to me. 'Contact an expert on card and palm reading and stick a brochure in her letterbox. You'll be surprised!' I did, and bingo, off she goes. Then I arranged it with that palm and card reading merchant. 'Predict such and such and tell her such and such!'

HEDDA. Tell me, what is this?

PAUL. Really amazing. 'Don't use the car tomorrow, danger.' And she really does use the bike. 'Don't do any shopping this week.' In the evenings she drives to Toni's takeaway. Suggestion. Influence.

HILDE (*on the stairs*). Can he just sit there telling all that? In cold blood. That must be some kind of game. Have I been played with like that?

ALFRED. He knows that you . . . He knows about some brochures.

PAUL. I know more.

HILDE. What am I supposed to do? What am I supposed to do about it? What must I do?

Exit HILDE, *in the direction of the kitchen,* GABY *appears at the top of the stairs,* HEDDA *goes up to* VICTOR.

HEDDA (*to* VICTOR). Your single-mindedness in the way you attack him sometimes really doesn't smack of conviction. You don't seem so sure of yourself. You won't accept that there are mistakes involved here. You keep dragging in irrelevant incidents. Your greatest weakness is you won't recognise his positive achievements. (*Follows* HILDE.)

VICTOR. If I don't say anything, it's not because I don't have anything to say.

GABY (*to* VICTOR). I want to tell you something. I'm ending it. It's over. Finished. Empty. I've had it.

While GABY *goes off to the terrace,* JOSEPH *enters, from under the stairs, and goes upstairs. In passing, to* GABY:

JOSEPH. It seems like a game, until you lose.

VICTOR (*gestures towards* GABY). She never changes. I'm still stumbling over the printing errors in the first edition.

HILDE *appears in the background, from the kitchen.* HEDDA *follows her.*

HEDDA. I really don't know what I'm hearing. But I am hearing it.

VICTOR (*to* PAUL). Why?

PAUL. Why? Exactly. I understand that question. I've been asking it myself the whole time.

HEDDA. I've suddenly got it all. Suddenly everything's fallen into place.

HILDE. She is abusing it. She has an account to settle.

HEDDA. Shouldn't we have a bit of a talk. Don't you think?

HILDE. No. Not now. Certainly not.

HEDDA. Oh no? Tell me, those little bits of advice you've been given now and then, may I know how extensive they were? Well? And how long you've been getting advice from the stars? How could I be so daft! All the absurdities I never understood! And I thought there was something sly behind it. How could I let myself be taken in time and again by moodiness, unpredictable behaviour, inexplicable reasons, unforeseeable results.

That arrogant conviction, what's it based on, I kept thinking.
And now it seems you're not actually responsible for your own
actions with your cosmic contacts. I shall have you certified.

HILDE. I knew you were going to say that.

HEDDA. Yes, that you can predict the future doesn't surprise me
at all.

HILDE. Must it be like this? Must that battle be fought out again
here? Haven't you any tact, any feeling? Nothing idiotic ever
happened. Everything I wanted happened the way I wanted it to
happen. What does it matter what reasons there were behind it?
What drove me! What inspired me! I know I've always been
very capable, and nobody has ever treated me as an imbecile.

HEDDA. But admit it. No, listen, don't admit it. You were caught
out. He fooled you. Your own husband! Having you followed!
Manipulated!

HILDE. I'm not talking any more. It's pointless talking like this.

HEDDA (*to* PAUL). Just tell it all to her again.

HILDE. No way. I'll start hitting somebody. Do you want me to
start hitting people?

HEDDA. That man. Ye gods, what a story. It doesn't surprise me
at all. (*To* PAUL.) That contact between you, how far did it go
actually?

HILDE. I'm going to hit out. I'm going to start hitting out, I warn
you.

HEDDA. The things that have still to come to light . . . We know.
Nothing surprises me any more. He behaved like a lunatic in
the last years. Driving the firm into bankruptcy. Forged stock
exchange quotations, incriminating facts.

ALFRED. I suggest that we continue to treat one another with a
minimum of respect. Anyone who can't manage to do that . . .

HILDE. If she would just keep her mouth shut.

HEDDA. Yes, this discussion is pointless. But I do have my own
power of judgment, as it happens!! (*Goes to the table, which
has meanwhile been laid, and sits down.*)

HILDE (*to* ALFRED). But what precisely is he supposed to have
known? What information did he have?

ALFRED. That we – (*Soundlessly.*) had an affair. (*Aloud.*) Yes, of
course.

HILDE. That man must have hated me.

ALFRED. But it's all in the past now.

HILDE. Yes, but there's the question. Who else knew all about it? And what has been said about it. And oh, and oh –

Enter GABY *from the terrace.*

GABY. I was looking for –

ALFRED. Yes?

GABY. You.

VICTOR. Some people's problem is they just can't escape their good luck.

Enter NATASJA *from the entrance hall, as though she has been standing there listening for some time.*

NATASJA (*to* HILDE). I understand how you feel. Do you understand that? Yes? Just think. I understand it.

HILDE. I don't know how I –

SONJA *is watching in the background.*

NATASJA. No?

HILDE. I really don't know how –

NATASJA. Good. OK then. That's fine.

NATASJA *goes off, while* MAX *appears at the top of the stairs in evening dress.*

SONJA (*to* HILDE). Watch out, she's difficult to pin down. I warn you, she bears grudges. (*Follows* NATASJA.)

HILDE. I'm totally dependent on her co-operation.

MARTHA *comes up to* HILDE.

MARTHA. Can I – Shall I – Must I –

HILDE. Yes.

Enter SONJA *and* NATASJA *from the kitchen,* NATASJA *goes to sit down at the table.* SONJA *and* MARTHA *put a screen round the table.*

ALFRED. Shouldn't we . . .

HILDE. No.

MAX. That seems to me the only correct solution.

HILDE. Yes. Let's not keep harping on. All that trouble. All these preparations. Everyone knows the real point of it all. Go and sit at the table everybody.

Music. GABY, MAX *and* SONJA *go and sit down at the table with* HEDDA *and* NATASJA.

MAX. That's turned out just right. I'm rather hungry by now.

GABY. It looks really lovely.

VICTOR *and* PAUL *watch the scene. During the following discussion* ALFRED *goes back and forth between the table and* VICTOR *and* PAUL. *He wants to have a serious word with them, but at the same time is concerned with the table discussion.*

MAX. You know, for him eating was part of the art of seduction.

NATASJA. At that time one party followed another.

MAX (*to* ALFRED). Yes, there was one party. Do you remember –

Excited, confused.

ALFRED. Yes, when he turned up in that tanker.

MAX. Exactly. Full, he said it was.

ALFRED. Full, he said. Yes, that was it.

GABY. Full. Really?

MAX. Honestly. And at that moment –

ALFRED. At that moment –

MAX. No, wait a minute. Now what exactly did happen?

ALFRED. No, look. It was after he had won with that hockey team.

MAX. Was that the same time as that business with the painter?

ALFRED. Yes, right. The same day he set fire to that painting.

MAX. Oh really? And at that moment he stands up and says in his well-known manner – 'And now you can all piss off, dammit.'

HILDE. Can I expect much more of this?

ALFRED (*at the same time, to* VICTOR *and* PAUL). If all the worms would now crawl back into the woodwork again . . .

HILDE (*to* PAUL). Just explain one thing to me – just explain one thing. How –

VICTOR (*to* PAUL). Let's just go walkies for a little while.

Exeunt VICTOR *and* PAUL *via the terrace. At the same time* GEORGE *and* JOSEPH *appear on the stairs.*

HILDE (*to* ALFRED). Painter? Was there something about a painter? (*To* MARTHA.) Wouldn't it be better if we –

(*To* ALFRED.) What should I do –

HILDE *and* ALFRED *go to the table. The hum of voices at the table continues.*

JOSEPH (*to* GEORGE, *on the stairs*). I find it upsetting. An overwhelming feeling of being in the wrong. As though I'm always in the wrong.

GEORGE. You know what the experts say about our existence.

JOSEPH. No, to be honest.

GEORGE (*going downstairs*). We reflect the image of the dismantling of modern man. That means we can no longer regard ourselves as people. Only as a series of quotations. Man has been banished from the centre of the action. The abstract forces of culture have joined battle, you see, and through our mouths they square up to one another. So people? Personalities? No, no. Refuse bins, chatterboxes, without background, depth or inner coherence.

JOSEPH. And can you just accept that?

GEORGE. I resist it. But seeing that everyone seems to have accepted that scenario I'm sure it'll take me over too. Oh, to be a man of the nineteenth century. (*Laughter at the table.*) To play the part of a genuine nineteenth-century man. Nineteenth-century joy. Violent forces, quelled by violent methods. Oh.

GABY (*has risen from the table, comes forward. To* GEORGE *and* JOSEPH). Are you coming? (*To* ALFRED *and* HILDE.) And you too?

ALFRED. Just give her a bit of time.

JOSEPH *goes to the table.*

HILDE (*to* ALFRED). I loved that man. But these are the antics of a lunatic. Is that meant as a punishment? Right now when I want to realise my plans.

GEORGE (*to* GABY). What do you think, weren't the cards all shuffled long ago?

HILDE (*to* ALFRED). I wanted to create something really new.

GEORGE (*to* GABY). Where life's concerned, I mean. That's a fear . . . Hopeless.

HILDE (*to* ALFRED). I'm sure there is a need for it.

GEORGE (*to* GABY). Take me, for example. Never master of ceremonies or referee. Always on the reserve-bench, me.

HILDE (*to* ALFRED). But what's left after something like that.

GEORGE (*to* GABY). The concept 'I' is actually misplaced, I've gathered.

ALFRED (*to* HILDE, *who is going up the stairs*). But look on me as a safe haven then.

GEORGE (*to* GABY, *who is constantly watching* ALFRED *and* HILDE). Because what is 'I' in the wrong costume, eh?

GABY (*to* ALFRED). Tell me, is this performance meant to be an educational exercise?

GEORGE *goes and sits down at the table,* ALFRED *follows* HILDE *up the stairs.*

ALFRED (*to* HILDE). Tell me honestly, do you really believe in all that – all those superstitions?

HILDE. No, please. (*Goes through the door, tries to close it behind her.*)

ALFRED (*tries to push the door open*). A bit more modesty. A somewhat less arrogant attitude, that wouldn't do any harm. You want to count on the loyalty of people who are under no obligation towards you. You really think you can drag people with you into some adventure.

HILDE (*from behind the door*). Why do you go along with what other people say?

Behind the screen MAX's *voice, understandable part of the table discussion.*

MAX. In general I say: whoever is dead has lost. Mourning is civilisation's attempt to suppress the primitive triumph in the fact that one has oneself survived. So we are here and now condemned to a profound joie de vivre, ladies and gentlemen.

HEDDA. Heh, wait a minute.

JOSEPH. Is that so? Is that really true?

NATASJA *appears in front of the screen.*

NATASJA (*to* GABY). Is it just me? Can't you smell it? (*Takes a piece of food out of her mouth.*) This food has the taste of his aftershave. I'm not rambling, am I? Am I rambling?

SONJA *appears in front of the screen.*

GABY. It may sound strange –

NATASJA. What?

GABY. When I see how attentive he is, how reliable. Your friend I mean.

NATASJA. Yes, bit of all right, eh?

JOSEPH *appears in front of the screen.*

GABY. You've struck lucky there though, haven't you? At least you haven't been wasting your time. Sometimes I get so sick of all the whole uncertain business.

Exit NATASJA, *to the terrace.*

JOSEPH. We were wondering where everybody was.

GABY. Yes, yes, I'm coming. I'm coming.

GABY *goes to the table.* SONJA *appears, sees* NATASJA *going away.*

SONJA (*to* JOSEPH). Just make sure you look after her, will you? It's all up to you now. Drastic measures, that's what she needs.

JOSEPH. Yes, what's going on now, tell me.

JOSEPH *goes to the table,* HEDDA *appears in front of the screen.*

HEDDA. That sister of mine, where on earth is she now?

SONJA (*to* HEDDA). I can see I haven't a leg to stand on where you lot are concerned.

HEDDA. How come?

SONJA. I just happen to believe in a certain degree of candour.

HEDDA. So?

SONJA. Her troubles have really got to me, do you realise that? I've identified with it all, tried to do something. And now she's doing the opposite of everything we decided on. I feel as if – Because – Oh, that morass you've all come out of, the mud. You! (*Cries.*) You lot have completely taken her in.

ALFRED (*at the top of the stairs, talking against the closed door*). But it can't go on like this! You've got the wrong man for that. Not as far as I'm concerned. This has been going on for three years now. I'd like a bit of certainty.

HEDDA. Oh, she'll always behave like that. (HILDE *suddenly appears.*) As though the world was created just for her sake. She studied art history, and after one and a half years at it she went to New York, so don't think you can tell her anything about life and art.

HILDE (*comes down the stairs*). Because I've shared my life with artists. Oldenburg. Rauschenberg, Ensor. Who wouldn't have wanted to meet them?

HEDDA. And that gives you the right to ill-treat and humiliate us.

HILDE. Do you have any right to say that?

HEDDA. I know you. And you won't pull the wool over her eyes just because she's in the way, if you don't get what you want.

HILDE. Just pull yourself together a bit, OK.

HEDDA. Self-control. Your life has been nothing but extreme self-control.

HILDE. You've always thought the worst of me. That was your weapon.

HEDDA. I do see some peculiar uncontrolled traits.

HILDE. That one day I won't be able to control myself any more, that's what I'm frightened of. That one day I'll –

HEDDA. Consult the stars then you'll see it coming.

HILDE. You can make fun of me, but leave art out of it.

HEDDA. Art! Art! If only it could save you from your sick fantasies. That idiotic admiration. I can't understand it. Admiration for whom or what? Who of these people do you respect? Who of us? Just what do you want?

JOSEPH (*behind the screen, table discussion*). Yes, just pile it on, please.

GABY. Would you like some more of this?

MARTHA. Does anyone else want anything?

JOSEPH. Tell me, I'd just like to ask. Are any topics for discussion taboo here?

MAX. Yes. Sexual diseases. (*Or another topical subject.*)

JOSEPH. Is there a reason for that?

MAX. So it doesn't ruin my apetite.

MARTHA *appears in front of the screen.*

MARTHA. Are you coming now? Otherwise it will all be gone.

HILDE. I'm not hungry, thank you.

MARTHA. But there are only four of them left sitting there.

HEDDA. Girl, eat a little something yourself too.

HILDE. I have a number of other things to do.

HEDDA. Yes, just go and inspect your circus.

MARTHA. Well, in that case I can start clearing away?

HILDE. I'll go and see how things are with – how things are with the various preparations. (*Exit to terrace.*)

MARTHA. Well then. Now I might as well put the screen away as well, don't you think?

GEORGE *and* MAX *appear in front of the screen.* MARTHA *and* SONJA *take the screen away.* HEDDA *goes to the table.*

GEORGE. You ask yourself, this collection of individuals, what are they after? Is there something binding them together, other than a few memories of a certain person? An arbitrary group photograph, or really something more than that?

MARTHA *starts clearing the table.*

MAX. I hesitate to say it, as though he could hear it. But his instinct for seeing through people, for being able to gauge their innermost desires, that was his most extraordinary feature. The way he confronted people with themselves, the pleasure he got out of it whenever he managed to embarrass somebody. The unexpected, that was the area he excelled in. At bottom he was the most complete charlatan. That's why we're not here just by chance. I have the feeling we are puppets in his puppet show. Use your instinct, your premonition, your intuition. Don't you feel there is something, something in the air? That everything that was murky for all those years ought to be cleared up now? As though all the secret feelings are reaching flash point? We are approaching a climax, my boy. Some things will come to an end, other things are just beginning. Desires, uncertainties, antipathies, don't you feel a sort of desperation? Don't you see that some of them are still trying to grab something from the flames? I, I, yes, I feel despair. Yes, yes. A general discontent. A powerless fanaticism, vague distrust, that uncertain balance between contempt and respect, you understand.

During this effusion JOSEPH *and* GABY *stand up and move closer.*

MAX. Feel, feel it. The intensity of all those feelings. Deadly. It piles up. I'm sorry. This is a meeting of players, monsters, people. In every sense of the word.

Enter PAUL, *from the terrace,* MARTHA *and* PAUL *are quietly discussing a broken lamp.* PAUL *disappears again. Meanwhile the others go on talking.*

JOSEPH. Even an outsider can feel it.

MAX. I can just see the conflicts that are going to break out.

JOSEPH. Well then, we as players should hang in there with a tidy bet.

GEORGE. Is this cynicism? I don't understand it.

GABY. Where there's play, there's cheating.

MAX. But if I've understood correctly, any moment now – (*Looks towards the terrace and sees* HILDE *collapsing, but this is not visible to the audience*). Oh God, oh. There you have it.

GEORGE. What? What?

MAX. I'll just go and have a look. I'm sorry I just must go. (*Exit to terrace.*)

GEORGE (*to* MARTHA). As far as I can see you're the only one of us who knows exactly what is going to happen next.

MARTHA. As far as I can see it's total chaos. As far as I can see none of it makes sense any more. (*Looks at a list, goes to the terrace, looks at her watch.*) Oh God! Can someone help me? I think I've forgotten something.

JOSEPH (*looks after her*). Am I seeing right? What's going to happen there now.

HEDDA. I think she might really need a bit of help.

JOSEPH, ALFRED *and* HEDDA *go off to the terrace, while* PAUL *enters with a stepladder and a lightbulb.* SONJA *remains seated.*

PAUL. Going up ladders is not my job. But what the hell, at least it gives me something to do.

PAUL *climbs up the stepladder, with the intention of replacing the broken lightbulb. The ladder threatens to collapse,* GEORGE *holds on to it.*

GEORGE. Do you know what I've heard about you? That you've been shadowing that poor woman.

PAUL. Terrible, yes. A disaster. That could really destroy you. You might look on it as a study in human behaviour, but you put yourself at the mercy of someone else's will. Why does she do this, for God's sake, and not that? And if you never get an answer to that sort of question . . . Well, I didn't want to scare her, but certain things I really had to get rid of.

The ladder has meanwhile ended up on GEORGE. *Only now does* PAUL *notice this.*

PAUL. Oh well, there you go.

Enter ALFRED, HEDDA *and* JOSEPH *from the terrace.*

ALFRED (*to* HEDDA). During dinner. That would have been exactly the right moment?

HEDDA. Amazing the way everything keeps turning out differently.

ALFRED. You discuss a matter like that during dinner.

Enter MARTHA *from the terrace.*

HEDDA (*about* PAUL). What's that man up to now? Who asked him to do that?

MARTHA. Well, I did.

PAUL disappears again. Enter MAX *and* HILDE *from the entrance hall.* HILDE *is in tears.*

HILDE. I can't. As though something is holding me back, as though something terrible is going to happen. As though it's slipping through my fingers. Right now, when I need it, I haven't the nerve.

VICTOR and JOSEPH also approach to listen.

SONJA (*to* HILDE). Would you like to say something now perhaps?

HILDE. Now? Can I, may I just ask once again for your support? It means realising a dream. I've always thought that – I believed in it so firmly. I – I, no.

HILDE breaks down. She is taken to her room by HEDDA.

JOSEPH. But what does she want exactly?

SONJA. She wants us all to join a sort of foundation or society, as a way to enable her to open up a gallery here. An amazing idea.

ALFRED. It certainly is.

SONJA. What's getting up her nose is, I think, the great success her little sister is having at the moment. You have to see this as an overtaking manoeuvre of hers.

GEORGE. The little sister? So what is that little sister doing then?

SONJA. She's getting to be a big name in the fashion world. Has her own shops, working on expansion plans, an extremely successful little monster.

VICTOR. Put five people together, mention the word art, and you have a festival, and a committee. That weird urge to get your

name linked with something artistic, the inclination to worm
your way in between artist and public, to open doors, to close
doors. And in most cases without any affinity. Do you
sometimes think that exists from the day you discovered it?

ALFRED. What are we getting now? Hold your tongue, you.
Artist? Are you one? Is he one, an artist? That man there? Is
that an artist? Do you call that an artist?

GABY. He's a failure. A joke.

ALFRED. One honest attempt to do something, and you're
mistrusted. Unjustified, that criticism. Artists? Restricted
vision, matey. Egocentric people. Ready to look down on
everybody. But unable to see they would be swept aside if other
people didn't look after their interests. Yes, I get angry. So
please let's not talk about art, today.

SONJA. It's best if we drop the whole subject.

*Exeunt SONJA, GABY, MAX, ALFRED and GEORGE to the
kitchen. Enter HEDDA, at the top of the stairs.*

HEDDA. Yet I wonder –

JOSEPH. I'll just go and see about these boxes here. What's
supposed to happen with them?

HEDDA. Boxes?

MARTHA. Yes, there are some boxes that seem to have been left
here.

HEDDA. Boxes have been left here?

MARTHA. Party jokes.

HEDDA *shrugs and disappears.*

JOSEPH. There were a load of funny things in them. Games and
tarot cards. I know how to read them.

Exeunt JOSEPH and MARTHA towards the entrance hall.

VICTOR (*alone on the stage, shouts*). I'm a joke, but I do practise
hard at it. I'm against successful people. Against them. Against
the so-called talented. Against that very specific idea of
success. No secondhand luck. Against it!

ALFRED (*offstage*). Look, during dinner would have been the
right time.

GEORGE (*offstage*). I don't know what to do about it either.

HEDDA (*in the doorway*). What was the whole thing planned for
anyway?

SONJA (*offstage*). Well, folks, don't let's discuss it now. We can still do something else.

Enter NATASJA *from the terrace,* MARTHA f*rom the hall.* MARTHA *continues clearing the table.*

VICTOR (*to* NATASJA). Well, yes, God Almighty, yes. That's often happened to me lately. Hearing myself blowing my top. It comes over me. Well, I'm not like – Well, yes, you get it – It's a matter of – We know one another, don't we? You do know me, don't you? I must admit, well.

Enter PAUL *from the terrace.*

VICTOR. Your father and mine, they were friends. We played together, as kids. Stuck things together and stuff, with spit.

NATASJA. I've got a headache from that shouting. Did you hear it? It hurts my ears. (*About* PAUL.) Do I know that man there? I do know that man, don't I?

PAUL. You look like him, certainly, certain features, yes, yes, she reminds me of him.

VICTOR (*about* PAUL). If I look carefully, I keep getting the feeling there's a dwarf in him having me on.

PAUL. Well, there you go.

MARTHA *finds a note on the table.*

NATASJA. Yes? Is he a murderer then?

PAUL. What? Me? Why? What? Oh, no, come on. (*Exit to terrace.*)

MARTHA. There's a note here. Here. What should I do with it?

VICTOR. For whom? A note? (*Reads note.*) No, not for me.

NATASJA (*reads note*). Well, no, not that I know.

MARTHA. No? And it was lying on the table here.

Enter GEORGE, *from the kitchen.*

VICTOR. There's a note for you.

GEORGE. A note? (*Reads note.*) Well no, not that I know. Where?

VICTOR. On the table. (*Puts the note back on the table.*)

GEORGE. Well, well. (*To* MARTHA.) A propos, I heard you did something in the artistic line.

MARTHA. I am an artist, yes.

GEORGE. You too?

MARTHA. You too?

GEORGE. No, not me.

MARTHA. Then why did you say: you too.

GEORGE. Oh, because I really admire them, artists. Oh, you know
– I sell antique weapons, but only if a genuine murder has been
done with them. Foreigner, eh?

MARTHA. Pardon?

GEORGE. You're from abroad.

MARTHA. Me foreign, yes.

Enter ALFRED, *from the kitchen.*

GEORGE. Where from then? Where from?

MARTHA. From Russia.

GEORGE (*to* ALFRED). A note for you. (*To* MARTHA.) Russia?
Well, well.

MARTHA. Yes, been through a lot, me. Yes.

GEORGE. Oh yes? Tell me.

ALFRED (*reads note*). Tell me, you trying to pull my leg? What
kind of rubbish is this. 'My love, after dinner joy is awaiting
here.' Are you lot all right in the head? Should I go? I haven't
eaten a bloody thing yet. (*Goes and sits at the head of the
table.*)

MARTHA. There is still a little bit left.

We now see GABY *crawling under the table from the other
side, half hidden by the tablecloth.*

GEORGE. Lovely. I still know a Russian proverb. 'He who
hesitates sleeps with the goats.'

ALFRED. Lyrical, poetic, tasteful.

GABY *continues crawling.*

MARTHA. Shall I teach you a song?

GEORGE. A song!

It looks as though ALFRED *feels his flies being opened.
During the following speech* ALFRED *begins a subdued
groaning.*

MARTHA. If you love colour
Then love gold.
If you love sweetness

Then use no salt.
Who in this life truly will learn
Knows one thing quickly:
Fortune is no gift
Fortune's a fault
Just remember that.

ALFRED. Yes –

Enter HEDDA *in a splendid robe, down the stairs.*

HEDDA. This is meant to open eyes and loosen tongues.

ALFRED. Yes. (*He comes.*) Oh good God Almighty!

Everyone looks at ALFRED, *who stands up and rearranges his clothes.*

ALFRED. It's nothing. I've just got to . . . Just a moment please.

Exit ALFRED *to the entrance hall. Outside, on the terrace, fireworks explode. There is a general movement in that direction. Blackout.*

ACT II

Darkness. Music and noise. Light. Dancing couples appear.
JOSEPH *with* GABY, GEORGE *with* MARTHA, SONJA *with*
VICTOR, MAX *with* HILDE, HEDDA *with* ALFRED. PAUL *gets*
in everyone's way. Gradually the couples disappear in the
direction of the terrace, where apparently the party is also going
on. On stage remain HILDE, HEDDA *and* PAUL. *A nervous*
atmosphere.

HEDDA (*to* HILDE, *about* PAUL). What's it all about? What's he
doing here! I can't understand why you don't chuck out people
like that.

PAUL. I'm not leaving before I know what my chances are.

Enter GEORGE, *from the terrace.*

PAUL (*to* GEORGE). I've come here today to wring something
from fate.

GEORGE. Oh, everyone has come here to settle a few crucial
matters.

PAUL. Christ, what a madhouse.

GEORGE. But I personally believe we are fated never to know the
results of our actions. We cannot gauge the full extent of our
behaviour. We wreak havoc, scamper from lust to gratification,
from gratification to lust. Destroy what is most dear to us.
Would like most of all to be liberated for a few hours from the
pitfalls, the barbs of our identity.

Enter GABY, *from entrance hall.*

GABY. Everyone's happy, everyone looks lovely, everyone's
having fun, we must do this more often.

Enter MAX *and* NATASJA, *from terrace.*

NATASJA (*to* MAX). Just come with me. I want to talk to you
about something.

NATASJA *and* MAX *go and sit at the table.* JOSEPH,
VICTOR, SONJA *and* ALFRED *enter from terrace.* JOSEPH
has a set of Tarot cards. He goes upstairs with GABY *and*
SONJA *in his wake.*

JOSEPH. Ladies and gentlemen, let me introduce the game in
which fate is heralded and determined. Death, disease, good

fortune, travel, meetings, inheritances. As you know, the cards can tell you about everything. Who will submit to prophecy, and dare ignore it. Ladies and gentlemen, here this evening you will meet destiny.

From this moment on, from upstairs behind the door a celebration can be heard.

VICTOR (*also going upstairs*). Love and art, last bulwarks in a culture of egoists, dropouts, maniacs and halfwits. (*Exit, closing door behind him.*)

ALFRED. Tell me, who got that idea?

PAUL (*to* HILDE). And is everything going more or less the way you wanted it?

HILDE. I've tried the cap on and now I'm going to have a go at wearing it.

Enter MARTHA, *from the kitchen, watches, together with* HEDDA.

PAUL. I understand exactly why you're doing this. I won't leave you in the lurch. Honest.

HILDE. What's this now? What do you mean exactly?

ALFRED *urges* PAUL *toward the terrace.* HEDDA *goes with them.*

PAUL. Well, if I don't get the chance to explain it . . .

GEORGE. I'm up to my eyes in criticism actually.

MARTHA. Are you drunk?

GEORGE. No. I'm up to my eyes in criticism. Simply constructively meant, sharp criticism, self-criticism.

HILDE *has meanwhile moved away, goes up the stairs.*

MARTHA. Why? If I might ask.

During the following monologue, MAX *and* NATASJA *go off towards the kitchen.* MARTHA *soon wishes to follow.*

GEORGE. Mankind, is there anything left to say about it? A human being without opinions, convictions, is that still a human being? Take me. Can I still be called human? Or is it just some misplaced anthropomorphic exaltation. Yes, I say. That description touches the core. Of course you flirt around with self-criticism. You're a child of your time. You expect of others that they have energy, and perspective. Inspiration, genuine inspiration.

Enter HEDDA *and* ALFRED *from the terrace. They adopt a festive pose and go upstairs. Together with* HILDE *they are welcomed by the partying group. They close the door on* GEORGE, *who tries to join in, and is now left on the stairs.*

GEORGE. I feel like a guest in a run-down hotel. I go out onto the street. I automatically assume that any directions I see are part of a scatterbrained puzzle. (*He catches sight of* MARTHA, *who is listening uncomfortably.*) Ha, ha, I've seen through them. They won't get me. I'm too tired to solve it. So back inside. The other guests justifiably speak in a lunatic code. On the ceiling there are peeling paintings of what was once called a golden age. The urge to keep looking upward is almost irresistible. But if I do, I'll fall down the stairs, or someone will secretly tie my shoelaces together. Do you get the picture? My problem?

MARTHA. Well, I'm only a simple soul.

HEDDA *comes downstairs nervously. The door remains open. Behind the door people are dancing and hopping.*

HEDDA. What a strangely nervous atmosphere. That must be because of her. I'm getting a whiff of excess, calamities. It's beginning to get on my nerves. (*To* MARTHA.) Is everything going as it should?

GEORGE (*continuing to hold forth*). Decay. A slight odour that you try to dispel, and yet it remains in the air. Oh, our lives, our lives, oh God Jesus, our lives. Seriously? (*Gestures to the party.*) My life, for example: not sharply defined, no. No. From time to time very frivolous. Oh yes. Yes. And yet, through the walls of existence laughter can always be heard. Oh yes, that's what I recognise, what we perhaps have in common. And drunk? Well no. Hardly. Drunk? No.

ALFRED *appears with* HILDE *at the top of the stairs, they watch.*

HEDDA; Yes? That's nice. That's nice.

MARTHA. Oh, it's really starting to get going now. Did you just see them necking? What a scream.

HEDDA. What? Who?

NATASJA *enters from the kitchen, looks at* HILDE. MAX *appears, looks at* HILDE. HILDE *goes to* MAX. ALFRED *follows.* NATASJA *keeps on looking. Meanwhile* VICTOR *and* SONJA *appear above, about to go downstairs.*

MARTHA. And outside they were going to start shooting, but I snatched the gun away.

HEDDA. Where? What?

VICTOR (*to* NATASJA). Good that I've seen you. According to the cards we're doomed to spend the evening together.

NATASJA. Then I'd look out if I were you.

> MAX *goes with* HEDDA *and* ALFRED *towards the entrance hall.* GEORGE *goes upstairs.* HILDE *has stopped still. In panic.*

HILDE. Well, girl, come on, girl. It's not just I don't have the nerve, but why do I have the feeling I have to get away, as quick as I can, away. If only I had never started it. But dammit, girl, girl, well.

MARTHA. Yes, I know that.

HILDE. What? (*Goes and sits in a corner.*)

SONJA (*to* VICTOR). Of course it's all bitchery. Being successful, travelling, becoming famous, me?

> *The party continues. Cheers are heard whenever anyone comes in. in this case* MARTHA.

SONJA. Good God, in no time flat I was completely on my beam ends. I'm practically without work. As a photographer I haven't had a decent commission for a year. I'm up to my ears in debt. He must have heard about it.

VICTOR. Then that's a pretty cynical prophecy he's just made.

SONJA. That will have been his sense of humour.

> *In the doorway people are blowing on tooters.*

SONJA. Some people here, well really.

VICTOR. But, eh . . .

> *Enter* HEDDA *and* ALFRED *from entrance hall,* MAX *follows at a distance.*

HEDDA (*to* HILDE). But if you just said what you wanted, for everybody that would be –

HILDE. Yes, I said. Yes. Yes.

ALFRED (*to* HEDDA). Why do you get so wound up?

HEDDA. That incredibly unpractical side. High-minded, long-winded. That lack of simplicity, of overview. That unworldliness.

ALFRED. Oh, it's never been any different. Although it did have its charms at the time.

HEDDA *moves away from* HILDE.

SONJA (*to* VICTOR). Perhaps I don't have the talent. Could that be it? Perhaps I'm no good at it, photography. All that competition. Perhaps I have to be that honest. I should advise anyone offering me a commission to steer clear of me.

VICTOR. Well, well.

SONJA. No really, there are so many people I know I'd really like to say the same to. All that bottled-up rage that makes them carry on kidding themselves.

JOSEPH (*in the doorway*). For Christ's sake, of course I realise I have to say something now. If you say something like that –

GABY (*in the doorway*). When you talk, I see in your eyes things that make me think: o . . .

JOSEPH. Is that so? Is that so?

GABY. Yes it is. I see things that make me . . .

GABY *pushes or pulls* JOSEPH *with her.* SONJA *continues talking.* NATASJA *listens.*

SONJA. Because this is unbearable. (*Cries.*) I can't stand it, anyway. I just can't cope any more. For years no prospects any more. I just don't see it. Again and again the same crisis.

HEDDA *goes up to* HILDE *again.* HILDE *disappears.*

SONJA. This crisis, it does pass, but it always comes back. Just think how I got to know her. Blind drunk, she was stubbing cigarettes out on her arm, because it gave her such a funny feeling. That's the state she was in.

HEDDA (*to* ALFRED). How can you ever – I mean, even though it's all terribly involved now, I still think . . .

HEDDA *looks at* SONJA *and* NATASJA *who have almost come to blows.*

NATASJA (*to* SONJA). Have you been talking about me?

HEDDA. But maybe I'm . . .

SONJA. Yes, you can't get away with this Cinderella bit.

NATASJA. No. Nor a dying swan either.

SONJA. Now listen . . .

NATASJA. No. (*Runs away.*)

HEDDA. Actually I'm a terribly sober type.

VICTOR (*about* NATASJA). But what's up with her?

MAX (*he has been at the refreshments; to* HEDDA). But that's true
... I hadn't congratulated you at all, had I? Those are really
successes. No, really. I read it recently. In the paper.

HEDDA. Oh well. A branch. Well yes. Heh –

*Meanwhile they are going upstairs together, and notice the
party.* HEDDA *goes in, is welcomed.*

SONJA (*to* VICTOR, *about* HEDDA). She opens up branches
abroad, while her cultural luggage consists of half a year's
piano lessons and elocution on Wednesday afternoons.

NATASJA (*to* SONJA). I'm neither aggressive, nor
overdemanding, nor spoiled, nor short-tempered, nor depraved.
Go away, go. Just clear off.

MAX *is at the top of the stairs, while* HEDDA *has entered the
room.*

MAX (*about* HEDDA). Of course she's grotesque and vulgar. And
of course it's just that sort of people who make it in life.

MARTHA (*in the doorway, as general announcement*). Russian
mothers, they're really the best. They don't use handkerchiefs,
they just suck their children's noses clean.

GEORGE, GABY and HEDDA *appear jigging at the top of the
stairs.* HILDE *starts talking through this. The noise dries up.
During the monologue those present –* ALFRED, SONJA,
VICTOR, HEDDA, NATASJA, MAX, GEORGE *and* GABY –
listen for longer or shorter periods, with fluctuating interest.

HILDE. A feeling of solidarity, conviction. I'm looking, I'm
looking for that spirit that . . . And I can't find it. Am I
mistaken? You've been our guests. For years we've met,
supported one another. You've kept coming. And it turned into
a sort of group, a club, how must you – I don't know any more.
Have we lost it all? Background, shelter. Is that all going to fall
apart? Does it have to now? Is that reality then? Isn't it possible
– something of the past – To work out a plan together, or to
take a step. Our today is our history, after all.

NATASJA (*screaming*). And I'm not unstable either. Perhaps,
perhaps I'm –

SONJA *intervenes and drags* NATASJA *by the hair off to the
terrace.* GEORGE *and* GABY *return to the party room.*

VICTOR (*to* HILDE). Just listen carefully, in my view you don't
have any right to anything. Not to any money, not to support or
co-operation.

HILDE. It looks as though I have lost my powers of discernment. You have passed your judgment, you put it all pretty clearly. Now you just have to tell me one thing. Why do you have to complicate things so much? Why? I sense Schadenfreude, revenge. What is it? Are you after my personal downfall?

VICTOR. I find your extravagance a pose, your ideas misplaced and outdated, and I simply don't believe in your so-called artistic inspiration.

HILDE. My dear man, I can't live any other way. My roots lie in this world. Incomprehensible but true. I come from a specific time, and my experiences are dear to me. It's my idea of adventure.

VICTOR. No more perverted world than that of so-called art. The greater the perversion, the more sterile the so-called adventure. Because the real aim smothers everything. And the real aim is, to create an alibi for yourself for a thoroughly perverted nature. And so ultimately art is a great collaborating bond of perverts all providing alibis for one another. Call it a game. You'll only lose.

GABY *appears in the doorway of the party room.*

GABY. Oh boy, how lovely it is.

ALFRED. O God!

Enter PAUL, *comes down the stairs.*

HILDE. Pervert? Perverted?

ALFRED. Oh yes?

During the following monologue there appears again in driblets a host of restless listeners; all except NATASJA. PAUL *too appears apparently unnoticed among those present.*

HILDE. To be able to stand eye to eye with the greatest? To be able to experience the greatest, and then use the word perverted? An artist wrestling with his material, perverted? Mercilessly destroying his failures, perverted? Fascination, ecstasy, shock. Berard, Picasso, Braque. (*Enter* JOSEPH.) The futility of words, compared with what really counts. We talk about art. (*Enter* GEORGE, MARTHA, SONJA.) Ernst, Cocteau, de Chirico. Art, a vehicle to paradise. Why love art? Why listen to music? Mondrian, Klee, Matisse, Monet, who paints water lilies the very moment cubism is discovered. Why get up early? (*Enter* MAX.) Need, dynamics, aggression. Someone asked me to go for it. I thought: a gallery? Art? Not for me. I started, and it erupted. Perversion? The knock-out effect, the punch, the theatricality. Just compare that with the unfulfilment of all things. Art. Fierce witness. Originality. Radicality. Manifesto. Art? In Tibet the word doesn't even exist. Art? The haven where civilisation is anchored. A poetic idea. (HEDDA *tries to calm* HILDE *down.*) How would we like to live? Lost dimensions. Hunger, desire, passion, untouched faith, the immoderate, excess. Pollock, Rothko, Warhol. Genius, charisma, imago, enthusiasm. The spirit of brilliant, endless improvisation. (*During the following* HILDE *arranges the circle of supporters:* GEORGE, ALFRED, SONJA, MAX *and* GABY, *which makes them embarrassed. Soon they spread out again. Then* HEDDA *busies herself with* HILDE *again.*) That's the spirit I want. In this place, in this building. Spontaneity, inspiration, the unexpected. The event, urge, need, surrender. A small circle of supporters, a few enthusiasts. Five interested people, six disciples, backers. A meeting place, a sort of salon. But deeper, more intense, more cosmopolitan. No provincialism, but East and West. I've always known what it should become.The plan is ripe. Haste is fatal. So I've been patient.

Giacometti, Ernst, Dubuffet. I'd like to have met them. Happenings at Oldenburg's. A visit to Rauschenberg's studio. I was there. Events. Traces we must keep on cherishing. Shaping your own time. Our today is our history. Is that perverse. Perverted?

VICTOR. It sounds like running the hundred metre hurdle in high heels.

NATASJA *appears on the terrace.* SONJA *goes to her.*

HEDDA. And all that because she was engaged to an American for a fortnight.

NATASJA (*to* SONJA). No, no. Maybe I – Just piss off. Maybe I – Maybe my figure's gone a bit, yes. But I'm not completely . . . No, honestly. Are you listening?

SONJA. OK, OK.

NATASJA. Never again. Never again will I ever let you –

Exeunt SONJA *and* NATASJA *to terrace. They soon re-enter, a stealthy pursuit.*

GEORGE. That from a certain moment what was happening imperceptibly stopped being real, we all do feel that, don't we? The oppressive feeling of hallucination. I notice you all devour faces as though they were genitals.

NATASJA (*childish, almost idiotic*). I love my daddy. But my daddy hits me. When daddy stops I'll want to see daddy.

NATASJA *goes upstairs,* SONJA *remains below.*

HILDE. I'm going crazy, I'm desperate. Last year I kept a diary. I didn't dare write words out fully, I used my own sort of shorthand. And now I can't read any of it any more. My past is wiped out. I'm a non-person.

HILDE *wants to go to the terrace. She bumps into* PAUL, *who makes the greatest possible effort to try to say something.*

PAUL. I –

GEORGE. What do you mean 'I'? You're all much too ugly to call yourselves 'I'.

PAUL (*screams*). I, yes. I! I! Now I!

A fight breaks out between GEORGE *and* PAUL, *the others watch, and make comments. The onlookers try to part them. Then confusion. Finally: bewildered silence.*

GEORGE (*softly*). Ugly sod.

MAX, VICTOR *and* MARTHA, *taken aback, go and sit at the table.*

HEDDA (*to* ALFRED, *exploding*). I have other things to do, I really have. She can make out she passionately wants something, but she creates situations where things have to fail. Has she just asked you for advice? I can't promise it will have got through to her. Ye gods, tell me.

ALFRED. No, she didn't ask me for advice. She rang me up in a panic after she had been told about the death. Whether I'd see to the most urgent things. Well, I agreed to, after that we spoke on the phone once more. A lot of emotion, confused talk. Then I couldn't get hold of her any more. I assumed you were with her.

HEDDA. I came as quickly as I could. I've been with her for three days now. But I'm only just beginning to realise what a tremendous blow it was to her. Ye gods. She seemed so calm. And now this.

ALFRED. She seems to have very little understanding of the consequences.

NATASJA *appears at the top of the stairs, with a written piece of paper.*

NATASJA. Ladies and gentlemen. And now my side of the affair. Ladies and gentlemen, do you have a moment for me now? Please follow me –

HILDE *sees that* NATASJA, GEORGE *and* MAX *are going upstairs.* SONJA *follows. At the top of the stairs there is a discussion.* NATASJA *tries to get people into the room.*

HILDE (*at the bottom of the stairs, to* SONJA). What kind of a state do you think she's in? Is she unpredictable? Does she think it's my fault? Is she resentful?

SONJA. I'm sorry, you fight your own battles. You with all those eternal relationships. What do you think? That no one knows anything? In your life everything is a public secret.

HILDE. Anyone talking about me by any chance?

SONJA. The denigrating way you talk about everybody . . . I was there. I was there, after all.

HILDE. Yes? Oh yes?

SONJA. Betrayal, that's your territory.

HILDE. Don't say that. You mustn't say that about me.

SONJA *and* HEDDA *move further up the stairs.* NATASJA *is standing at the top.*

VICTOR (*to* NATASJA). This evening I feel as though I'm constantly being drawn towards you. Really. We really ought to have a good talk sometime.

NATASJA. Oh yes? Of our own free will, or because we're forced to?

VICTOR. What the hell do you mean by that?

NATASJA, VICTOR *and* ALFRED *disappear. A propos these events,* GEORGE *says:*

GEORGE. But nothing's expected of me, is it? Is anything expected of me? I do get that impression. But I just don't want to get involved. Not in that way. I'd really like – Most of all I'd like – If I can help if need be. You know that I'd do anything – anything – But I don't want that. I can't do that.

GEORGE *stumbles. While upstairs in the room the discussion continues,* GEORGE *falls painfully down the stairs. The door is closed.*

GABY (*to* GEORGE). For God's sake, haven't you learned yet how to go up and down stairs?

GEORGE. I'm going outside to put a bullet through my head.

JOSEPH. Of course that is more effective.

Exit GEORGE *in a very upset state, followed by* GABY *and* JOSEPH.

MAX (*to* HILDE). I can't really understand this business. Whether this obsessiveness is not doomed to failure, is still an open question for me.

HILDE. Oh God, Oh God.

PAUL. I completely understand you. I understand exactly why you're doing this. Why you do what you do, even though maybe you don't understand it yourself.

HILDE. How do you manage that?

PAUL. I understand you are thinking of giving up your original plans.

HILDE. How can you know that? Apparently discussions have been earholed here. Who did you get that from?

PAUL. You are even toying with the idea of going away. Are you afraid of something, I wonder.

HILDE. Is there really so much talk? It's staggering. Just leave me in peace. It really looks as though there's a curse on this evening. The same curse that gradually infected the whole relationship –

PAUL. But that's true. That's true. What's been happening here is really all part of the power of a curse pronounced against you by your husband in my presence.

HILDE. What are you saying there?

PAUL. As soon as you have time, I'd like to talk to you more fully.

HILDE. A curse? Come on. Now I really don't know what I'm supposed to feel. As though someone is trying to grab me, from the darkness. Inescapable. Inescapable all this. Thank you, that's yet another revenge. A punishment. Marked, scourged, humiliated. I did try for you. Nobody could help you. I felt so hounded, so guilty.

PAUL. Look, if you are really seriously thinking of going away, first listen to me. Now I have to lay bare my soul. You don't realise what was going on in the background. It could look as though I was following you, in fact I was protecting you. Do you realise what that means, to get involved in someone's life in that way. Do you think you owe me nothing at all? The mental pressure I had to put up with, because I could not, would not say everything you – I couldn't. And whatever I did, I knew that I always had to betray someone. Because I for you – no, for

THE STENDHAL SYNDROME 277

him – Because I – There is a kind of love that demands a fantastic input. That is loving without a counterpart. (*Grabs her.*) The longing to be the destiny of the other. To become the event the other is immersed in. The feeling you are enshrouding someone in an occult power. It happened to me. The game I had to play for it . . . It destroyed me. Please. Please don't misunderstand me. Do you understand me? Do you understand the significance? We are being tested together. You understand. I know you understand me. I know you. Don't be angry. You do understand me? Resistance is useless. You believe in that power too. And that can't be a coincidence. You must know I don't want to be a punishment, not a sentence. But I can't just let you go this time.

HILDE *tries to get away.* PAUL *pursues her. Upstairs the door opens.* MARTHA *appears.*

HILDE. I'm speechless.

MARTHA. Speechless? Well, somebody else certainly isn't. There's no stopping her.

HILDE. I'm so afraid she – Has she already said anything?

MARTHA. She's just standing there giving a speech.

NATASJA, SONJA, ALFRED, HEDDA *and* VICTOR *come out of the room.*

HILDE. But what's she saying? I'm frightened she'll –

HEDDA. I really think you have to forget that plan of yours.

NATASJA (*runs downstairs*). So what did you expect from me? You can't expect anything else from me, can you? Don't expect anything else from me. Don't expect anything from me. It's pointless to say any more. Our presence here is useless. There's no hope. It'll never be any good again. I'll wreck it. I'll do everything to to to . . .

Exit NATASJA *to the kitchen, where crockery is thrown.*

NATASJA (*from the kitchen*). I won't go along with it.

The rest of the company standing or sitting on the stairs.

HILDE. Then I've had it. Standstill. Impasse. Wiped out. Done away with.

MARTHA *tries to go into the kitchen.* NATASJA a*ppears again.*

HEDDA. But it's really time I left. I've still got loads of things to sort out. What a heap of disasters, what a mess.

Gradually the company gets moving again.

ALFRED. If she doesn't play along the whole thing is going to get even more complicated.

HEDDA. Open a gallery? As far as I can see you couldn't even run a bar in Torremolinos.

HILDE. My gallery. Haven't I a hope? Just tell me. It's your field, isn't it?

ALFRED. All those years I looked after your private finances, I talked to him about a sound will and testament. What do I find? A fireplace full of half burned paper. An indescribable mess. I'm sorry, but you have to get this into your head. Marriage certificate, insurance policies, bank statements, those sorts of papers you bung in a safe. I haven't been able to find any key. Of course, the universally admired letter in flowery language I sent you, that was lying there for all to see.

HILDE. Don't be vulgar, please.

ALFRED. But no trace of a will.

HILDE. Is that allowed? Can that happen?

ALFRED. Now his daughter has rights too. And what her rights are, that must be explained to her.

MARTHA starts clearing up.

HILDE. God, God.

ALFRED. Yes, God. I'm willing to put up with a lot. But I don't want my name involved in a big scandal. I'm beginning to notice that a lot of things don't square up. That suicide, the circumstances, the fudging, it's just a confession of guilt on his part, don't you see that? Can't you see you're tempting fate? You have never listened to me and now it's too late.

Meanwhile JOSEPH and GABY have entered, with GEORGE, who looks terrible. The company moves towards them.

GEORGE. What a day. What a day. What a day.

HEDDA. What's up with him?

JOSEPH. Doesn't feel well.

HEDDA. He's not the only one.

JOSEPH (*about* HILDE). But maybe she'd rather be alone.

HILDE is crying. HEDDA goes to her.

HEDDA. Yes, what a day this has been. Yes. Of course you want to be able to cope with it all, I can understand that, and then finally it's just all too much, isn't it? Well, you did your best, but now it must stop. Over, finished. Come on.

GEORGE *goes slowly up to* HILDE.

HILDE. I can't go on.

GEORGE. But we have to maintain the circle. We form a circle. A link has gone, so what? We've learned something, haven't we? We have to go farther, farther, farther? Look farther than –

PAUL (*pointing to* HILDE). She's crying. That's terrible.

MAX (*to* PAUL). So, young man . . .

PAUL. What?

MAX. I'm still wondering about that story of yours. Tell me some more. I'm intrigued.

PAUL. What do you mean, tell? What?

MAX. I have a sort of idea that it comes into my field. The Stendhal syndrome. The mentally disturbed, people with psychological problems, unstable characters, very fascinating, that they need help again and again. Lovely story, that case of yours. Have you, if I may ask, ever needed psychiatric help?

PAUL. How? What? But – Well, no. No, in fact. Not that. Oh God, so you know? Not again, OK. I – Oh God, yes, yes, yes, yes.

PAUL *panics, makes ghostly lunges at the other guests, who shrink back and run away.* PAUL *comes to.*

PAUL. Just look at me. I can't help it, can I? Oh shit, shit, I'm just a wreck as well.

MAX. That's really not what I was aiming for.

SONJA. Oh well. Couldn't you see that straight away? A real mess. Thicko! Fool!

The company keeps moving, now in the direction of the kitchen.

MAX. No, that really amazes me. I didn't think of that for a moment. My goodness, what a really peculiar case.

GABY (*to* SONJA). What are you looking so happy about?

SONJA. Shall I tell you something? Little sister has made me an offer. Fantastic. I'm going on a trip. Great.

GABY. Jesus, that's great.

SONJA. I'm going to photograph collections. Well, what do you say? That's what you call work, heh? What a break. That really gets you going again, doesn't it. (*Disappears in the direction of the kitchen.*)

GABY. Yes, I can understand that. (*To* JOSEPH.) Getting going, that's my department, after all.

Meanwhile HILDE, GEORGE, VICTOR, ALFRED, HEDDA, MAX, PAUL *and* NATASJA *have disappeared into the kitchen.*

SONJA (*at the kitchen*). Then I'll just go and settle some other things first. This all fits in fantastically well for me.

SONJA *disappears into the kitchen. From the kitchen now and then couples appear, who calmly move or dance upstage. Some of them could be drinking.*

JOSEPH (*to* GABY). Well now, here we are then, eh? Yes. You have to realise that, don't you? That I look on this as a joke, as a bit of fun. I have other commitments for the moment. You know that. You must have seen that too? It was nice, but I'm afraid that's where it has to stop for the time being. That's just the way it is. Do you understand? Where is she, by the way? The headstrong poor little rich girl. Miss Over-the-top?

NATASJA *moves downstage together with* VICTOR.

GABY. That friend of yours, I think he's looking for you.

NATASJA. That friend of mine? (*Pushes* JOSEPH *away.*) He's just a walking example of people's inability to get the point.

VICTOR. The other thing I wanted to say, I find your attitude fantastic. Great. Lot of guts. Totally justified.

GABY *now pulls* JOSEPH *with her upstage.*

NATASJA. Actually it won't make any difference at all. By the way, I hope there's no misunderstanding.

VICTOR. Misunderstanding?

NATASJA. I keep having this dream that I'm a princess. That frightens you, doesn't it? A princess like in a fairy story.

VICTOR. Yes, and then what?

NATASJA. The princess meets a prince, and that prince turns out to be a princess. Could that mean anything? Those two princesses are seen by a coarse woodcutter, who gives everything away. (*Starts to sob.*) The one princess is thrown straight into a dungeon, under permanent guard, and in the end disinherited.

VICTOR. So yet again everything looks quite a bit more complicated than we thought.

ALFRED and HILDE move downstage. A little later GEORGE too. NATASJA and VICTOR move upstage.

GEORGE. It's extraordinary the way everyone is just aimlessly wandering around.

NATASJA (*to* VICTOR). I see you understand my story.

GEORGE. What kind of behaviour is that?

NATASJA. Lovely.

GEORGE. I don't feel well. Can't we think of something? What kind of atmosphere is this.

In the background people are still calmly dancing or moving about. GEORGE joins them.

HILDE. What's left for us, in terms of inspiration? Do you know? Where's the enthusiasm, the longing? I feel death around me.

ALFRED. Just shut up about death.

HILDE. There is a curse on me.

ALFRED. It's in you yourself. It's not something around you. It's not cosmic. You're your own curse.

HILDE. That I could be so convinced of myself.

ALFRED. You're heading for a disastrous mental breakdown, if you don't watch out. I know you.

HILDE. I have to be alone. A long time alone.

ALFRED. You can't be alone. You'll always keep on looking for protection and security from others. That's what you're like. What you call independence is just a smart way of getting other people to look after you. Yes, I'm bitter.

GEORGE (*imitating*). Oh, he's bitter.

ALFRED. Yes! I feel misused!

HILDE. Oh, you . . .

HILDE moves upstage, to MARTHA, who has put some food on the table. HILDE, MARTHA, SONJA, NATASJA, VICTOR, GEORGE, GABY and JOSEPH go to the table. MAX is talking to PAUL. HEDDA goes to ALFRED.

ALFRED (*shouting at* HILDE). Go on, say it. I know it anyway.

NATASJA. Then I'll go in search of that other princess.

HEDDA (*to* ALFRED). What do you think? I value your opinion. I, I'd like – I feel – I'm glad I've got to know you better. I think –

ALFRED. Yes?

HEDDA. At least one normal person here. What a failure, what a disaster. I have the feeling, it's really strange, that I can trust you. Nice. A lovely feeling.

ALFRED. Don't forget the risk.

HEDDA. I don't see any risk.

ALFRED. Aren't I running a risk?

HEDDA. I'd really love to get the chance to let you see how much I trust you.

ALFRED. I can't do more than let you know the risk I'm running.

HEDDA. Your manner of speaking is shameless.

ALFRED. Yet I'm always the loser.

HEDDA. If you don't want to lose you have to show initiative.

ALFRED (*increasingly bewildered*). I'm someone who suffers to a terrible degree from self-criticism. I don't say what I would like to say, I don't write what I would like to write, I have the feeling I have to constantly watch my step. That my remarks are always being twisted. I feel the malice when people look at me. That I am kind is not believed. People want to see proof that I'm harmful. People want to see me unmasked as a shit. I am under suspicion. In fact I live in secrecy. I keep quiet. I'm not allowed to do anything. The age we're living in is driving me crazy. My job is driving me crazy.

The dancing in the background has begun again.

HEDDA. I don't think I understand what you mean.

ALFRED. I'm tired. I've been on the go for a long time, and so much has still to happen. A complete breakdown of the property, who gets clobbered with that? Who asks the notary to sort out the estate? And this building, and all the debts, what's to happen to them? Oh, after that bankruptcy to have to wade through a pile of horrors again. I have to make sure it doesn't get totally out of hand.

HILDE *listened to part of this, and now has gone past them and run up the stairs. She disappears behind the door.*

HEDDA. Poor man.

ALFRED. And what if everything has to be sorted out in the shadow of an enormous debt?

HEDDA. Yes? Do you think?

ALFRED. We're nearing the end. We must draw up a plan. Then we can save ourselves a heap of trouble.

HEDDA. Well, why don't we do that?

ALFRED. Because no one wants to listen to me.

HEDDA. Yes they do. I certainly know someone who'll listen to you.

HEDDA *and* ALFRED *go up the stairs, to the top.* PAUL *comes out of the kitchen with* MAX.

PAUL (*to* MAX). But why couldn't you help me then? Can't you answer my questions?

MAX. I seriously doubt it.

PAUL. You're the one who spoke on the telephone last with my employer.

MAX. How do you know that?

PAUL. With ears like mine, and – Well. At a certain moment it was said: 'During a telephone conversation with his psychiatrist he stabbed himself in the heart with a knife'.

MAX. I can't help anybody. I'm not a therapist. I write books. The superficiality of such information is typical. I don't practise. Haven't for years. I give lectures. I'm interested in tangents between psychoanalysis and art. Well. And then you're a friend who helps, even though it doesn't help. Death here was an imminent event. Only the date was missing. You've got problems. We've all got problems. No one who can help. Just go and sit down. And just look at it all.

MAX *and* PAUL *go and sit at the table. In the background the dancing continues.* VICTOR, MARTHA, GABY *and* GEORGE. NATASJA *and* SONJA *are talking together.* JOSEPH *is listening.*

NATASJA. And is that what you want to tell me?

SONJA (*comes downstage*). Yes. It's no longer my choice, so let's switch off. I'm afraid it's too deep. I can't reach it. Then for a while it's OK again, and then again and again that relapse. If you say that deep inside you're not rotten, then I believe it. But again and again the fear of that moment when I have to say: You can't talk to her, because she screams. You can't touch her because she hits out. Do I have to tell you what it's like for me?

How miserable, how tired, how powerless I feel? How irritated? That obstinate resistance to good advice, while today of all days there was a perfect reason to change your behaviour.

NATASJA. Yes, I understood all that.

NATASJA *goes into the entrance hall,* SONJA *continues.*

SONJA. Those crazy contradictions you fill your life with. Stuffing yourself with cakes in the morning, desperately exercising in the afternoon. And you thought you'd got yourself together enough to take her on.

Meanwhile HILDE *has appeared in the doorway at the top of the stairs. She makes a sign to* JOSEPH, *and is ready to make a speech.* SONJA *holds her head between her hands, hears nothing.*

SONJA. We've been at it for months. All those evenings we stood or sat in the kitchen talking, and washing up, without having to look at one another. I read to you, as though you were a child. While you lay in bed smoking and couldn't sleep.

They stand still and look at HILDE.

JOSEPH. The lady of the house has an announcement to make to us any moment, she said. (*To* SONJA, *about* NATASJA.) What's up with her?

SONJA. Just leave her alone.

JOSEPH (*goes to* SONJA). Just between ourselves. I've been watching it all today. I should tell you I'm not her own choice. I forced myself on her.

SONJA. That's none of my business.

JOSEPH. It's an impossible position I'm in. To put it briefly, I give up.

HILDE. Listen, I've come to a decision. There's no reason at all for me to stay here, so I'm not going to lose any more time.

HEDDA *and* ALFRED, *who have been sitting talking at the top of the stairs, go to* HILDE.

SONJA. So?

HILDE. So now I'm announcing my departure.

JOSEPH. Aha.

HILDE (*to* MAX). Ah, there you are. I want some advice. From you.

MAX. My dear lady, it's late. I'm too old for a lot of adventures.

HILDE. Yes. You heard. What do you think of it?

Enter NATASJA, *from the terrace.*

MAX (*quoting*). 'How fluid once a world that now congealing its great weight laments.' (*Then very directly.*) Just realize there's one thing we have to get clear. none of us knows what's to happen with her. (*Meaning* NATASJA, *no one realises she is present.*)

SONJA. But do I have to explain it all again to her?

HILDE. We've all tried to talk to her.

MAX. She just can't bring herself, in a decent way –

JOSEPH. And what's more, she's standing there listening.

SONJA. Oh God.

NATASJA. I'll say goodbye. There's really not much to say. We're ready. Completely ready.

HILDE. We –

NATASJA. Yes, we are.

SONJA. Wait a minute now.

NATASJA. I'll just go and pack.

The company breaks up. NATASJA, MARTHA, MAX *and* GEORGE *go off under the stairs.* PAUL *goes to the kitchen,* SONJA *goes to the terrace.*

HILDE. Yes, yes. Me too. Me too.

Exeunt HILDE *and* HEDDA *via the stairs.*

ALFRED (*at the bottom of the stairs*). Ladies and gentlemen, can we now please just discuss what's going to happen? Where have they all gone to suddenly?

JOSEPH (*on his way to the hall with* GABY). There, and there, and there and there, and everywhere.

ALFRED exits shaking his head, via the stairs, enter GEORGE *from the kitchen, and he blocks* JOSEPH's *path.*

GEORGE. Tell me, what have I just been hearing about you, about all of you?

JOSEPH. Yes, that's how stories get spread about.

JOSEPH and GABY *change course and go to the kitchen.*

GEORGE. Goodness me.

VICTOR (*has remained behind*). I want clarification. Clarity. Above all. Why all this?

GEORGE. There are some stubborn characters who act the part of unmaskers. They have to expose something at all costs. They have to uncover horrendous truths. But I wonder: does there have to be exposure to explain, to clarify, or is it all just for the sake of moral cleansing? In other words, just to be able to wade in.

VICTOR. To forbid, to prevent. To prevent everything still being attacked with such impunity. So that whip stops lashing out. I see my father, wrung dry. And I read his diaries. And I want punishment, I want retribution. I want a liar able to be called a liar.

GEORGE. You know, today we are commemorating a suicide committed with an antique knife. And that knife was supplied by me.

VICTOR. What kind of a story is this now?

GEORGE. There was a guarantee on that knife that a genuine murder had been committed with it. He must have found out that I, well, swindled him.

VICTOR. Is that true?

GEORGE. Just imagine a liar being called a liar by a liar. What do you do then?

VICTOR. A paradox. Yes. But I don't believe in paradoxes, because I don't believe in language either. I studied the philosophy of language, and I know that you can't trust language.

Enter GABY *from the kitchen.*

GEORGE. But you didn't finish, did you?

VICTOR. Is she going around saying that?

GABY. What am I supposed to be saying? I have something to tell you.

GEORGE. Oh yes? Did you manage it?

GABY. Yes. I'm so happy. We've just, eh, how do you say?

GEORGE. Rigged up something?

GABY. Made plans.

VICTOR. I'm kept out of everything. For God's sake. What's happening now?

GEORGE. Some people can't escape their good luck. Others manage to escape nearly everything. In my view we're about to learn something extremely unsavoury about you. (*He beats a hasty retreat.*)

VICTOR. Have you told him that? That I didn't finish . . .

GABY. Me? Of course not. Why?

VICTOR. I don't get it. Today cynicism is the passport photo of truth.

GABY. That's a good one.

VICTOR. Oh for God's sake.

Enter JOSEPH *from the kitchen.*

GABY. Really, you ought to be a writer.

Enter HEDDA, *with jacket and bag.*

VICTOR. Not for anything. Writing's to do with language, so – Although . . .

JOSEPH (*to* GABY). You coming?

GABY. Yes, I'm coming.

Exeunt GABY *and* JOSEPH *via entrance hall.*

VICTOR. What's she doing with him now?

Enter MARTHA, *with suitcase.*

MARTHA. Nice, eh? What a nice pair.

VICTOR. What? Them? Together? A . . . You don't mean?

HEDDA (*shows her bag*). Look at this, made out of the skin of a Mexican butterfly fish. Tough as suede.

Enter HILDE, *at the top of the stairs,* NATASJA *enters from under the stairs,* MARTHA *goes off towards the entrance hall.*

HILDE. Heh, it's just like a burst boil. All that hysterical tension, completely gone. Let's all just go and sit down together for a bit.

HEDDA. So you're going as well?

HILDE. Yes, I'm going as well. And when I've finally achieved peace, I know an old monastery on an island. An enclave. It's still around there, the atmosphere I'm looking for. Night-long stimulating discussions. But that atmosphere will never go. Yes, I'm ready.

Enter ALFRED *with car keys, makes a questioning gesture to* HEDDA, *which is understood by her as 'How many people will be in the car with us?'*

HEDDA (*to* HILDE). Great, great. Then we know something. (*To* ALFRED.) Four, yes. Four.

HILDE. And have you asked if some photos could still be taken?

HEDDA. That's been sorted out.

Enter MAX *from the kitchen.*

HILDE. But let's just dwell again for a moment on this wonderful, strange man. The memories. The gambling. The cars. The friends. The nights. The desperate monologues. The lies. And the bankruptcy. And the end.

MAX. And his enormous addiction to people, to meetings. His enormous energy. His gigantic curiosity.

HILDE. But he remained a man who had difficulty sorting out his life.

NATASJA. A dying man. Constantly pursued by fear.

HILDE (*to* NATASJA). But where did it start? Why was he so possessed by thoughts of wealth? Hurled himself on shares and options. Seemed to be overcome by panic. Bought, sold. Reacted to every rumour. Acted according to unfathomable logic, that guided his behaviour more and more. When that firm no longer paid its way he started speculating with borrowed money. Waste, unstoppable. And just sat at that telephone.

NATASJA (*tight-lipped*). All feverish energy frittered away, those long, mad monologues.The cry for revenge. Injury that turned into rage. 'I saved that woman's life,' he kept repeating it.

Enter SONJA *from the entrance hall.*

MAX. He was convinced he would be left in the lurch.

HILDE (*passionately*). What we had was too involved. An idiotic intermezzo. I saw it go up in flames.

NATASJA. And then you got another confusing telephone call, and you go there again, and you find him in bed again, dried scabs on his legs. In his hair: vomit and shit. I tried to look after him. And when he started to scream, I screamed back that I was ill too. 'I'm sick too, for Christ's sake.' I am sick, aren't I? It was almost funny. His mood changed so quickly, I thought he was joking. After a while he started to annoy the neighbours.

HILDE. He couldn't be left alone any more.

NATASJA. Total destruction. Everything in ruins.

HILDE (*passionately*). That you want to lay at my door. And I'd be quite willing to spend time mending what's broken, but I can't keep on facing the past all the time.There's such a sharp wind blowing from that past.

Enter GEORGE *from the terrace.*

VICTOR. I can't identify with your problems. But when I've settled with all of you, then you'll all know who you are. I shall unravel a few of your gripping biographies. Throw the spotlight on a few of you. I'll shout it from the rooftop and turn you into nailbiters.

NATASJA. I must go.

SONJA. You know, I really can't take any photos now. I just have to be left in peace.

Enter PAUL, *from the kitchen.*

NATASJA (*to* SONJA). I feel panic-stricken, you know? I've become so dependent on you. I always thought when anything happened to me: thank God I can tell her about it tomorrow. I don't have to be treated very harshly. If you say something nice to me, then I start to feel sorry for myself. And I really can't do anything about it, can I?

ALFRED. Have definite arrangements been made? Does everyone know where they're going? And with whom?

Enter MARTHA *from the entrance hall.*

GEORGE (*goes up to* HILDE). Tell me, that famous knife, what happened to it?

HILDE. That knife. Do you think I ever want to see it again?

GEORGE. It's become valuable. A curiosity. Something like that represents a certain value.

HILDE. If you really know anyone who's interested in it, then you can make me an offer.

Enter GABY *and* JOSEPH *from the entrance hall. Now everyone is onstage. Thoughtful music, for example a string quartet by Beethoven, Opus 130, slow movement. They all begin moving in a circle, to say goodbye to one another. In the movement at a certain moment there is a collective standstill, a pause for thought, when* ALFRED *talks about the inheritance.*

NATASJA. I must go.

HEDDA. Well, we're ready anyway.

ALFRED. I'll look for a notary. I'll see to it that we find out how big the debts are. And how we can settle them. I hope we can assess the amount of the remaining debts, so that you all know where you are. You have to think out what you want to do with this inheritance. I'll keep you up to date about everything. And where this building is concerned – Yes, is anybody listening? If you want to go, then make arrangements among yourselves. There's bound to be trouble.

NATASJA. Yes, I'm going.

JOSEPH. We have an interesting plan for this space. We're seriously interested in it.

HILDE. Who do you mean, we?

GABY. Well, we. (*Points to* JOSEPH.)

HILDE. Just sort everything out. Sort it out, go on. I'm not taking anything. I don't want anything. I'm leaving everything behind.

While ALFRED *discusses with* JOSEPH, *new groups form here and there.*

HEDDA (*about* SONJA). She's going to work for me, did you know that? Yes, she moved fast there.

HILDE. Was that possibly the reason why she came here today?

HEDDA. Now, you mustn't start spreading nasty stories.

NATASJA. Good. Then I'm going. 'All fails, until I desist', as the poet said.

HILDE. It's as though the echoes of time are expanding, and finally threaten to fall silent. Any moment we will be swept away by history.

HEDDA. You remind me of an actress on her farewell tour. We get all the highpoints and a bit extra.

JOSEPH. Ladies and gentlemen, for the moment I am assuming control of this room. We mustn't stay here too much longer. When we come back I expect I can close the joint.

GEORGE. Who exactly is leaving now? Where to?

GABY. We're going together to sort out a few things.

Exeunt JOSEPH, GABY *and* ALFRED *under the stairs.*

MAX. What am I hearing now? A ballroom? A dance-hall? Are they going to turn it into that?

Exit MARTHA *towards the entrance hall.*

VICTOR. That is a more sensible plan than all the others I've heard today.

Exeunt VICTOR *and* SONJA *towards the terrace.*

HILDE (*to* NATASJA). He just couldn't have loved me. You meant everything. You meant everything to him. For him you were everything.

Exeunt HILDE *and* HEDDA *via the stairs.*

PAUL (*to* MAX). But you knew him well, didn't you?

MAX. I don't know. I studied him.

HILDE (*in the doorway*). Do you still remember the talks then? So and so's coming, and she is, and he is . . . Oh, yes, so festive.

MAX. That man could be touched. Deeply touched like a child. A painting, a work of art could affect him profoundly. He was extraordinarily receptive. A special instance of the Stendhal syndrome. (*Enter* MARTHA, *with jackets.*) I wrote a book about him. A dwindling human species. (*Enter* GABY *and* JOSEPH.) A dwindling disease too, that syndrome of mine. But will that make the world more healthy? That's the question I ask myself, as who can still be moved? He was energetic, loved plans, took big risks, wanted panoramas. Looked for a travel guide for an optimistic imagination. (*Enter* SONJA *and* VICTOR.) Needed people and wanted something from them. Passionate, that man was. Impetuous. With a wide circle of friends and stimulating ideas. Ultimately though I still didn't fully understand what his selection was based on. I saw people coming and thought: that can't last. But no. Was there actually calculation behind his friendship? I felt more and more arbitrariness and lack of control. We shared less than we thought. Yes – arbitrariness, pitifulness, sought and found nothing. Parting, misunderstanding.

Exit MAX *to entrance hall. People put coats on.*

VICTOR. Was this the last madness the legend had to offer his worshippers? Is everyone going now? Everyone?

GEORGE. I'm sure you get satisfaction out of it that everyone's leaving empty-handed.

Exeunt PAUL *and* MARTHA *towards entrance hall.*

VICTOR. I'll write the records. I can say I had a front seat. I observed it closely, I saw through it. If this had been Olympus, how I'd defy the gods.

SONJA. I'm not going. I've got to sort out a few other things.

Enter ALFRED *from the kitchen.*

ALFRED. For the last time, if people want to leave, then I won't stop you. But I hope you all realise that I need an answer. (*Exit via stairs.*)

VICTOR. You've all disappeared from my sight. There may not be an adequate version of the truth available, so, as if I were the story-teller, for artistic reasons I'll see to a conclusion.

GEORGE. What did you want to inform mankind about?

HILDE *appears in the doorway with a half-burned toy peepshow* (*diorama*).

HILDE. Who's been using my peepshow as an ashtray? Just look at this. (*Exit.*)

VICTOR. I'm gradually inclining to an ending with the following drift: that man appears, contrary to the general idea, not so much the victim of himself as of a large assembly of show-off cry-babies and hysterics.

GEORGE. As I said. The art of narration must be encouraged. It would be unsporting to retract that statement. A cry-baby, you said? I'll see what I can do for you. You talk about an ending, and I start to tremble. But not a horrible ending? Please, I plead for a human ending. An ending that justifies our presence here.

A shot sounds. ALFRED, HILDE *and* HEDDA *enter terrified.*

ALFRED. What's happened?

Enter MARTHA *and* PAUL *from the entrance hall,* PAUL *has an antique pistol in his hand.*

MARTHA. Give it to me, come on.

PAUL. How did that happen?

MARTHA. He was standing there with that pistol in his hand. I didn't know – I thought . . .

PAUL (*about the pistol*). Now I see it. Is it a real one?

GEORGE. No, young man. Valuable object. An antique. Stage pistol. Belonged to Bassermann. Classical talent. Generations back. Stage prop. Give it to me, I say.

PAUL (*to himself*). What now? No solution? Give in? Hm. Well? What?

Exeunt MARTHA, HILDE *and* HEDDA *via the stairs.*

ALFRED (*about* VICTOR). This gentleman promised to arrange a common ending for us. So don't suddenly make up your own ending.

Exeunt SONJA *and* ALFRED *via the stairs.*

JOSEPH. Please, people. A cheap attempt to imitate what I did with the cards.

VICTOR. So you think you can escape the past?

GEORGE. Never. Whenever I get a good price for some knick-knack or other, I think thank God, we can't escape the past.

JOSEPH. But doesn't anyone want to take anything from here? The dustman can have the lot?

Enter SONJA, *with a roll of film.*

SONJA (*destroys the film*). Good. Then we have carefully and consistently erased all traces. No memories. No obstacles.

JOSEPH. Jesus Christ, so I got into that bloody typhus-ridden bath for nothing, shit.

Exeunt JOSEPH, GABY, GEORGE *and* VICTOR, *towards the entrance hall.*

NATASJA. That story about the princess, you know the one, don't you? She had to run round an enormous wall. For years. Round an enormous wall. Till she reached a little door. Then she was in a wintery garden. And she didn't want to freeze. Then she found an entry to a vault, went down the steps till she came to the crypt. On the table was a book, and on the cover her name. Oh, of course: the book of her life. She picked up the book, and when she went to read the last page, the door suddenly slammed. It became pitch dark.

ALFRED, HILDE, HEDDA *and* MARTHA *come down the stairs, with coats and suitcases.*

ALFRED. The only thing really of any use is a legal ruling. For the very last time. I simply must know what is to happen with the inheritance. What if there is a large debt left?

HILDE. Speaking for myself, I haven't lost my marbles, you know. You think it probable debts might be left, you say? Apart from that, after what has happened I say: I don't need that inheritance. I don't want it. I don't have to accept it. I know my rights and I'm not accepting it. I reject it.

ALFRED. Finally. Then I'll write. You reject it.

HILDE. Oh, the thought that I have owned this building and that it will now have to be sold. For a few days this building was mine. It wanted to belong to me, I felt that.

ALFRED. What do you mean?

HILDE. The day after his suicide I went to the bank. I paid off all the debts. The feeling of having been without debts for a few days, I have never known that before.

ALFRED. What did you do? You redeemed the whole mortgage?

HILDE. He had written in his letter, 'Don't forget the mortgage'. It was the date fixed. I always did it myself. The wonderful feeling that it would one day be mine.

ALFRED. You were authorised to do that? Oh my God, now I get it.

HILDE. The trust he put in me. He wanted to share everything with me.

ALFRED. But you don't want his inheritance?

HILDE. I can't answer for the rest of my life for those debts? I don't accept it. I have the right to reject it.

HEDDA. Let him sort that out for you. We should go.

Exeunt HILDE *and* HEDDA *to the entrance hall.*

ALFRED. I daren't tell her that.

SONJA. What's up then?

ALFRED. In the eyes of the law, and that is the only thing that counts, she has accepted the inheritance by doing that. Fatal and inescapable. There's nothing to be done about it now. She has accepted. She has become administrator of the estate. His revenge. His curse. One day before the redemption date, he puts an end to it. And he writes in a letter . . .

SONJA. I see what you mean.

ALFRED. But who's going to tell her that?

SONJA. Oh no.

NATASJA. No.

PAUL. I want – shall I – shall I – Shall I break it to her? (*Exit towards entrance hall.*)

ALFRED. Somebody has to do it. There's nothing else for it.

NATASJA *and* SONJA *take their leave.*

NATASJA. It has to be. Bye, see you. Cheerio.

SONJA. It's better that way. Better.

Enter GABY *and* VICTOR *from the entrance hall, they take their leave.*

GABY. It's better if we don't see one another any more.

VICTOR. How did you work that out? If this is the ending you wanted . . .

Enter JOSEPH, MAX *and* GEORGE *from the entrance hall.* MAX *and* GEORGE *take their leave.*

MAX. All the best. We've known one another a long time.

GEORGE. Abroad again. But I just want to thank her. She was so friendly and hospitable.

Enter MARTHA *from the entrance hall.*

MARTHA. Watch out.

Enter HEDDA *and* HILDE *from entrance hall.*

HILDE. Is that true? Is what I've been told the truth?

ALFRED. Now I see what's been going on.

HILDE. Aren't I free any more? Aren't I a free being any more?

ALFRED. The pitfall you had to fall into.

HEDDA. Well no. He's making that up. He doesn't know anything. Just check it all out.

HILDE. Oh no. That man. It's true. Yes, of course.

HEDDA. Listen. Tomorrow morning ring up a lawyer.

HILDE. Oh no. Not another sleepless night. Not that permanent doubt again. (*Exit, towards the terrace.*)

ALFRED. It's the truth. Really. She's now – Can anyone . . .

A shot is heard. They look behind the scenes.

NATASJA. Oh no.

ALFRED. Oh no. Now it's all starting again from the beginning.

SONJA. Terrible. Not again. Not another time.

VICTOR. Am I glad I didn't think up this ending.

GABY. My God.

MAX. There's nothing for it now but to stay.

GEORGE. No, of course we can't leave now.

MARTHA (*pointing to the kitchen*). Coffee and rolls?

Blackout. Requiem.

End.